Bread - The Scripts

Bread - The Scripts

Carla Lane

BBC BOOKS

Published by BBC Books,
A division of BBC Enterprises Ltd
Woodlands, 80 Wood Lane, London W12 0TT

First published 1990

© Aromandys Ltd, 1986, 1987

ISBN 0 563 20919 4

Typeset by Ace Filmsetting Ltd, Frome
Printed and bound in Great Britain by Redwood Press Ltd, Melksham
Cover printed by Richard Clay Ltd, Norwich

Contents

Cast list

MRS BOSWELL	Jean Boht
MR BOSWELL	Ronald Forfar
JOEY BOSWELL	Peter Howitt
JACK BOSWELL	Vic McGuire
ADRIAN BOSWELL	Jonathon Morris
AVELINE BOSWELL	Gilly Coman
BILLY BOSWELL	Nick Conway
JULIE	Caroline Milmoe
GRANDAD	Kenneth Waller
CARMEN	Jenny Jay
MARTINA (*usual DHSS girl*)	Pamela Power
FATHER DOOLEY	J. G. Devlin
RSPCA WORKER	Barry McCarthy
YIZZEL	Charles Lawson
MR WILSON (*man in DHSS*)	Chris Ellison
CYCLIST	Roy Brandon
Produced by	Robin Nash
Directed by	Susan Belbin

Series One
Episode One

MR KELLY	Eddie Ross
FLORENCE	Josie Kidd
EDIE	Jan Davies
VAN DRIVER	Tony Scoggo
KID AT DHSS	Ben Davies

Episode Two

MAY	Pamela Sholto
MAY'S NEIGHBOUR	Barbara New
DHSS GIRL	Ishia Bennison
BENNY	Paul Beringer
FIRST YOUNG MAN	Phil Mulhaire
RADIO ANNOUNCER	John Livesey

Episode Three

OLD MAN (*George*)	Tom Ryan
LADY	Georgina Smith
CHILD JACK'S VOICE	Ross Dawse
MAN (*Docks*)	Robbie Dee
MAN (*Voice off*)	John Livesey
WOMAN (*Voice off*) (*Docks*)	Beryl Nesbitt
LADY (*Voice off*) (*Flats*)	Pamela Power
OPERATOR (*Voice off*)	Lorraine Ashbourne

Episode Four

ANDRÉ	Michael J. Jackson
GIRL SINGER	Susanna Page

Episode Five

FIRST BEARER	Al T. Kossy
LADY SWEEPING	Mandy Walsh
FIRST LADY (*Voice off*)	Beryl Nesbitt
SECOND LADY (*Voice off*)	Josie Kidd
MAN (*Voice off*)	Phil Ryan

Episode Six

YIZZEL'S MATE	Simon Rousse
MR HAYWORTH	Noel Collins
FIRST BOY	Danny Cunningham
SECOND BOY	Tom Price
DOG'S HOME ATTENDANT	Barry McCarthy

Series Two
Episode One

FIRST MAN	Tim Dantay
SECOND MAN	John Wild
OTHER DHSS GIRL	Joanne Zorian
TAXI DRIVER	Harry Goodier

Episode Two

CHAP IN DHSS	Charles Pemberton
SISTER	Shevaun Bryers
MAN WITH BANGLE	Roy Brandon
MILKMAN	Jimmy Wilde
WOMAN	Georgina Smith
FIRST AMBULANCE MAN	John Thomolla
SECOND AMBULANCE MAN	Michael Atkinson

Episode Three

MRS STEVENSON	Dorothy Mawdsley
ROBBER	Brian Croucher
OLD MAN	Eric Wyn
ROBBER'S MATE	Derek Deadman

Episode Four

MAN IN DHSS	Tommy Wright
1ST KID	Christian Ealey
2ND KID	Alex Green
1ST LADY	Viv Molyneux
2ND LADY	Marie Jelliman
3RD LADY	Mandy Walsh
4TH LADY	Sharon Power
BUTLER	David Hanson
DOG'S HOME ATTENDANT	Peter Terry
YIZZEL'S MATE	Simon Rouse
NEIGHBOUR	Jo Manning Wilson

Episode Five

WOMAN	Georgina Smith
ALICE	Gina Maher

Episode Six

RECEPTIONIST	Cathy Flanagan

Foreword

For those of you who want to be a writer for television, and judging by the letters I receive there are many, here they are – the finished ramblings of a none-the-wiser comedy writer.

The ingredients of successful comedy hide themselves in the nooks and crannies of reasoning. My own theory is that apart from the essential humour itself, a combination of truth and pathos, threaded with identifiable situations and scaffolded with deeply drawn characters, should do it.

If these facts exhaust you, then I can cheer you by saying that in the beginning, my own scripts contained none of these things. Indeed, they were fashioned with endless self-indulgent dialogue and not a single stage instruction to break up the monotony. I had no idea what the word 'fade' meant and I expected cameras to perform impossible feats; so success was not instant, it came with trial and disaster, tears and pain – the important thing is, it did come.

These are good days for the writer, particularly the comedy writer. Somewhere along the way we have become a rare species. Our voices listened to, we are no longer barred from the Rehearsal Rooms, we are no longer verbally inhibited, we can at last deviate from the dark path of cliché. Indeed, a successful comedy writer sits on the high throne of respectability.

There are rules of course and it has always given me great pleasure to break most of them, but a certain amount of caution is valuable. Subtlety is always desirable, as is dialogue as opposed to jokes and gags. The ability to make the viewer or reader identify with the words, the feelings, even the rage, and if you are very lucky, a loud smile in between would not go amiss.

So – read the scripts – either for learning or for pleasure. It is a large arena out here, closed to no-one and yet, strangely, occupied by very few.

Carla Lane

Series One

Aveline

Episode One

The Boswells' living room (*early evening*)

Joey, Jack, Adrian and Aveline are lounging around, as if waiting for their meal. Joey is reading the paper, and Adrian is reading an estate agents' magazine. Jack is repairing his watch, kneeling at the table. Aveline is filing her nails.

MRS BOSWELL. (*Appearing at door.*) It's nearly done.

ADRIAN. Oh God, must she always be filing her nails?

JOEY. Leave her – she's a girl.

ADRIAN. Her whole life is spent doing herself up.

AVELINE. I'm a model, aren't I?

ADRIAN. If it's not filing nails, it's plucking eyebrows, shaving legs, dabbing spots. Nothing's allowed to grow on her.

AVELINE. Models have to look unblemished.

ADRIAN. Why don't you just give yourself a quick going over with a sanding machine?

AVELINE. Models have to look smooth like bathroom tiles.

JACK. This imitation Cartier watch is rubbish.

JOEY. The real thing sweetheart – you should always wait until you can afford the real thing.

Jack sighs, puts his watch on and sits on sofa.

JACK. I'll just have to wear it and guess the time.

AVELINE. I'll have a real fur coat one day, when I've done more modelling.

Jack is feeling down the side of the sofa and he brings out a dirty magazine which is obviously always kept there.

JACK. (*Flipping through the pages of the magazine.*) It doesn't seem fair – fur.

AVELINE. What d'you mean?

JACK. It's animals isn't it? How would you like someone to grab you by the arse and peel you like a banana?

AVELINE. I wouldn't mind would I, if I was dead.

JACK. How do you know?

AVELINE. 'Cos I've seen dead things, haven't I?

JACK. And anyway you would start off being alive, wouldn't you? You'd have to be rendered dead and no matter how carefully they render you it's not very nice.

ADRIAN. Shut up you two! You depress me the pair of you.

AVELINE. (*Ignoring Adrian.*) Everything can't live, can it? There would be no room on the earth and anyway what would we eat?

JACK. Each other, the way animals do.

AVELINE. Sometimes I think your bolt's undone.

JACK. It works in the jungle, doesn't it? There's no unemployment there, no housing lists. If you want somewhere to live you turf someone out. If you're hungry you eat your neighbour.

AVELINE. I'm starving. (*She shouts.*) How long will it be Mam?

Joey, sensing that Mrs Boswell is coming into the room, warns Jack to hide the magazine. Jack stuffs it down the side of the sofa.

MRS BOSWELL. (*Calling.*) Nearly done.

AVELINE. I've been thinking.

ADRIAN. Oh God! The four-minute warning.

AVELINE. I won't have a fur. I'll have diamonds instead – big diamonds – one in each ear like wing-mirrors. (*She turns to Joey.*) You don't have to do murder for diamonds.

JOEY. All this talk about death. Why don't we talk about life? Instead of nightmares why don't we dream?

JACK. One day I'm going to walk into someone's attic and there in the corner will be a Leonardo, a pale maiden with hands clasped and an enigmatic smile.

AVELINE. I thought somebody had already found that one.

JACK. 'Oh!' I'll say, 'What a nice little print – I'll give you a tenner darling and take it off your hands,' then off I'll go to Sotheby's, Christie's and the Bahamas.

ADRIAN. I'm going to open my own business in London.

JACK. Why London? They're all show-offs.

ADRIAN. The metropolis, the centre of history, the heartbeat of the universe.

AVELINE. They're all funny down there, they have a bath every day. (*She turns to Jack.*) Anyway, we haven't heard what our Joey dreams about.

JOEY. I dream about keeping the art of dreaming, sweetheart.

AVELINE. Oh God! Isn't he deep?

The bedroom in Julie's parents' house (*early morning*)

Billy is in bed and Julie is seated on the bed.

JULIE. You know the thing about men – they can't really look after themselves. They're like hedgehogs – the minute they leave their mother they get run over.

BILLY. I don't know where you get these theories from – they just come out, one after the other, and all about men. Haven't you got any theories about anything else?

JULIE. You've started wearing black underpants.

BILLY. I mean, what about . . . flowers, animals, God?

JULIE. God is a man – he's included in me theories. (*Julie lies back.*)

BILLY. Don't you like men?

JULIE. Men who wear black underpants are devious.

BILLY. Me mam bought them for me – so she can put them in with the socks.

JULIE. I'm surprised she hasn't got two washing-machines – one for black, one for white. She's got everything else.

BILLY. She's a good woman – she came up the hard way, my mam.

JULIE. They *all* came up the hard way in this street Billy – and they've all got sons and daughters like your mam – but they haven't *all* got a magic wand.

BILLY. The magic wand, as you call it, is unity – that's what it is – family solidarity – human bondage. (*Pause.*) The family pot.

JULIE. You sound as if you're talking about the sex life of the Mohicans.

BILLY. The family is disappearing – mothers and fathers are getting divorced, kids are leaving home. I mean look at you – there were seven of you – you're the only one left, and you only stay here because you've got the place to yourself. Your dad's at sea and when your mam goes to the pub she can't find her way home.

JULIE. (*Sitting up and kissing him.*) We wouldn't be able to do this if she could, would we?

BILLY. (*Reflectively.*) Our Joey will be on his way home now. He's got style our Joey, he doesn't walk, he sort of oozes.

JULIE. The thing that worries me about your Joey is where does he ooze? I mean, when he borrows the family wand, where does he wave it?

BILLY. Our Jack will be on the way back with something bought, something sold and something in his back pocket. (*Julie lies back.*) Our Aveline will be in the bathroom with her bath oil and her apricot body scrub. (*Pause.*) And our Adrian—

JULIE. Adrian! Who's Adrian?

BILLY. Jimmy – he prefers to be called Adrian.

JULIE. Oh I see – Jimmy not good enough for him then?

BILLY. Well he does work in real estate. And our Adrian (*Julie rises and crosses*) will be sitting at the breakfast table with his serviette (no, napkin, that's the word), with his napkin tucked in his suit.

JULIE. (*Angry now.*) And our Billy will be over the road screwing Julie Jefferson. (*Billy stares at her.*) Well, that's how it is, isn't it?

BILLY. No. (*Pause.*) No.

   Pause.

JULIE. You never mention anything, Billy.

BILLY. Like what?

   Julie rises and moves to the bed.

JULIE. Like living together – like marrying each other.

BILLY. I will marry you one day Julie, when I've got a job.

JULIE. Job – you'll never get a job. There aren't any jobs. (*She sighs.*) And even if we did get married you'd probably sleep here at No. 41 and go and have your breakfast at No. 30 . . . (*emphatically*) with your mam.

BILLY. I don't like you talking about my mam, Julie.

JULIE. (*Shouting.*) Of course you don't, Billy. She's the boss, that's why. She squats in your bloody house like the Queen of Tonga.

BILLY. (*Lying back.*) I'll get organised one day, you'll see.

JULIE. (*Sitting.*) You – you're about as organised as a tossed salad. I hate your family, Billy. I hate this street – I hate this city – I hate this life. (*Pause*) and I hate the fact that I don't hate you. It's time to get dressed – me mam'll be here in a minute – unless you want to hear 'Nellie Dean' again.

BILLY. (*Laughing.*) I'm sorry about your mam.

JULIE. (*Beginning to giggle.*) At least she won't stand in our way.

   She goes to him. They both laugh now.

She might *lie* in it though.

BILLY. (*Stops laughing and looks at Julie.*) Come here.

   They kiss passionately.

Outside in the Boswells' street (early morning)

Silence as we see a row of terraced houses with doors opening on to the street. A lone postman goes from door to door with the post. Along the street, there is a milk float.

We come to No. 30 which has two Police 'No Parking' cones in front of it. The milk float draws up and the milkman gets out. He fills a tray with milk bottles and goes to Nos. 34 and 32, placing a pint of milk on each step. When he comes to No. 30 he places eight bottles there and goes back to his float whistling. He drives off. And there is a morning silence again.

Now, coming towards us, there is a big black car. It is an old Jaguar, and it comes slowly and quietly, suggesting style and composure, eventually pulling up near No. 30.

The car door opens and Joey gets out. He is dressed very smartly in a black leather jacket, black leather trousers and all the trappings (a noticeable gold watch, a gold ring, dark glasses and a black cigarette in his mouth). He strolls over to one of the cones, picks it up and places it on the pavement, rubbing his fingers together afterwards to remove any dirt. Then he parks his car, locks it, picks up the cone, puts a key in the door of No. 30 and lets himself in, closing the door quietly after him.

At this moment an old van comes screeching along the road. It is falling to pieces, and is very noisy. Painted across each side is a huge rainbow. It pulls up quickly and out comes Jack, wearing jeans and a T-shirt. He rushes to a cone, picks it up, puts it on the pavement and parks his van. He opens the house door, then rushes to the back of the van and gets out a large box which has written on the side 'Italian Tomatoes'. Jack goes in and out of the house at top speed with four large boxes of these tomatoes. As he carries the last one in, a tomato drops to the ground. He kicks it out of the way, dumps the last box in the hall, closes the van door and goes inside the house, closing the door with a bang.

The door of No. 32 opens. The neighbour, Mr Kelly, comes out in his dressing-gown. He picks up his milk and is about to go in again when Julie's door opens – No. 41. It is further along on the other side. Billy comes out, followed by Julie who is in her dressing-gown. They go into a passionate clinch on the doorstep. Finally Billy leaves her. She gives a little wave, and he wanders across the road towards No. 30 – tall, thin, hunched shoulders, wearing a denim jacket and jeans. He yawns as he walks.

MR KELLY. (*To himself.*) Oh God – here he comes – Paradise on a stick. (*He closes his door.*)

Pause – silence – and then a mongrel dog comes trotting along the road. It stops at No. 30 and scratches the door. The door opens – the dog goes in. The door closes again.

Silence and the street.

The Boswells' kitchen (*a little later*)

The family are having breakfast. The table has a large pot of honey, a glass jug of orange juice and a big box of de luxe muesli on it. There is also a pineapple in a dish.

Mrs Boswell is frying eggs and tomatoes in a large electric frying pan. Nearby is a microwave oven – the bacon is in there. She is humming.

Billy, Jack, Joey and Adrian are sitting around the table. They are drinking orange juice while they wait. Jack goes to pick up a piece of toast.

MRS BOSWELL. (*To Jack.*) Leave the toast alone.

Billy yawns. Jack puts the toast back. Mrs Boswell takes a dish with bacon on it from the microwave, places it on the table and goes back to her frying pan.

(*To Billy.*) Cover your mouth.

He does so. He then picks up his fork.

Leave the bacon alone!

He puts the fork down again.

JOEY. (*To Billy.*) You should get some more shuteye sweetheart – a growing lad.

BILLY. (*To Joey.*) So where've you been all night then? (*Pause.*) I saw you coming home.

MRS BOSWELL. (*Reprimanding him.*) Billy, we don't ask each other personal questions. All right?

BILLY. Everybody asks me personal questions.

MRS BOSWELL. About your private life – yes. But not work – we don't talk about work.

ADRIAN. That could be due to the fact that apart from me nobody *does* work.

MRS BOSWELL. (*Being conciliatory.*) We all work – in our different ways – we do what we can for the family.

ADRIAN. (*Pointing at Billy.*) How does he work? Will somebody explain to me how he fits into the rich embroidery of our family life?

MRS BOSWELL. He's a growing lad – he's learning the trade.

ADRIAN. What trade? Nobody in this house has got a trade.

JOEY. He's learning about survival – it begins with women.

ADRIAN. Mine began with school and exams.

MRS BOSWELL. You've got a headful of capacity, that's why.

JOEY. At least he's got a steady relationship. I don't see anybody else around this table with one. Who knows, the magic might all dry up? The universe might be short of Boswells. At least he'll rectify the situation. (*To Mrs Boswell.*) Give him an egg.

BILLY. So what am I then – the family stud?

JOEY. You're a member of the work force now Billy – you go out there with the rest of us.

BILLY. (*Enthusiastically.*) I'm meeting this chap today – on the Dock Road. (*To Joey.*) You know, the one our Jack . . .

JOEY. Why don't you just do it – OK?

MRS BOSWELL. We don't talk about work, Billy.

JACK. You go out there – make your pennies – and come home, all right?

BILLY. I wish I had a proper job . . . (*looking at Adrian*) . . . like him.

JOEY. He buys and sells houses. People with proper jobs can't afford houses, so – in effect – he's working for us.

BILLY. You mean when we move to Gatacre?

JACK. Who wants to live there? They're all posh there. (*Pointing at the dog.*) Where's our Mongy going to pee? He can't pee in Gatacre.

BILLY. Julie likes it there.

JACK. What about when you sign on? You can't give an address in Gatacre.

BILLY. Well, we won't be signing on for ever, will we?

They all glance at each other.

MRS BOSWELL. Of course we won't son, of course we won't.

Aveline comes rushing in. She is wearing a very tight skirt, an equally tight sweater, a band across her head and huge earrings.

AVELINE. Mam – I'm late.

She reaches for a piece of toast and eats it standing up.

JACK. Where are you going then?

AVELINE. I've got a modelling job.

JACK. Modelling what?

AVELINE. It doesn't matter *what* I'm modelling – I'm just modelling.

JOEY. Sink units. (*They all look at him.*) She's modelling sink units.

AVELINE. Oh very hilarious. At least I'm open about my job – nobody *knows* what *you* do.

She drinks some coffee.

BILLY. I thought models walked about in fancy clothes so people could buy them.

AVELINE. I do walk around in fancy clothes.

JACK. Only people don't buy *them* – they buy sinks.

AVELINE. (*Putting her cup down.*) I'll see you, Mam.

MRS BOSWELL. Have you got your whistle, Aveline?

Aveline shows her the little chain around her neck with a small whistle on it, and exits.

JACK. I don't see what good the whistle is with those clothes on. Supposing she has to run for her life, that band round her head has only got to slip down and she's bound and gagged herself.

MRS BOSWELL. She'll be in *Vogue* one day.

BILLY. (*With innocent joy.*)Yeah – and we'll all move to Gatacre.

ADRIAN. And when we do, will Gatacre move to somewhere else, I ask myself.

All the breakfasts are now served. Mrs Boswell sits down in front of them. Jack has started his, Mrs Boswell stares at him. Jack puts his knife and fork down.

MRS BOSWELL. Prayers.

JACK. I don't know why we have to have prayers.

MRS BOSWELL. We have prayers because we're thanking God for what we are about to receive.

JACK. But we've earned the money to buy it. I went to the market to fetch it – you cooked it. What's God got to do with it?

Mrs Boswell stares at him, then closes here eyes. Everybody else does, except Jack.

MRS BOSWELL. (*Without opening her eyes.*) Close your eyes Jack. (*He does so.*) We thank Thee, oh God, for giving us the skill to earn the money to buy the food, for giving our Jack the strength to carry it from the market, for giving me the will to cook it, and for giving us all a gob to eat it. Send us, oh Lord, good health, good heart and good thoughts. Amen.

They all acknowledge silently.

JOEY. (*Continuing the prayer, in fun.*) But please don't send us any more tomatoes!

JACK. (*To Joey.*) OK, OK – so I got paid in tomatoes – we don't all have your luck.

JOEY. Not luck sunshine – skill.

MRS BOSWELL. (*Rising.*) Shut it you two – it doesn't matter what you bring home as long as you bring something. (*The phone rings.*) That'll be yer grandad – he wants his breakfast. (*Holding the cordless phone.*) Hello – yes love – it's coming now. Adrian will bring it in on the way to work. Yes, I'll put plenty of sauce on. OK love. I'll do your shopping later. Tarra.

Putting away the cordless phone, she sits at the table.

ADRIAN. Does Grandad really need to phone? I mean, he only lives next door. Couldn't he hammer on the wall, or walk even?

JOEY. He's our grandad – the rare species, the founder member, the hierarchy. Don't you know the rules yet? In order of importance (*pointing to next door*) him, (*to Mrs Boswell*) her, (*to those around the table*) us, (*to Billy*) and him.

Outside in the Boswells' street (*a little later*)

Adrian comes out of the house carrying his briefcase and a tray with a covered plate on it. He puts his briefcase down and knocks on No. 28. After a moment Grandad opens the door.

ADRIAN. Breakfast, Grandad.

GRANDAD. Ta.

He takes the tray and closes the door before Adrian can even pick up his briefcase. Adrian shrugs, picks up the case and gets into a shiny old Volkswagen which is parked in front of the Jaguar.
He drives away.
As soon as he does this, Jack comes out of the house with a Police cone. He places it in the space left by Adrian's car. He goes back inside.

Outside the DHSS building

A large queue has formed outside the building.

Inside the DHSS building

There are rows of red plastic chairs and three serving windows opposite. Behind these, girls are preparing to open up. The 'Position Closed' signs are still displayed.

There is a ticket machine and notice which reads 'Please take your ticket and wait for your number to be called'.

A little kid comes creeping in and takes the first ticket. Just as he does so, one of the girls sees him. She shouts through the window.

DHSS GIRL (MARTINA). Hey – out! Go on.

The kid runs for it.

Little bastard.

As the kid runs, he encounters the first rush of people who are in the queue outside and are now entering the office. They each go to the ticket machine, take a ticket and sit down. There are quite a number standing around the ticket machine.

Outside the DHSS building

Joey comes strolling along in his black leather and gold. The kid runs to him with the ticket. Joey takes a pound note out of his pocket and gives it to the lad who runs off. Joey goes into the building.

Inside the DHSS building

Everybody is sitting down waiting. Two women start talking.

FLORENCE. Jesus – how long are they going to be?

EDIE. (*Two seats away.*) I spend me whole life here. I met me husband here – I went into labour here. (*Pause.*) I'll bleedin' die here.

FLORENCE. They've got to have their Earl Grey teabreak.

EDIE. That one on the left is all right. At least she smiles at you when she says 'On yer bike'.

FLORENCE. The others look like they've got their foot trapped in a mangle.

EDIE. Look at that one over there. Her face isn't used to good news, is it?

FLORENCE. The trouble is, you grow to look like your job, don't you?

EDIE. Yeah.

FLORENCE. I mean, people who sell flowers look peaceful, don't they?

EDIE. Yeah and men that do funerals, they have a sort of mortuary look.

FLORENCE. Yeah, you only have to look at Dr Palmer down the street – he's ravaged, he's pale, he's haggard, he coughs and he limps.

EDIE. God works in a mysterious way, Florence.

FLORENCE. I know this much – he doesn't work here. (*To the counter.*) Come on, for God's sake.

A few people start to sing 'land of hope and glory', with others joining in, including an old man.

DHSS GIRL (MARTINA). All right, all right – we 'eard yer.

They continue to sing.

We won't start until you stop.

EDIE. (*To herself.*) Who does she think she is?

Bit by bit the singing stops.

MARTINA. Thank you.

EDIE. (*To herself.*) Don't mention it – frosty-faced cow.

The 'Position Closed' signs are removed one by one.

MARTINA. (*Calling.*) No. 1!

At this moment Joey comes strolling through the door holding his ticket aloft.

JOEY. House!

He goes to the window whilst other girls call. A woman gets up and goes to window two. A man gets up and goes to window three. We concentrate on window two.

FLORENCE. (*To Martina.*) All me clothes 'ave been stolen from me washing line – everything – the entire lot.

We go back to window one, to the first DHSS girl and Joey.

MARTINA. Haven't you found work yet, Mr Boswell?

JOEY. Tell me where, sweetheart, tell me where.

MARTINA. (*Writing.*) Is that your Jaguar outside?

JOEY. Actually I meandered here – I like to take in the lead-laden air, and fill my soul with the sound of sparrows queuing up for a tree.

MARTINA. By outside I mean two blocks away, round a corner, in a street – *hidden.* (*He starts to speak.*) I *saw* you Mr Boswell.

JOEY. Oh – *that* Jaguar. It's my mate's – he's doing very well in videos.

MARTINA. Did he lend you the gear to go with it?

JOEY. There's no law against having style, sweetheart. 'We may be lying in the gutter – but some of us are looking at the stars.'

MARTINA. Is that so?

JOEY. Oscar Wilde.

MARTINA. Was he on social security too then?

She pushes a form towards him.

JOEY. Oh, I forgot to mention – my mother doesn't like to talk about this – but we have a case of incontinence in the family and I was told that you give a special allowance for it.

MARTINA. We do – yes. But owing to the sudden rush of incontinent nineteen-year-olds we're only giving it to those who qualify.

JOEY. Does my grandad qualify? He's seventy-four.

MARTINA. Then tell your mother to make an application – we give a special grant of thirty pounds a week to cover laundry expenses in severe cases.

JOEY. I'll tell her – thank you. It's very severe. We er – we have to keep buying him a new bed. (*The girl looks at him for a very long time.*) Only it's all right – we club together – you know, the family. We muddle through. After all he is our grandad, the leader of the pack must have his place.

MARTINA. Has he got a garden your grandad?

JOEY. (*With mock sadness.*) No, no – just a little window box.

MARTINA. Then perhaps you could use the money he claimed for a set of garden tools and a wheelbarrow . . . (*Pause*) . . . to buy a bed. (*She pushes the form nearer to him.*)

Joey gives in – he gets a gold pen out of his pocket and signs a great, flowing signature. Then he closes his fist and stamps the form with it, back and forth as if using a rubber stamp and an ink pad. He pushes it towards the girl.

JOEY. Will you marry me? With your charm and my academics we could live in Gatacre.

He smiles and walks away.

MARTINA. (*Edie comes up to the window.*) Yes, love?

EDIE. I want to report something stolen.

EDIE/MARTINA. From me/your washing line.

Martina reaches for a form.

At the dogs' home

Joey is walking slowly past the cages. He is very moved by these animals, but he walks with his head up and controlled composure. As he comes to the end of the line of kennels he sees an RSPCA worker.

RSPCA MAN. Morning Mr Boswell.

Joey puts his hand in his pocket, brings out his wallet and gives the man several notes amounting to about twenty pounds.

Thank you Mr Boswell, thank you for your support.

Joey just wanders out, saying nothing. We hear the dogs barking.

A back street

Billy's old van is parked at the side of the road. He is sitting in the driver's seat waiting. Shortly another van comes along quietly. It stops behind Billy's van. A chap of about 40 gets out. Billy gets out of his van and the two men walk towards each other. A vicious dog barks and growls from the window of the other man's van.

MAN. Shut up Saviour!

BILLY. What have you got?

The man slowly lights a pipe.

MAN. (*Speaking with teeth clenched on his pipe.*) Historical trappings, bits of heritage. (*Pause.*) A chandelier, a little something from a cathedral, the odd garden statue. (*He draws the smoke in.*) A bit of stained glass.

BILLY. They weren't stolen, were they?

MAN. (*Casually.*) No, no, no.

BILLY. I don't buy anything that's stolen.

MAN. I don't *sell* anything that's stolen. (*They look at each other.*) They belong to me granny . . .

BILLY. Where did she get them from?

MAN. Her dog brought them in.

A look passes between them. They walk towards the van. The man opens the back doors, revealing all the items. Most noticeable is the garden statue which stands in front of the pile. It is a woman with an urn, or something of that kind, on her shoulder – about four feet high.

BILLY. How much?

MAN. Two hundred quid.

BILLY. I'll give you a hundred an fifty.

MAN. A hundred and fifty!! (*He looks at the statue.*) The urn she's carrying is worth more than that.

BILLY. A hundred and seventy.

MAN. You're looking at a bit of Renaissance there, mate. (*Casually.*) It has all the artistic ingredients of Donatello – fifteenth century – probably shipped from Rome.

BILLY. (*Firmly.*) A hundred and seventy-five.

MAN. (*Relenting.*) A hundred and seventy-five.

Billy gives him the money, counting it in tens first, then handing the whole lot to the man.

MAN. Done!

BILLY. Done. (*Pause.*) It's all I've got. Took me four months to make that. Still – when I sell the statue.

MAN. I er – I think I know someone who'd be interested.

BILLY. Oh yeah.

MAN. No. 144, Sefton Park Road – she's a customer of mine.

BILLY. Why didn't you sell it to her then?

MAN. Personal.

BILLY. (*Trying to be worldly, a lot of gestures and winking.*) Oh – right.

They set about lifting the statue.

Alderstone park

There are beds of flowers beautifully laid out, and a couple of Parks and Gardens workers weeding.

Joey's car pulls up nearby. Joey gets out and walks towards them slowly. As he does so he stops to admire a row of window boxes on the ground filled with flowers.

He takes out a black cigarette and a golden lighter, lights up, inhales and blows out smoke.

JOEY. (*To the men.*) Good morning.

FIRST MAN. Yeah.

JOEY. Nature's tapestry, wouldn't you say?

SECOND MAN. Oh yeah.

Sefton Park Road

Billy's van comes hurtling along – he is looking for No. 144. After a moment he draws up outside a large house. He gazes at it. There is a row of six statues along the front of the garden. The fifth one is noticeably missing.

The Boswells' kitchen

The family are settling themselves around the table.

MRS BOSWELL. Prayers.

AVELINE. Oh Mam, I'm starving.

MRS BOSWELL. (*Emphatically.*) We thank Thee, oh Lord . . .

They all put their hands together and close their eyes.

. . . for what we are about to receive, and we ask Thee, dear Father, to forgive those who put their bellies before their faith and those who do us harm and swindle us.

Billy opens his eyes suddenly, then closes them.

And those who read dirty books.

Jack shifts uncomfortably.

Amen.

JOEY. (*Raising his glass.*) To us.

ALL TOGETHER. To us.

They all drink, then they eat silently.

BILLY. (*Suddenly.*) I didn't know it was from someone's garden. (*Nobody speaks.*) He said it was Renaissance. What does Renaissance mean? (*Pause.*) Well, it is me first day.

MRS BOSWELL. (*Casually.*) Potatoes, Adrian?

ADRIAN. Thanks.

BILLY. I've no money left now.

Pause. Then Joey takes a ten pound note out of his pocket and puts it in front of Billy. Jack takes a five pound note out of his pocket and puts it in front of Billy. Adrian sighs, then takes a pound note and passes it to Joey who puts it in front of Billy. They all look at Aveline.

AVELINE. I'm broke – I had to have me legs waxed yesterday.

They all look at her. She eventually gets out fifty pence and puts it in front of Billy. They eat silently.

MRS BOSWELL. (*Casually.*) Has anybody fed the dog?

JOEY. Yes I have.

JACK. Yeah.

AVELINE. Me too.

ADRIAN. I didn't know he'd been fed.

BILLY. (*Looking at the money, then speaking in a fit of emotion.*) There are starving people in this world.

MRS BOSWELL. There are starving people in this street.

BILLY. (*Pointing at the dog.*) And he's been fed four times.

JOEY. That's because he's *our* dog.

JACK. It's called luck.

BILLY. All this talk about 'here's to us' – what's so special about us?

AVELINE. We pull together Billy. We all work and I model.

BILLY. All right – so we pull together. Who's on the other end of the rope?

They ignore Billy now.

MRS BOSWELL. The priest came today. He was looking for something for his flock. (*Pause.*) I gave him some tomatoes.

JOEY. Oh by the way, I enquired about an allowance for Grandad.

MRS BOSWELL. What for? He's getting three allowances already.

JOEY. Incontinence.

BILLY. But . . .

The family stare.

ADRIAN. But he's not incontinent.

BILLY. That's what I was going to say.

JOEY. But he might be – one day.

ADRIAN. (*Looking at Jack.*) The only incontinent thing in this house is the shower *he* brought in.

JACK. That is a de luxe shower – you'd pay over a hundred quid for that in the shops.

ADRIAN. But it doesn't turn on, and it doesn't turn off – it just drips.

AVELINE. It'll come on eventually.

ADRIAN. You say that about everything in this house – I hope they don't all come on together – we could all dissolve.

BILLY. (*Standing up.*) I asked a question! (*Silence. They all look at him. Then, quietly.*) Who's on the other end of the rope?

Pause.

JOEY. (*Eventually.*) *They* are, sunshine, *they* are.

MRS BOSWELL. It's a bad world out there Billy – you can't trust anyone. Here is where you're safe – in this house. You only go out there to beat them at their own game.

Billy thinks.

BILLY. That bastard said it was Renaissance.

JOEY. (*Casually.*) Well, after we've put it back tonight, Jack and I will give him a little call.

ADRIAN. You're not going to do anything violent, are you? I've got a respectable job to keep.

JACK. We're going to get our money back, that's all.

JOEY. Plus twenty quid for the safe return of the said 'antiquity'.

The phone rings.

MRS BOSWELL. Oh God it's yer grandad – he's smelt the caviar. Joey, it's your turn to take him his dinner. (*To Grandad.*) OK love, it's on it's way.

Outside the Boswells' house

The Boswells' house is bedecked with flower boxes – Grandad's house too – a colourful sight.
    The Boswells' door opens and Joey comes out with the tray. He has a napkin over his arm. He knocks at Grandad's door and after a moment it opens. Grandad snatches the tray and Joey bows and presents him with the napkin.

GRANDAD. Piss off.

He closes the door.

JOEY. (*To the door.*) No style. No style.

He strolls back home.

Grandad

Episode Two

Outside the Boswells' and Grandad's house (*lunch time*)

Grandad is sitting outside his house in an old wicker chair. Nailed on to the wall nearby is a small canary cage with a singing bird in it. Grandad is nodding off intermittently.

After a moment Jack comes rushing out of the Boswells' house. He slams the door. Grandad winces.

JACK. Hi Grandad – all right?

He goes to his van, opens the back door and brings out a small old music box. He goes back to Grandad with it.

I bought you something.

He hands the box to Grandad, who gazes at it.

Look.

Jack turns the key and it plays an old tune.

GRANDAD. I hate that song.

JACK. Don't play it then – just look at it.

GRANDAD. Is me dinner coming?

JACK. (*Gazing heavenwards.*) Mam's doing it now. See yer Grandad.

He gets into his van and drives away.

Billy comes out yawning, with one hand in his pocket. He carries a Police cone in the other. He places it in position outside No. 30, then slouches back towards the house.

BILLY. OK, Grandad?

GRANDAD AND BILLY TOGETHER. Where's me dinner?

Billy closes the door and Grandad looks at the music box. He turns it over, switches it on and switches it off again.

Just then Aveline comes out of the Boswells' house. She is wearing a short tight leather skirt, high-heeled boots, long earrings and a tight (not plunging) sweater.

AVELINE. Tarra Grandad. I'm going modelling.

Mrs Boswell appears at the door.

MRS BOSWELL. (*Shouting.*) Aveline!

Aveline stops.

MRS BOSWELL. You've forgotten your whistle.

Aveline sighs and goes and takes the whistle from her. It's on a cord.

AVELINE. Oh Mam, it's daylight. (*Putting it round her neck, she walks off muttering.*) It clashes with me beads.

> *Mrs Boswell goes inside. Grandad takes his music box and also goes inside.*
> *At this moment Joey's black Jaguar comes slowly, quietly, intriguingly up the road. Inside is the enigmatic Joey with his black clothes, his single gold earring, gold watch and black cigarette. He pulls up outside the house and gives a discreet beep on the car horn.*
> *Billy comes out yawning, picks up the Police cone and takes it indoors.*
> *Joey parks his car, gets out slowly and gracefully, and locks his car with an enormous bunch of keys. He strolls towards the house.*

JOEY. (*Calling into Grandad's house.*) All right there, Grandad?

> *He looks up at the cage and gives a few tweet tweet sounds. Standing on the step for a moment, he looks up and down the street rather like a lord surveying his property. Then he goes into the house.*

The Boswells' kitchen

Mrs Boswell is just putting the cutlery on Grandad's tray. His dinner is already on it and nearby there is a row of dinners on plates on the kitchen counter. They are all covered with clingfilm. Adrian is seated at the table. Joey enters.

MRS BOSWELL. Are you here to eat yer dinner or not?

JOEY. I'll eat it.

MRS BOSWELL. (*Indicating the row of dinners.*) It's there.

JOEY. (*Inspecting the row.*) Which one?

MRS BOSWELL. The one with no onions, no meat and two ton of cabbage.

> *She picks up Grandad's tray. Joey puts his plate into the microwave and siwtches on.*

JOEY. I'll take Grandad's.

MRS BOSWELL. Tell him not to wipe his nose on his serviette.

> *Joey takes the tray and goes out. Mrs Boswell continues to set a place for Joey.*
> *Billy comes into the room. He looks worn out as usual, and sits.*

MRS BOSWELL. Are you here to eat yer dinner or not?

BILLY. I'll eat it.

MRS BOSWELL. It's there.

BILLY. Which one?

MRS BOSWELL. The one with no gravy. Don't move, son, I'll do it.

She then puts his meal in the microwave, muttering.

I've ordered yer wheelchair.

Jack comes in through the back door.

What are you doing back?

JACK. I ran out of petrol.

MRS BOSWELL. Are you going to eat your dinner or not?

JACK. I might as well eat it now I'm here.

MRS BOSWELL. It's there.

JACK. Which one is it?

MRS BOSWELL. The biggest one, the one that looks like a high rise.

Jack goes to the sink to wash his hands. Joey comes in and sits at the table.

MRS BOSWELL. Is he all right, our grandad?

JOEY. (*Throwing Grandad's serviette on the table.*) Yeah he's fine but he says serviettes are for poofs. (*He begins to eat, then turns to Billy.*) So, my old son, how are things? I see you spent the night at Julie's again.

Billy starts to speak.

MRS BOSWELL. You'll have to talk to him Joey. He's overdoing it.

BILLY. What do you mean – I'm overdoing it?

MRS BOSWELL. I mean that whatever you're doing over there, it doesn't leave you with enough strength to do anything over here.

JOEY. Having a girlfriend is fine, Billy. It's good for the soul.

ADRIAN. It's not his soul we're worrying about.

JOEY. But don't put all your energies into one thing. Do you know what I mean? Save some for the ordinary everyday, nitty gritty, mundane, hour to hour existence.

BILLY. I don't understand women.

JOEY. You're not meant to understand them, son. They're put on this earth to baffle you.

BILLY. How d'you know? You and Jack never bother with girls.

JACK. Because we've done it all, that's how we know. When we were your age there wasn't a girl in this city, we hadn't clocked. We spent our entire lives in the horizontal position and we made an amazing discovery – a spectacular, scientific, biological fact. It makes you tired.

MRS BOSWELL. I don't mind you being normal, Billy. I don't mind you tasting the wine of life. It's now you're becoming an alcoholic I start worrying.

JOEY. (*In fatherly fashion.*) We need you to pull your weight, son. Prices are going up, things don't drop from the sky. (*Rubbing his fingers together.*) We need the pennies, sunshine.

BILLY. I want to get a proper job, like our Adrian.

MRS BOSWELL. Our Adrian's got brains, he's got a mathematical head.

JOEY. In this life Billy . . . you don't need A-levels, you don't need academia. Those days have gone. We live in a world of science, machinery, technology. All around us is buzz buzz, ding ding, tap tap and 'Next please'. Man is obsolete Billy, so he's had to get a new set of rules: 'Take what you can, when you can, how you can'. And that means you've got to go out there (*pointing outside*) with your wits and you grab the next fella by his wits and you shake him until his balls drop off.

Adrian winces.

JOEY. Put your potato down. I'm talking. Now we – we are lucky. We have got a family. And that's it Billy, that's our strength, because nobody out there cares a monkey's willy about us. The only people who care about us are us.

BILLY. What about the priest?

Mrs Boswell and Joey glance at each other.

MRS BOSWELL. He's in a different situation – he's God's messenger.

JACK. You know, when there's a war and no matter whose side you're on, if you're an ambulance they let you through. (*Billy looks at him.*) Well, he's like that.

JOEY. So, what I'm saying, our Billy, is: pleasure – yes; work – not if you can help it; but shake him until . . .

BILLY. . . . . his balls drop off – I know.

JOEY. Yes – definitely yes. (*He dips his fingers in his bowl.*) And you don't let go until you hear them clank to the ground.

ADRIAN. Oh God, must we have all this detail? Why don't you just drag someone in off the street and show us how it's done?

BILLY. The trouble is I'm no good at buying and selling things.

JOEY. You don't have to be good at buying and selling things. Yo\
to be good at selling things.

BILLY. I'm no good at getting things to sell.

JOEY. Oh (*tut tut tut*) Billy, you're a Boswell. You know the family mott\
'The best things in life are expensive.' (*Indicating across the road.*) So, less\
over there and more over here. OK?

The telephone rings – Mrs Boswell answers it.

MRS BOSWELL. Hello? (*She rises.*) What do you mean, Grandad? (*Pause.*) Are
you sure? (*She sighs.*) I've told you – haven't I told you? I'll come, yes, I'll
come round. (*She puts the phone down and looks at the other two.*) His
canary's gone – pinched.

Joey's face sets.

BILLY. I've told him about putting that bird cage in the street.

MRS BOSWELL. We've all told him. They'd pinch the pennies off a dead man's
eyes round here.

JACK. What did I say? I told you, didn't I? Everybody's getting guard dogs
round here – we'll have to get him a bloody big buzzard!

JOEY. (*With suppressed anger.*) So you see how it is, Billy. See how they are
out there. If they can't pinch your money or your food or your furniture . . .

ADRIAN. I hope you're not going to get over-emotional about this. My job is
hanging by a thread, hanging by a thread, with this lot.

MRS BOSWELL. Now Joey, I don't want any trouble – it's only a canary.

JOEY. It's not 'only a canary', it's our grandad's canary. (*He gets up and looks
at them.*) It's family.

Mrs Boswell and Joey leave.

Outside in the Boswells' street

*Grandad is standing on the kerbside waving his arms about and addressing the
entire world.*

GRANDAD. I'll kill them, I'll kill them all, the bastards. I'm not afraid, I've
fought in two world wars.

A cyclist passes – he calls out as he rides.

CYCLIST. Go on there, Grandad, give it to them son!

GRANDAD. I'll terminate the whole bloody lot of them.

CYCLIST. (*Ringing his bell and calling.*) Go to it there, lad!

Mrs Boswell and Joey come out of the house. Mrs Boswell goes to Grandad and ushers him towards the door of his own house. Joey is silently looking around for evidence.

MRS BOSWELL. (*To Grandad.*) Come on love, don't upset yerself.

Joey is looking on the wicker chair now.

GRANDAD. (*Waving his arms about.*) I fought for that lot out there, I fought for them.

MRS BOSWELL. Of course you did love. Don't you worry – we'll get you another canary.

GRANDAD. (*As she pushes him inside.*) I don't want another canary – I want *that* canary.

Joey has picked something up from the wicker chair. It is a gold earring, quite large, in the shape of a cross. Joey tosses it slightly into the air, then pockets it. He walks towards his car, whistling softly.

A street

Billy is slouching along with some papers in his hand. He stops by a lamp post and sellotapes one of the notices to it. It reads:

'LOST'
'Stolen from Hope Street, yellow canary
in cage. Reward. Ring 708 0298.'

Billy trudges on with the other notices.

Outside the DHSS building

Joey is putting a notice up by the entrance. He steps back and looks at it, smiles, then walks into the building. The notice reads:

'FOUND – Gold earring, shape of a cross.
Ring 708 0298
ask for Joey.'

The late Mrs Conlan's parlour ·

The parlour is stacked with bits of Victoriana. Mrs Conlan's sister May is having tea with a neighbour.

NEIGHBOUR. Lovely woman your Cissy, God rest her soul.

MAY. Called suddenly.

NEIGHBOUR. Yeah – but it's the best way.

MAY. She was wearing an old nightie – she wouldn't like that.

NEIGHBOUR. (*Pointing upwards.*) He doesn't mind.

MAY. Funny thing the heart. Like a rubber ball, you never know when it's going to stop bouncing.

NEIGHBOUR. She looked blue, you know. I told our Nellie that.

MAY. Sitting up, she was, her purse open in front of her.

NEIGHBOUR. Checking her pension.

MAY. Always checking her pension. (*Pause.*) She'd got her teeth in.

NEIGHBOUR. Oh thank God.

MAY. She wouldn't have gone without her teeth.

There is a knock at the door.

NEIGHBOUR. I'll go, love.

She pats May on the shoulder and goes to the door. We hear Jack's voice.

JACK. (*Putting on the charm.*) How d'you do? I'm Jack Boswell. I believe you have some things to sell.

NEIGHBOUR. Oh yeah – come in will you. (*Calling to May.*) It's the furniture man, May.

JACK. After you, my sweetheart.

They come back into the room. Whilst talking Jack is taking stock of the contents.

NEIGHBOUR. This is the bereaved sister.

JACK. (*He shakes her hand and bows a little.*) How do you do?

MAY. (*Holding back the tears.*) I – I haven't room for her stuff you see.

JACK. Don't upset yourself my love. Let friendly Jack take all the strain. I'll just have a look round, all right?

The two women sit down again and Jack looks around the room.

MAY. (*To neighbour.*) I don't know what she did with her money, you know. There was no Post Office, no bank, not even a pig.

Jack purposely kicks a table. A vase falls off which Jack catches.

NEIGHBOUR. Is that so?

MAY. No will – she left no will.

NEIGHBOUR. She should have done, you know. She should have left a will – save everybody fighting.

MAY. She had her old age pension, her Cammell Laird's pension, a supplement – and she had no electricity to pay because Screwdriver Liz used to come and fix the meter for her.

NEIGHBOUR. Lovely woman, Liz – robs the rich to heat the poor.

The neighbour addresses Jack now.

NEIGHBOUR. She was a beautiful woman was Cissy.

MAY. Called suddenly.

JACK. Better be called suddenly, love, than to sit there with Him waggling his finger at you. (*He looks round.*) Now then, what have we here?

He walks around and weighs up various items, including a still life picture of a brace of pheasants and a dead rabbit.

JACK. Not bad, not bad.

MAY. (*To neighbour.*) She loved that picture. Reminded her of her husband.

JACK. Hmm, I'll tell you what, I'll take the picture and the small table. (*He picks up a teapot.*) And I'll give you a fiver for this.

MAY. But that's our teapot!

JACK. It was a joke – to take your mind off things!

MAY. What about the bookcase?

JACK. (*Shaking his head.*) No, love, I'm sorry – it's rubbish you see. (*Hits it.*) I have to sell these things again. (*Then, quietly.*) Right. So how about fifteen for the picture, ten for the table and a fiver for this (*indicating the ornament*) – that's thirty quid (*Pause*) in the hand.

The two ladies look at each other.

JACK. I'll tell you what – I feel a favour coming on. I'll relieve you of the bookcase. Another tenner – that's forty quid.

They look at each other again. Jack takes May's hand, and begins to count the money into it. She looks at the money and looks at him.

JACK. And not a word to the Social Security! (*Jack goes to the bookcase and finds he can't lift it.*) You couldn't . . .

The ladies look.

The street outside Mrs Conlan's house

Jack is loading the things into his van. He closes the doors, gets in and drives away very fast.

He screeches round the corner, pulls up and gets out of the van. Then he goes to the back, opens the doors, gets in and closes the doors.

He takes one of the books from the bookcase and shakes it. Nothing. He takes another, shakes it and a five pound note drops out. He takes the books one by one and a note falls out of approximately every other one. Jubilantly he counts the money.

JACK. (*Counting money.*) Ten, twenty, twenty-one, twenty-two, twenty-seven, thirty-two, forty-two. (*To himself.*) It never fails. (*Looking upwards.*) God bless you, darling.

He pockets the money and gets out of the van.

Inside the DHSS building

There are several people there. Joey is sitting opposite a service window quietly watching the girl behind it as she writes.

After a moment of this she suddenly shouts.

DHSS GIRL. Next!

She looks up and sees Joey.

GIRL. Oh you're there.

JOEY. I want to make a claim.

GIRL. What for?

JOEY. My grandad had his canary pinched this morning from outside his house.

GIRL. We're not responsible for canaries. Canaries are not regarded as an essential part of life.

JOEY. *And* . . .

GIRL. We're here to . . .

JOEY. *And.* (*Pause. Quietly.*) His suit was hanging on the cage.

GIRL. Why?

JOEY. He was airing it.

GIRL. Why was he airing it on the bird cage?

JOEY. Because there's only one nail in the wall.

GIRL. Why couldn't he air it in the house?

JOEY. Because that's where it got damp in the first place.

GIRL. He'll have to come and make his own claim. Next! (*She starts writing, then looks up.*)

JOEY. (*Moving his chair in.*) He can't.

GIRL. Why?

JOEY. He hasn't got a suit to wear.

GIRL. So what does he do when his suit's at the cleaner's?

JOEY. He stays in bed.

She looks through some papers.

GIRL. You're already claiming for his incontinence.

JOEY. We are – yes – very unfortunate.

GIRL. That money is to cover the cost of laundering expenses. If he's only got one suit there can't be many laundering expenses, can there?

JOEY. I've already told you – because he's only got one suit he stays in bed a lot. It's the bed we have to launder.

She looks at him for a long time – she's heard it all before. She picks up a form and pushes it towards him.

GIRL. Fill this in.

JOEY. Thanks. (*Pause.*) Oh, by the way . . . (*He feels in his pocket, brings out a little gold earring and holds it up.*) You haven't seen anybody wearing one of these, have you?

She looks at it.

GIRL. It's gold!

JOEY. (*Tut-tutting.*) Well, it wouldn't be anyone coming in here then, would it?

He gets out his gold pen and, with a deliberate gesture, fills in his form.

GIRL. It's only a form, Mr Boswell, not the Magna Carta.

The living room at Julie's parents' house (*that night*)

Julie and Billy are kissing on the settee. Billy breaks off suddenly.

BILLY. I gorra go, Julie. I've gorra get an early night.

JULIE. You don't have to go to have an early night – we can have an early night here.

BILLY. I *mean* an early night. You know (*pause*), a night that's (*pause*), early.

JULIE. (*Thwarted.*) If you're talking about sex we won't have sex. I don't have to have sex, I only have it because I think you want it. See if I care about sex.

BILLY. I've got to start pulling my weight, our Joey said.

JULIE. I can get sex anywhere. (*She stands and moves to the mirror.*)

BILLY. I'm the only one in the family who's living on Social Security alone. All the others earn money as well.

JULIE. In fact I looked in the mirror this morning and I thought, 'Who's that lovely person I can see in the mirror, with the face and the hair and the body?' 'I wish I was as lovely as that,' I thought. And then I looked again and I thought, 'Oh it's me – aren't I lucky!'

Billy sighs.

JULIE. (*Walking round sofa.*) When a girl is in love with someone, Billy, she doesn't look at other fellas. She brings down a barrier between her and the rest of the randy army. And they know it's there so they don't bother.

BILLY. I don't know why you're telling me all this – all I said was I wanted an early night.

JULIE. But I'm going to lift that barrier Billy – I'm going to send out little 'come and get me' vibes. And when all the fairy princes are on their knees pleading for me hand and kissing me flip-flops, I'll wave them all aside (*she sits*) and I'll point to one, the one with the handsomest face and the whitest horse and the gold American Express card and I'll . . .

BILLY. (*Rising and moving to Julie, then suddenly.*) I'm going to buy you a ring.

She stops, open-mouthed.

JULIE. What kind of a ring?

BILLY. A round one.

JULIE. (*Agitated.*) A friendship ring? A 'be mine for ever' ring? A 'will you marry me' ring? Or a 'put the bolt back on your barrier, I haven't finished with you yet' ring?

A long pause.

BILLY. (*Quietly.*) Just a ring.

JULIE. (*Elated.*) An engagement ring!

BILLY. (*Sitting on a chair.*) No – just a ring.

JULIE. (*Rising.*) Well, it's got to have a meaning. I can't go round telling all me friends 'Billy's bought me a ring but we haven't decided what it's for yet', can I?

BILLY. (*Tenderly.*) Please yourself.

JULIE. Where're you getting the money from?

BILLY. Grandad gave me a musical box – I sold it for thirty quid.

JULIE. Why did he give you a musical box?

BILLY. He didn't like the tune.

JULIE. It frightens me when I think of your grandad.

Julie sits on the sofa.

BILLY. Why?

JULIE. I could end up like that. When you and I have been married for hundreds of years and our kids have got kids and you're dead and I'm left with my arthritis and my supplementary benefit they'll put me outside the house in a wicker chair with my cellular blanket, pointing south, and they'll put a big hat on me to keep the pigeons off . . . (*Pause.*) We must get away from this street Billy – this city.

BILLY. I don't see the point. If I'm going to die – you'll be all alone in a strange street. (*Billy goes back to the sofa.*) We will one day when my ship comes in.

JULIE. Ships don't come here any more, Billy.

Outside the Boswells' house (lunchtime, next day)

Billy comes out of the Boswells' house carrying a tray with Grandad's lunch on it. He knocks on Grandad's door and waits.
    Grandad opens the door, grabs the tray and closes the door again.
    Billy knocks again.

BILLY. Grandad!

He knocks again. The door opens and Grandad looks at him.

BILLY. I bought a ring. (*He opens a little box and shows Grandad the ring.*) Isn't it great?

> Grandad stares at it for a moment, and his face freezes. He looks at Billy, horror-stricken. Then he closes the door fearfully.
> We hear all kinds of bolts and locks being shot from the inside.
> Billy gazes at the door for a moment, shrugs his shoulders, puts the ring back in his pocket and goes back into his own house.

The Boswells' kitchen

The entire family are about to have lunch. Mrs Boswell, Adrian, Jack and Aveline are sitting round the table. Joey is pouring the wine, and the table is laden as usual, a picture of plenty. In the centre is a huge dish with a cockerel for its lid. In front of each member of the family is a plate covered with a lid.
Billy comes in.

MRS BOSWELL. Just in time for prayers, our Billy. Sit down. (*He does so.*) Has anyone got anything to be especially thankful for?

ADRIAN. I might get a rise actually.

AVELINE. 'Actually' – why does he have to say 'actually'? Big poof!

MRS BOSWELL. He's got brains. People who've got brains say 'actually'.

AVELINE. We've all got brains.

MRS BOSWELL. He *uses* his.

AVELINE. What do you think I use when I go out every day trying to get work?

> *Jack starts to speak.*

And don't say it's my body. The moment I was born I was warned about my body in this family. I'm so aware of the perils of my body that if somebody at the studio asks me to take my coat off, I blow my whistle.

MRS BOSWELL. We're looking after you, that's all. How much did you get?

AVELINE. Twenty quid and the promise of a glossy magazine.

JACK. I've done well. I've had to pit my wits against these two sharp customers but I outwitted them.

JOEY. I put a claim in at the Social Security for Grandad's suit.

> *They all look at him.*

The one that was hanging on the bird cage when it was stolen.

ADRIAN. (*Interrupting*.) But there wasn't a suit hanging on the bird cage when it was stolen.

JOEY. I know but there might be one day. Might as well claim while we're claiming for the cage. Saves paperwork.

MRS BOSWELL. I must get on to the insurance about that suit.

Adrian stares at her.

ADRIAN. You'll all end up in court one day.

AVELINE. Well at least Grandad will have a suit to wear. Oh, I've lost one of me false nails.

ADRIAN. Oh God, search the salad.

Mrs Boswell takes the lid off the huge cockerel and looks at them all.

JOEY. It came my way.

> *Joey puts in fifteen pounds.*
> *Jack puts a five pound note in. They all stare at him. He puts another fiver in.*
> *Mrs Boswell looks at Adrian. He puts a one pound coin in.*

ADRIAN. I haven't got my rise yet actually.

AVELINE. (*Putting two one-pound coins in.*) I need new glitter tights, and I'm a nail short. (*She looks at Adrian.*)

JACK. That's not fair – I need all sorts.

MRS BOSWELL. Tools of the trade, Jack, tools of the trade. (*She puts the lid back on the pot.*) And now we'll pray.

BILLY. (*Suddenly.*) I've got something.

> *They all look at him. He brings out of his pocket a £5 note, takes the lid off the pot and drops it in.*

BILLY. Grandad gave me a music box.

JACK. A music box! I gave him that.

BILLY. He didn't like the tune. I sold it for thirty quid.

JACK. Thirty quid!

JOEY. (*To Jack.*) You'll have to take another look at the *Antique Year Book*, sunshine, won't you? (*To Billy.*) Well done, son.

BILLY. (*Proudly.*) I bought a ring with the rest . . . (*Pause*) for Julie.

They all glance at each other anxiously.

MRS BOSWELL. A ring.

AVELINE. Oh, isn't he dead romantic?

MRS BOSWELL. What kind of a ring?

BILLY. Why does everybody ask what kind of a ring?

MRS BOSWELL. It's not an engagement ring, is it?

BILLY. No, just a ring.

JOEY. (*Brightly.*) And why not? We've all bought rings for people, haven't we?

JACK. (*Muttering.*) And we've all had them thrown back at us. I've still got the mark.

Billy gets the little box out and opens it. He hands it to Mrs Boswell who gazes at it horror-stricken. She closes the box and hands it to Joey. He opens it, looks very grave and closes it again.

MRS BOSWELL. Dear God – it's an opal.

They all cringe except Billy, who is open-mouthed. Joey gets up. He raises his hands to the rest of the family as if to calm them.

JOEY. It's OK, it's OK.

Joey goes out of the room with the ring. Billy gazes at them all.

BILLY. What's wrong?

JACK. It's an opal, soft-head!

BILLY. I know it is.

MRS BOSWELL. Never bring an opal to this house, Billy – never.

AVELINE. No wonder I'm having all these disasters this morning with my shoulder blades.

BILLY. What disasters?

AVELINE. The photographer said they didn't match, and I'm a model, aren't I? Everything has to be a pair.

BILLY. How can it be the opal? I only got it today.

AVELINE. My shoulder blades were all right yesterday, weren't they?

Joey returns and sits down.

JOEY. It's OK, it's in the yard.

MRS BOSWELL. What about the dog?

JOEY. He's in with Grandad. (*He turns to Billy.*) Now then, the thing is, sunshine, the opal is bad news.

BILLY. Why?

JOEY. Why, he says! If we knew the answer to that we'd be able to buy opals, eliminate our rivals and take over the world, wouldn't we? The fact is that for some – and especially us – the opal is bad, really bad, Billy. OK?

ADRIAN. I don't believe all that hysterical rubbish.

BILLY. (*Bravely.*) Neither do I.

JOEY. (*Looking straight at Adrian.*) It's in the yard. You can have it if you want it.

ADRIAN. I don't suit rings, do I?

BILLY. No, he doesn't. Can't we sell it?

JACK. I'm not carrying it to the gold depot, my van's already looking for an excuse to disintegrate.

BILLY. Ask the priest to buy it, he's always saying he fears no evil.

MRS BOSWELL. But he does fear dry rot in his church, Billy.

JOEY. (*Enigmatically.*) I've got a better plan. (*He takes twenty-five pounds out of his wallet.*) Here – buy another ring.

BILLY. It was only twenty.

They all look at each other and each one says to the other and in general they all say:

ALL. Very good, oh very good.

ADRIAN. Oh yeah, honesty's very good.

JOEY. You're learning, son. Honesty at home, save all the skulduggery for the bastards outside. (*He adjusts the money.*)

The telephone rings. Mrs Boswell answers it.

MRS BOSWELL. All right, Grandad? Oh it's for you Joey.

Joey takes the phone.

JOEY. Hello, yes. (*Pause.*) Yes, that's it, yes. Oh, I found it in the park. Yeah, yeah, it is gold – a cross, yes. (*Pause.*) Look I've got to go somewhere tonight, I'll drop it off if you like – 19 Phythian Street about seven. OK. Ciao.

He puts the phone down, sits at the table, smiles and looks at the others.

JOEY. Let us pray, shall we?

They put their hands together.

MRS BOSWELL. We thank Thee, oh God, for what we are about to receive, for bringing our Billy safely home from the jeweller's.

BILLY. (*Opening his eyes.*) I got it from the pawn shop.

They all ignore him. He closes his eyes again – she continues.

MRS BOSWELL. We ask Thee, oh Lord, to look down on us with thy favour and deliver us from the opal. Amen.

Outside No. 19, Phythian Street

Jack's van arrives. It comes unusually slowly and quietly, pulling up outside No. 19.
    Then Joey's black car arrives, slowly, quietly.
    The door of the van opens. Jack, Billy and Aveline get out. They stand in a group staring at the door of No. 19.
    Joey's car door opens. Joey and Adrian get out. Adrian is carrying a briefcase and he's rather nervous.
    The group walk forward in Mafia fashion towards the steps of No. 19.
    We see their feet as they walk – Joey's shiny black shoes with embellishments, Billy's pumps, Jack's Kickers, Adrian's lace-ups and Aveline's high heels and black stockings with bright red ankle socks over them.
    Joey knocks. Silence.
    The door opens. A young man of about 24, dressed in leather and black studded belt, opens the door. He tries to look tough and eyes the family up.

YOUNG MAN. (*Calling.*) Benny!

Benny, another young man, of equal pseudo-toughness, appears. The family and the duo stare at each other.

JOEY. (*Charmingly.*) Good evening.

He holds his hand out to Adrian who opens his briefcase and brings out a little box. Joey hands it to Benny.

Yours, I believe.

Benny takes it with caution, opens the box and holds up the earring.

BENNY. Thanks.

JOEY. (*Charmingly again.*) I – er – found it in Hope Street, not the park. How silly of me to mislead you that way.

BENNY. Would you like a drink?

A canary tweets in the background. Benny gives an awkward little laugh.

JOEY. (*Through his teeth in suppressed fury.*) Fetch it!

BENNY. Fetch what?

JOEY. Fetch it, I said.

The two young men clench their fists.

BENNY. What do you think I am – a bloody dog?

The whole family take a menacing step forward.
The two young men back down.
Benny turns to his mate and gestures for him to go and get the canary.
Joey relaxes.

JOEY. (*Looking around casually.*) Animal lover?

BENNY. Yeah. (*Pause.*) I saw this fella so I chased him, you know.

Joey nods. The whole family nod, not believing him.
The other young man comes back now, holding the cage. He hands it to
Joey who briefly inspects it, then hands it to Billy.

JOEY. It says on my notice: 'Reward'.

BENNY. (*Closing the door, glad to be getting away.*) It's OK. I don't want
nothing.

JOEY. (*Putting his foot against the door.*) I am an honourable man. When I
say reward I mean reward.

He holds his hand out to Adrian who gets the little ring box out of his
briefcase. He hands it to Joey who hands it to Benny, who takes it somewhat
dubiously. He opens it, looks pleased, picks up the ring, inspects it and shows
it to his mate.

JOEY. You know how it is, who's got money. We do what we can.

BENNY. Yeah – thanks.

Benny and his mate shuffle away and close the door.

JOEY. (*To Billy.*) Take the bird back to Grandad.

They silently go back to their van and their car and drive away.

The dogs' home

Joey walks along the row of cages quietly, with his head high, saying nothing,
just looking at the the dogs.
The warden joins him.

WARDEN. Afternoon, Mr Boswell.

He walks behind Joey until they come to a cage with a little mongrel in it.
  Joey just stops and looks.

WARDEN. It's his last day, I'm afraid.

  Joey slowly takes out his wallet, gives the man two ten-pound notes and puts the wallet away again.

WARDEN. Thank you Mr Boswell, thank you. I'll see to it Mr Boswell. Thank you. (*Then, to the dog.*) You're all right, son.

  The warden hurries away and Joey walks out of the dogs' home to his waiting car.
  He switches on the engine, switches on the radio and there is music playing as Joey pulls away.
  Now we hear an announcer on the radio.

ANNOUNCER. We interrupt this music to bring you a newsflash. There has been a gas explosion on Phythian Street. The area is cordoned off. . . So those of you travelling in the city centre please look out for the diversion. There are no casualties. . . The explosion happened only a few minutes ago. Apparently it was totally unexpected. There had been no reports of a gas smell and residents of No. 19 found themselves suddenly sitting in the open air as their bay window simply disappeared. Said a spokesman for the Gas Board. . .

  Joey reaches over and switches radio off.

JOEY. (*Smiling to himself.*) Oh dearie, dearie me!

In the kitchen

Episode Three

The Boswells' kitchen (*morning*)

Mrs Boswell is getting Grandad's breakfast tray ready and at the same time attending to an enormous toaster which does about six rounds at a time. Adrian is sitting at the breakfast table. He is reading the paper. The table is laden as usual, and on a tray with a cloth there are about eight different jars of jam.

MRS BOSWELL. I don't know why you read the papers, Adrian – there's enough to worry about. (*The toaster pops, she clutches her chest.*) Oh dear God, it's got a savage streak this toaster.

ADRIAN. I read the papers because I like to know what's going on, that's all.

MRS BOSWELL. I can tell you what's going on: killing, robbing, bombing, starving – and some bloody fool trying to cross the Atlantic on a dinner mat.

Billy comes into the room – he is wearing a pair of striped pyjama bottoms and a plain yellow top.

ADRIAN. Oh – here he comes – the resident wasp.

Mrs Boswell is making orange juice with the orange squeezer.

MRS BOSWELL. Billy, why don't you put the right pyjama legs with the right top?

Jack wanders in – he has the plain yellow bottoms and striped top. She looks – Billy starts to speak.

Oh don't bother, son.

Jack sits down and inspects the jars on the tray.

JACK. Any loganberry conserve?

MRS BOSWELL. (*Sarcastically.*) No, but we'll have some flown in.

JACK. (*Stretching.*) Oh God.

MRS BOSWELL. Well, let's hope God's not trying to have a lie-in.

JACK. Another day.

MRS BOSWELL. It's no good moaning to him about another day – you should be thanking him. Lots of people are waking up to their last day. (*A dog barks in the hall.*) There's the post.

Aveline comes in – she is wearing a tight T-shirt and jeans. She has little glitter stars on her cheeks.

AVELINE. Morning, Mam. (*She sits down.*) I'll have my diet drink – pineapple flavour 'cos I'm modelling.

Mrs Boswell begins to prepare this – it is in a packet. She puts the contents into a cup and adds water.

JACK. (*To Aveline.*) Do you go to bed with that stuff on your face?

AVELINE. None of your business.

BILLY. She goes through the car wash once a week.

AVELINE. At least it would solve the bathroom problem in this house.

JACK. I haven't been able to get in the bathroom for two weeks.

BILLY. You can't do anything if you do get in – it's like an intensive care unit for tights and bras.

MRS BOSWELL. Will somebody get the post?

ADRIAN. (*Looking up from his paper.*) Any Earl Grey tea on?

MRS BOSWELL. I've got one pair of hands, that's all, and I'm doing Aveline's diet drink with one and getting your Grandad's tray with the other.

Joey comes in – he has been out all night. He is carrying the post.

JOEY. Greetings.

He throws three envelopes on to the table.

MRS BOSWELL. Joey – here – sit down – you must be worn out. Did you have a good night?

JOEY. Not bad, not bad.

He takes his wallet out, takes five ten-pound notes out, holds them up for all to see, then lifts the cockerel dish lid and drops them in.
Joey takes his coat off.

ADRIAN. Fifty pounds! I have to work half a week for that.

JOEY. That's the difference between working for others and working for yourself.

He sits down.

BILLY. What did you do to get that much?

MRS BOSWELL. (*Smacking Billy across the head.*) I've told you – we don't talk about *work*. You just put the money in the pot and shut your gob.

Mrs Boswell sits down.

AVELINE. You all talk about my work.

MRS BOSWELL. You're a girl – it's different – we have to know what you're going to do so we can stop you doing it.

AVELINE. Mr Julian said I'll be a famous model one day.

JACK. He's been saying that for years – you'll be modelling surgical stockings soon.

MRS BOSWELL. (*To Billy, handing him a bill.*) Pass the phone bill round.

Billy looks at it.

BILLY. Who do I phone?

He passes it to Adrian.

ADRIAN. (*Looking at it.*) I use the office phone.

He passes it to Aveline.

AVELINE. It's not me – I never use the phone.

She passes it to Jack.

JACK. (*Looking at it.*) It's not me either.

He passes it to Joey, who passes it to Mrs Boswell.

MRS BOSWELL. (*To Joey.*) You'd better get on to the Telecom people, Joey. Tell them to take the phone away – nobody uses it.

ADRIAN. *It!* We've got *four* phones – the rents must be fifteen pounds each. No wonder . . .

JOEY. We've got *one* phone Adrian. The other three are personal connections brought about by the fact that Jack has a lot of friends in British Telecom – and I'm very good with wires. OK?

MRS BOSWELL. (*About the letter.*) It's the insurance form for our Grandad's suit.

ADRIAN. What suit?

JACK. The one that was hanging on the bird cage when it was stolen.

ADRIAN. But he claimed for a suit a month ago when his armchair caught fire.

JOEY. (*Looking straight at Adrian.*) He's very careless – our Grandad.

ADRIAN. I don't approve – I want you to know that – it's cheating.

JACK. Of course you don't approve. You've got a job, that's why. All you've got to do is go (*he rubs his fingers together*) here pussy cat, here pussy cat – and your wage packet comes leaping into your hand. Our pussy cat keeps leaving home.

ADRIAN. You claim for Grandad's incontinence – he went all the way to

Edinburgh for the bowls trip and they didn't have to stop the coach once –
he's as tough as a camel's hump.

JOEY. And do you know why? Because we look after him. Instead of letting
him become knackered and then claiming for him, we claim for him first and
use the money to stop him becoming knackered.

ADRIAN. It's dishonest. Still, you all go running to confession I suppose:
'Forgive me Father for I have sinned. Apart from collecting Social Security
for Grandad's mythical incontinence, and claiming money for the
maintenance of a guard dog that never comes home and pees himself if he
meets you in the hall with a new hat on, I've claimed from the insurance for
a suit that wasn't on the chair when it caught fire, and the same suit which
wasn't hanging on the bird cage when it was stolen.'

MRS BOSWELL. (*Putting final letter down.*) It's time for prayers.

AVELINE. Oh shurrup Adrian. I can't stand all this purity first thing in the
morning, I'd rather pray.

ADRIAN. (*To Aveline.*) I'd like to know what you get up to down at the
photographic studio as well. I mean nobody actually *knows*, do they? You
walk in and out of here with your short skirts and inadequate knickers.

AVELINE. I'm a model, aren't I? So, what I'm doing is modelling.

BILLY. Her voice gets on my nerves. (*He mimics her.*) 'I'm modelling'.

JACK. I'm going back to bed.

He stands up.

JOEY. Nobody's going back to bed.

Jack sits down again. Pause.

Right, Mam.

Mrs Boswell clasps her hands and closes her eyes. They all do the same.

MRS BOSWELL. We thank Thee, oh Lord, for the food on this table, and for
the unity of this family.

*Billy opens his eyes and looks quickly around. He is met by Mrs Boswell's
eyes. He closes his again.*

We ask thee to bless our minds so that they might be strong enough to
outwit our enemies, and sharp enough to keep an eye on our friends. God
bless us and ours. (*Pause.*) Including our dad.

They all open their eyes and stare at her.

Amen.

AVELINE. (*Eventually.*) I thought we weren't supposed to mention our dad. 'Don't ever mention his name in this house,' you said.

MRS BOSWELL. (*Indicating the third letter.*) He's coming to see us.

ADRIAN. Oh – well – that's very considerate of him. It's only been three years.

JACK. Has his fancy woman left him then?

BILLY. I'll stay at Julie's when he comes.

JACK. I'll move in with Grandad.

AVELINE. I'll have to stay here. Grandad hasn't got a full-length mirror.

JOEY. We'll *all* stay here.

JACK. He left us – walked out – not a word to our mam – and all for some blonde with a runaway chest.

AVELINE. He's right – and another thing . . .

JOEY. We'll all be here when he comes. (*Pause.*) He's Family.

Outside in the street

A bit further along from the Boswells' house, a small, dapper man, with a modern cap and a sailor's walk, comes along the road. He is pushing a Corporation cleaning cart. There is a radio attached to the cart, it is playing pop music, and the man is whistling to it.

An old man stands in a doorway lighting a pipe.

MAN. Hello Freddie. All right there, mate?

FREDDIE. Blue as the sky, George – blue as the sky.

He moves on. A lady putting milk bottles out stops, looks at him.

LADY. Freddie, is it? Freddie Boswell?

FREDDIE. It is Mary, it is.

LADY. How are you love?

FREDDIE. Green as a tree Mary, green as a tree.

LADY. Come back to us, have you?

FREDDIE. On me white horse, on me white horse.

LADY. Still the devil Freddie Boswell.

She goes into her house. Freddie walks on and comes to the Boswells' house.

He stands outside weighing it up, whistling. Then he switches off the radio, puts the cart amongst the Boswell cars and knocks at the door.

After a moment the door opens, Joey is there. The two men are silent. Then Joey stretches his hand out.

JOEY. Dad.

They shake hands, Joey indicates that Freddie should go inside, which he does. Joey looks around the street in his usual way, sees the dustcart, raises his eyes to heaven and closes the door.

The Boswells' kitchen

The family are still sitting round the breakfast table. Joey and Freddie enter. there is a stony silence for a moment.

FREDDIE. I was in the area.

Mrs Boswell and Freddie Boswell exchange a long look.

JOEY. Cup of tea, Dad?

FREDDIE. Ta. So what have you all been up to then?

He looks at Adrian.

ADRIAN. I'm in property investment.

Freddie looks at Aveline.

AVELINE. I'm a model – I do modelling.

JACK. I dabble in antiques, and things.

BILLY. I – I – haven't thought yet.

FREDDIE. (*Looking at Joey.*) Joey?

JOEY. Oh – this and that.

FREDDIE. All yellow as the sun eh! Yellow as the sun.

MRS BOSWELL. You haven't changed have you Freddie Boswell – the talking colour chart.

JOEY. (*To ease the tension.*) What about you?

FREDDIE. I've got a job, I'm an environmental hygiene officer with the corp., I've got a flat – a high rise. On a clear day I can see British Airways. (*He looks around.*) It looks nice – well-equipped.

BILLY. Mam does the house.

JACK. Like she always did.

FREDDIE. Got all the gear.

MRS BOSWELL. We stuck together.

JACK. We had to really, didn't we?

FREDDIE. (*To Mrs Boswell, with affection.*) These mams and their lads.

MRS BOSWELL. Pity it isn't these dads and their lads.

FREDDIE. (*Looking at Mrs Boswell.*) Always got a cob on. (*To the others.*) Remember breakfast, in the old days. I'd be slaving my guts out, burning the toast, spilling the cornflakes, and in she'd come . . . (*Pause.*) Rambo in a frock.

> *They all laugh, but they are stopped in their tracks by a glare from Mrs Boswell.*

MRS BOSWELL. (*To Freddie*) We run a business in this house – a survival business. Everyone pulls their weight – we don't want any weak links in the chain.

FREDDIE. Just passing through that's all. Just taking a look at me family – seeing what colour they are.

> *He puts his hand in his pocket, takes out a fifty pence piece, takes the lid off the cockerel dish, drops the fifty pence in and puts the lid back.*

Tarra.

> *He goes to leave.*

ADRIAN/AVELINE. Tarra.

BILLY. (*In a sudden burst.*) Where do you live Dad?

> *The family look at Billy.*

FREDDIE. Ask a pigeon son, ask a pigeon.

> *He walks out.*

MRS BOSWELL. (*To Joey.*) Grandad's tray is ready Joey. Take it out, will you.

> *Joey picks up the prepared tray and goes out.*
> *Mrs Boswell looks around the table, she can see that the family didn't really want their father to go*

MRS BOSWELL. You'll be late for work, our Adrian.

ADRIAN. Oh – oh yes.

> *They all start to eat. Silence.*

Outside in the street

Mr Boswell is just starting off with his cart. He pushes it along jauntily, whistling as he goes.

Joey is standing watching him rather sadly with the tray in his hand. Grandad's door opens and Grandad comes out. He is in his pyjamas.

GRANDAD. What's up? Staff shortage!

He grabs the tray and goes back into his house, closing the door.
Joey keeps watching his father.

At church, in the confessional box (*later the same day*)

The priest, Father Dooley, is sitting in his section of the box. He is just unwrapping a sweet and puts it into his mouth when he hears someone come into the adjoining section. He doesn't panic – he just chews for a moment.

MRS BOSWELL. Are you there, Father?

FATHER DOOLEY. (*Swallowing.*) I'm sorry, my child, I was just indulging in the sins of the stomach.

MRS BOSWELL. I'll give you time to swallow it, Father.

Pause.

FATHER DOOLEY. Thank you, my child. Speak now.

MRS BOSWELL. I am a good person, Father.

FATHER DOOLEY. Indeed, indeed.

MRS BOSWELL. I've steered my lads and my girl through all the hazards of life's motorway – and I've cried Father – (*with emphasis*) I – have – cried.

FATHER DOOLEY. Ah! A heart full of love is a heart full of tears.

MRS BOSWELL. My husband left me, as you know Father, three years ago.

FATHER DOOLEY. May he be forgiven for his sins.

MRS BOSWELL. He left me for . . . (*Pause.*) I am a good person, Father, with good thoughts – I speak as I find. (*Pause.*) A tart.

FATHER DOOLEY. Oh foolish sheep.

MRS BOSWELL. Now – he's back.

FATHER DOOLEY. (*Praying, with closed eyes*) Dear Father, we thank Thee for the safe return of thy foolish sheep to the fold.

MRS BOSWELL. I don't want him back.

FATHER DOOLEY. And we ask Thee to forgive and to guide him . . .

MRS BOSWELL. As far away from our house as possible.

FATHER DOOLEY. As far away from (*pause*) sin – as possible.

MRS BOSWELL. When he went, Father, my lads and me was like a maypole that had toppled over – nothing for us to hold on to – ribbons in the wind. Now we're strong again, we're a team. We ask no favours, we harvest what the good Lord provides and we read the small print on the Social Security forms.

FATHER DOOLEY. The family unit – a blessed, most desirable thing.

MRS BOSWELL. I feel like someone who has spent years knitting a life, Father, and now he comes along and sits there, unravelling it.

FATHER DOOLEY. Sometimes in life my child we are crippled with disappointment and made weak with anger. Let us call upon our Father to fill your heart with tolerance and love – to help . . .

MRS BOSWELL. Forgive me, Father, for having bad thoughts.

FATHER DOOLEY. Perhaps in your wisdom and with your great understanding, my child, you might find it in your heart to see in this man's weaknesses a thing to be loved. And you might, with God's help, welcome him back to the family fold.

MRS BOSWELL. I might, Father, I might.

FATHER DOOLEY. Compassion, my child, is a rare gift.

MRS BOSWELL. On the other hand, I might punch his gob right through the back of his head.

Mrs Boswell gets up and leaves the confessional box.

FATHER DOOLEY. (*Pleading with the Almighty.*) Where has the fear gone!!

The dock road

Jack's van is coming along the road. It turns into one of the great stone gateways of the docks, drives into the open square and stops. Jack gets out of the van, and looks around, awestruck and thoughtful. We hear the voices of Mr Boswell and Jack as a child.

CHILD JACK'S VOICE. I'm going to be a docker like you one day, Dad.

MR BOSWELL. You're going to be a captain, son, with shiny black shoes and braid as golden as a buttercup.

Jack walks slowly and we see through his eyes the panorama of dockland –

the arches, the great walls, the cranes and the cobbled ground, the storehouses, and the rope winches. As Jack is standing by a rail gazing at the water, he hears a voice.

MAN. Want to buy a radio?

Jack turns and sees a man of about thirty standing beside him. He is dressed in jeans and a leather jacket. He is smoking a cigarette and blowing the smoke as far as possible.

JACK. (*With fright.*) Jesus.

MAN. The last dozen – never to be repeated.

JACK. How much?

MAN. A tenner each.

JACK. On yer bike.

MAN. Thirty-five in the shops.

From a pocket inside his jacket, he takes a brochure and hands it to Jack.

Details of the aforesaid.

JACK. (*Looks through the brochure briefly.*) Where?

The man indicates with his head a car which is parked next to Jack's van in the distance. Silently they walk back to the vehicles and as they do Jack thinks again of his father and his father's voice.

MR BOSWELL'S VOICE. And you'll come in with the pilot boats and I'll be waiting for you, son, with your mam in her best stockings and her flowered frock. And they'll pipe us aboard, and we'll be proud and as pink as a monkey's bum.

They have arrived at the cars. The man silently opens his boot. There is a big cardboard box inside. He lifts the top, revealing about three large double speaker radios. They are neatly packed in plastic wrapping.

MAN. Last dozen – one-twenty.

JACK. A hundred.

MAN. Look mate, I haven't just come over on the boat yer know.

JACK. A hundred.

MAN. Piss off.

JACK. One-ten.

MAN. (*Muttering.*) Keep the kids in bloody dolly mixtures.

JACK. Done?

MAN. (*Reluctantly.*) Done.

JACK. (*Looking around.*) Do you take American Express?

MAN. (*Impatiently, with his hand out.*) Only if it's the gold card – we have to be careful – know what I mean!

He goes to take the money but Jack snatches it away and indicates that he should first transfer the box from his boot to Jack's van. The man does so, muttering and grumbling.

MAN. Would that be all? Or would yer like a police escort?

He holds his hand out again.

JACK. I haven't heard them play yet.

The man puts his hand into one of the plastic bags and turns a knob. We hear a phone-in.

MAN'S VOICE. Now then Winnie, how are you, blossom?

WOMAN'S VOICE. I'm seventy-five, love. All me extremities have gone, but I've got me pension and I've got me lads.

He switches that one off and switches the second one on. We hear a brass band. He switches the third one on. We hear Spanish music.
  Jack immediately springs into a Spanish dance with the money in his mouth. The man raises his eyes to heaven and switches off. Jack stops like a statue, then goes back to normal, strolling up to the man.

JACK. I saw me dad today.

The man looks away, bored.

I suppose you see your dad every day.

MAN. He's in the clink – robbery with stupidity. (*Pause.*) He thought he'd do a bit of breaking and entering – you know – to relieve the redundancy. He broke his arm entering, saw the guard dog and broke his leg exiting. (*He holds his hand out again, Jack gives him the money.*) Ta.

The man strolls away, gets into his car and drives off.
  Jack goes to the boot of his van and is just going to close it when he notices something odd about the box. He lifts the radio out, then the other, then the third one. Packed beneath them is a mass of apples.

Outside a high rise block

We see a general view of a group of high rise buildings, and hear the following dialogue.

BILLY. (*On the telephone.*) Hello – is that the Liverpool Corporation Cleaning Department?

LADY. Can I help you?

BILLY. I'm trying to find the address of a Mr Freddie Boswell – he works for you.

Pause.

LADY. I'm sorry we don't give addresses . . .

BILLY. He's me dad you see – and I'm his son – and I've come from Australia to see him.

We now see Billy and Julie. They are standing in front of one of the high rise buildings gazing up. Billy is out of breath.

BILLY. He's not in.

JULIE. I told you he'd be at work.

BILLY. He's on the eleventh floor – the lifts aren't working.

JULIE. I think it's disgusting, putting people that high up, we're land creatures.

BILLY. (*Gazing up*) I suppose they all adapt.

JULIE. It's disgusting. I mean, supposing there was an emergency, supposing your dad had a heart attack, by the time the medical team got up there they'd all be having one.

BILLY. (*Still gazing up.*) I suppose they don't go to bed like the rest of us – they go to roost.

JULIE. Supposing there was a fire – he'd go right through the tarpaulin.

BILLY. (*Taking her arm.*) Come on.

She follows him, clip-clopping along in high-heeled shoes.

JULIE. (*As they go.*) Is he still with his girlfriend?

BILLY. He didn't say. (*Pause.*) I wish he'd come home.

JULIE. What do you want him to come home for? You've got your mother.

BILLY. That's a daft thing to say isn't it – we're supposed to have a mother *and* a father.

JULIE. With *your* mother you've *got* a mother and a father.

BILLY. (*Stopping and turning towards her.*) Now look, Julie, I've told you – I won't have you talking about our mam.

They go on.

JULIE. You know what happens to fellows that idolise their mothers – they turn into poofs.

BILLY. Oh yeah – I'm a poof aren't I? Pass me me hair band.

JULIE. We'd get married if it wasn't for your mother.

BILLY. It's got nothing to do with me mam. I haven't got anything to get married with, have I? (*He walks on, talking to himself.*) It was fun when me dad was at home.

JULIE. (*Calling after him.*) What's wrong with your grandad's house? He doesn't need all that space.

BILLY. (*Muttering.*) Oh God – she's off!

JULIE. I mean, there's only him and the canary.

Billy put on some speed, Julie has difficulty keeping up with him in her heels.

Now I know why some people spend their lives on the housing list – they haven't got canaries. (*She shouts.*) Billy! (*He walks on – she shouts louder.*) Billy!!

BILLY. (*Turning briefly.*) I'll ring you later.

JULIE. (*In a rage.*) Don't bother to ring me later – I won't answer anyway. See if I care about you, Billy Boswell. (*Pause.*) You'll be walking through these streets with your flat feet and your hands in your pockets 20 years from now. And don't expect me to wave when I pass you in me Rolls!

The Boswells' living room

Joey is sitting on the settee reading the Financial Times. *The expensive stereo is playing. He reaches out to a silver tray which has cut-glass decanters on it, and pours himself a drink. Then he takes a bite from a sandwich on a plate nearby.*

Mrs Boswell comes downstairs, she is dressed to go out.

MRS BOSWELL. (*Getting a tissue out from her bag.*) I wish you wouldn't spill that Coke everywhere Joey – it takes the hallmark off the silver.

JOEY. Then we'll get a gold one, Mam, we'll get a gold one.

MRS BOSWELL. Aren't you going to get some sleep? You don't get enough rest Joey – up all night, up all day – it's bad enough living like a barn owl, you'll look like one soon.

JOEY. (*Reading.*) Later, Mam, later.

MRS BOSWELL. I'm going out – don't forget to feed the dog.

JOEY. OK, OK.

MRS BOSWELL. (*Handing the phone bill to Joey.*) Pay that for me Joey, will you? I know who it is who runs the phone bill up, you know. It's our Billy. If he's not over there with Julie he's over here on the phone to her.

He is not listening, she hesitates.

He looked well, didn't he?

JOEY. (*Looking up, casually.*) Who?

Mrs Boswell is relieved that his father seems to be unimportant to Joey after all.

MRS BOSWELL. Nothing. I won't be long. Oh, there's a plate of sandwiches for your grandad. Take them in to him, will you?

She goes. Joey puts the paper down, looks at the bill, stretches a little, then reaches for the phone. He dials and waits.

OPERATOR. Operator – can I help you?

JOEY. Hello. Yes, this is 708 0298. I've been trying to reach London but I keep getting the wrong number.

OPERATOR. What number do you want?

JOEY. Oh it's all right – I got it eventually. But I did get the wrong one three times.

OPERATOR. All right caller – I'll credit you with that amount.

JOEY. Thank you, Operator. (*He puts the phone down.*) It all helps.

He smiles and picks up the paper again, but his mind is on his father. We see the superimposed picture of Mr Boswell leaving the house, pushing his cart, the way Joey last saw him.

Joey puts the paper down, goes to the kitchen, picks up the plate of sandwiches and leaves.

Outside the Boswells' house

Joey comes out with the sandwiches and knocks on Grandad's door. The door opens, a hand comes out to snatch, but Joey pulls the plate away. Grandad emerges reluctantly.

JOEY. Oh, it's you Grandad. I thought it was a praying mantis.

GRANDAD. (*Looking scornfully at the sandwiches.*) Where's me lunch?

JOEY. This is your lunch, Grandad.

GRANDAD. Sandwiches! For me lunch! I'm going to complain to the Social Security.

He grabs the plate and closes the door. Joey smiles and walks towards the house. He sees Billy coming along, kicking a Coke tin, hands in pockets, shoulders hunched.

JOEY. Hey come on, Billy. Straighten yourself up. Where do you think you are? Notre Dame!

BILLY. I'm pissed off.

JOEY. Where've you been?

BILLY. (*Cagily.*) Nowhere.

JOEY. Ah – that's why you're pissed off. You should never come home lad unless you've been *some*where!

They go into the house and close the door.

Outside in a street

Aveline is strutting along in her high heels and her wide belt, and her earrings. She is carrying a large box of chocolates. We hear this dialogue over her walking.

AVELINE'S VOICE. Hello – is that the Liverpool Council Offices Cleansing Department?

OPERATOR. Can I help you?

AVELINE. Oh yes. My name is Aveline Boswell, I do modelling, and my dad works for you.

OPERATOR. (*Muttering.*) Oh not again.

AVELINE. Do you think you could tell me where he's sweeping? Only I'm his daughter you see, and I've come all the way from America to see him.

Mr Boswell's cart is parked in the street and Mr Boswell is nowhere to be seen.

Aveline goes to the cart and looks around for a moment, then she places the box of chocolates on the cart, and goes away again. The note reads: 'love, Aveline'.

As she goes out of sight Mr Boswell comes out of a cigarette shop. He goes to the cart, sees the chocolates, picks up the note. As he reads it, a group of four young men, all wearing suits and white collars, approach. Adrian is amongst them. They are about to turn into the estate offices where Adrian works.

They are all sharing a joke. Adrian catches sight of his father. He waves the others in without him. Then he goes to his father rather secretly, checking now and then that no one is watching.

ADRIAN. Hello . . . (*Pause.*) Dad.

MR BOSWELL. Hello, son.

ADRIAN. Are you all right?

MR BOSWELL. Bright as a brothel's lamp, son, bright as a brothel's lamp.

He tips his cap and walks off with his cart.
Adrian watches for a moment.

ADRIAN. Dad!

Mr Boswell looks back.

P'raps you could call in again sometime – on your way round.

MR BOSWELL. I will, lad, I will.

He continues sweeping and Adrian goes into the office building.

The Boswells' kitchen (*that evening*)

The family are seated around the table for dinner, the room is full of dishes with apples in them. There is a curious silence as Mrs Boswell places the various dishes of food on the table. Billy takes the lid off one and picks up a potato. She slaps his hand, he drops it back in the dish again. The final tureen is placed. Mrs Boswell pulls out her chair and sits down. She looks at them all, takes the lid off the cockerel dish and places it down. They all shift uncomfortably, she looks at each one in turn.

JACK. I'll have something tomorrow.

AVELINE. I had to buy a present for a friend.

ADRIAN. The cashpoint was out of order.

BILLY. I didn't make any money today. But I know where there's a decorating job – I'm going tomorrow.

ADRIAN. (*Looking at Billy.*) Decorating! What does he know about decorating?

BILLY. I've watched our Joey, haven't I?

ADRIAN. I've watched the aeroplanes flying overhead – it doesn't make me a pilot, does it?

MRS BOSWELL. The family pot would be empty if it weren't for Joey's fifty pounds this morning.

BILLY. And the fifty pence me dad . . .

She glares at him. He stops.

MRS BOSWELL. So what have you all been doing?

JACK. We told you, didn't we? (*About Billy.*) *He* didn't do anything. *His* cashpoint was out of order, *she's* buying pressies and I bought some (*pause*) radios.

MRS BOSWELL. You mean, you paid for radios and you got apples.

JACK. I wasn't concentrating.

MRS BOSWELL. It was tomatoes last time.

JOEY. Pull your fist out, sunshine, will you? What do you think you are? A greengrocer?

Billy starts to giggle and Jack glares at him.

BILLY. (*Trying to make up for it.*) Oh, eh, it's not easy, this buying and selling game. Remember the bike?

JACK. I'd rather not talk about the bike.

BILLY. (*To the others.*) He bought a bike from this fella. He tried to sell it to the priest.

MRS BOSWELL. We all know about it, Billy.

BILLY. And it turned out . . .

JACK. (*Butting in.*) How was I to know they nicked it from the priest in the first place?

JOEY. OK, you two, OK!

Billy starts to open his mouth.

JOEY. Billy . . .

MRS BOSWELL. Did anybody feed the dog?

JOEY. Sorry I forgot.

JACK. So did I.

AVELINE. Me too.

ADRIAN. I thought they were doing it.

BILLY. Nobody asked me to.

MRS BOSWELL. Either he gets fed four times or not at all. You know what'll happen now, he'll go down to the delicatessèn and pinch the Stilton. (*She sighs.*) We've had a bad day, haven't we? An empty pot, an empty dog and I made sandwiches for lunch. *Me – sandwiches!*

AVELINE. Don't worry, Mam, when I get in the glossies, with me modelling, you won't be able to get the lid on that pot.

Pause. Suddenly Mrs Boswell bangs her fist on the table.

MRS BOSWELL. There's never been a day of *nothing* – not since he went, not *ever*.

JOEY. (*Quickly.*) Mam, don't upset yourself.

MRS BOSWELL. I have to upset myself, Joey. We're a team, a business. We survive becuase we're a family and we have a plan. You work yourself to death, I cook myself to death – and the reward is money in that pot! Never an empty day.

A brief silence.

AVELINE. (*Blurting it out.*) I didn't buy a present for a friend – I bought chocolates – for me dad. (*They all stare at her.*) Well – he is my – dad. He's *our* dad. It's no good boasting about a family if we're going to leave him out of it.

Pause.

JACK. I was down at the docks. I kept remembering – when he worked there.

MRS BOSWELL. He didn't *work* there – he played cards there. He was in the queue with his bike an hour before knocking-off time.

JACK. (*Calming her.*) It was a good place, Mam, the docks – the ships sailed . . .

MRS BOSWELL. Aye well your father didn't help them to sail. When he was on nights his mates used to have to scoop him up off the dock road and pour him on board. He'd book himself into a first class cabin, set the alarm for five minutes before the boss came in the morning – get up, collect his tins of ham and his danger money, bribe the gate policeman and come home in time to watch racing on television.

BILLY. (*Suddenly.*) I went to see him today. (*Pause.*) He wasn't there. (*Pause.*) But I went.

ADRIAN. I had a word with him – he was outside our office building. (*Pause.*) Just a word.

MRS BOSWELL. (*Looking at them all helplessly.*) You don't know, do you? You just don't know.

JACK. Know what?

MRS BOSWELL. He's bad for us, that what.

AVELINE. But he's our dad. (*Pause.*) Isn't he?

MRS BOSWELL. (*Glaring at her.*) Wash your mouth out, my girl.

JACK. He's not the only man who's gone off with another woman, Mam.

MRS BOSWELL. *Tart* – she's a tart.

JOEY. It's his age, isn't it? He's – well he's like an old car, he's doing his last bit of revving before his engine packs up.

BILLY. (*Innocently.*) Why don't you get back together?

MRS BOSWELL. (*To herself.*) Oh God – when *is* he going to let go of his rattle?

JACK. Look – let's get on with the prayers, shall we? I'm going down with malnutrition here.

JOEY. Let's talk about it after some wine – it'll all seem much better then.

MRS BOSWELL. (*She puts her hands together – they all close their eyes.*) We thank Thee, oh God, for the food on the table, and pray that we'll be able to replace the food in the cupboard. Keep us together, dear Lord, and keep us safe from evil influences.

There is a knock on the door, they all open their eyes and Mrs Boswell glares at them. They close them again.

Amen.

They open their eyes again.

BILLY. I'll go.

The rest all start serving themselves food. Billy goes to the door. Within a moment he comes back.

It's me dad – I saw him through the letter-box.

Mrs Boswell and Joey exchange looks.

JOEY. Invite him in for dinner.

The rest all smile with relief, Billy races back to the door.

AVELINE. Mam, you're great.

Outside the Boswells' house (*later*)

The door opens and Mr Boswell comes out. He is carrying a see-through plastic bag of apples, and one of Jack's radios. Aveline and Billy have come to see him off. He turns to them.

MR BOSWELL. That was a multi-coloured meal, a multi-coloured meal.

The two laugh. Mr Boswell goes to his cart, positions his new radio and switches it on. He hangs his bag of apples on the handle, puts his box of chocolates in it, and off he goes with a jaunty step.

AVELINE. Tarra, Dad!

BILLY. Tarra!

Mr Boswell waves his hand without looking round. The two close the door.

The Boswells' living room

We see Mrs Boswell clearing coffee cups from the coffee table. Jack is sitting in the armchair and Adrian is sitting on the sofa. Billy and Aveline come in and sit on the sofa.

AVELINE. Aye man that was fantastic – I've never laughed so much.

JACK. He was always good fun, me dad, always full of tricks.

Mrs Boswell rises and goes out.

BILLY. Hey wouldn't it be great? Now that she's left him, if he lived next door with Grandad, we'd all be together then, and yet separate.

Joey comes downstairs and sits on the arm of the sofa.

JOEY. Enough is enough Billy, just cool it – OK?

AVELINE. It was nice seeing him go with his bag of apples, and his chocolates, and his new radio. I gorra lump in me throat just watching him.

BILLY. (*About Joey.*) Should we tell him now?

AVELINE. It's about your pet spider.

JACK. It was in the sink.

JOEY. I told you to check the sink.

JACK. I did, it got mixed up with the tea leaves.

JOEY. Tea leaves don't have eight legs, do they?

JACK. No, but it was very deceiving. His body's black and his eight legs are black. I just thought I'd got nine extra tea leaves. Anyway, he survived that.

JOEY. And . . .

JACK. I put him on the draining board to dry out. (*Pause.*) Then I put the teapot down on him.

Joey starts to say something but Billy interrupts.

BILLY. It's only a spider.

ADRIAN. It's not only a spider, it's Joey's spider.

ALL. It's family.

Mrs Boswell comes in.

MRS BOSWELL. He's pinched the money, and the fifty pence he put in.

JACK. The bastard.

MRS BOSWELL. He was always good fun your dad – always full of tricks.

Joey

Episode Four

The Boswells' living room (*morning*)

Jack is sitting on the settee studying a book. Propped up in front of him is a watercolour painting. It is out of its frame, which is on a chair. It is a picture of sky and sea. Nearby is a piece of hardboard with black oil paint squirted on it, and a fine brush.

JACK. (*Reading aloud.*) Henry Moore was a popular Victorian painter. He was best known for his seascapes. Born in the year 1831, he died in 1895. (*He puts the book down.*) He'll do. (*He picks up the brush and begins to sign the picture, saying as he does.*) H – (*Pause.*) – E – N – R –

> *Mrs Boswell enters. She is carrying a brown paper bag. Jack hides what he is doing by putting the palette and brush underneath the coffee table.*

MRS BOSWELL. The lunch is ready . . . There's a pan of scouse on – help yourselves. I've given Grandad his.

JACK. OK Mam – thanks.

> *She takes apples, pears and oranges out of the bag and fills a large wooden fruit bowl.*

MRS BOSWELL. (*Looking at the painting.*) I don't think much of it.

JACK. It's a good picture that – it's a Henry Moore.

MRS BOSWELL. I thought he did those people with holes in them.

JACK. This is the Victorian Henry Moore – the painter, not the sculptor.

MRS BOSWELL. It's just waves.

JACK. It's hard to paint waves – waves are moving things – you have to give the impression of movement.

MRS BOSWELL. My impression is boredom – there's not even a boat.

JACK. (*Pointing.*) What's that? What's that?

MRS BOSWELL. (*Peering at it.*) Oh, is that a boat?

JACK. It's distance – it's subtle you see.

MRS BOSWELL. I don't see the point of having a picture of a boat if you've got to get a pair of binoculars to see it.

> *She walks out of the room to the kitchen.*

The Boswells' kitchen

Mrs Boswell comes in. Billy is there, he is drinking milk from the bottle. Mrs Boswell smacks his head.

MRS BOSWELL. Other people have to drink that.

He finishes the milk off.

BILLY. They haven't now.

He walks towards the door. There is a clanging sound. Billy has a cymbal tied to each knee.

Have you seen my mouth organ?

MRS BOSWELL. Must you wear them things in the house? Can't you wait until you get to your pitch?

BILLY. It's too much messing. (*He takes his mouth organ out of his pocket.*) Oh, here it is. (*He blows it.*)

MRS BOSWELL. The dog hasn't come home since you put those things on Billy.

BILLY. He'll have to get used to it – it's me living.

Mrs Boswell raises her eyes to heaven.

I'm putting money in the family pot, aren't I? *And* it's bought me car. I'm going out in it now.

He clanks off.

MRS BOSWELL. Where to?

BILLY. Julie's.

MRS BOSWELL. Why are you going in the car? She only lives across the road.

BILLY. Tarra, Mam.

The door shuts, Mrs Boswell shrugs.

Outside the Boswells' house

Grandad is sitting in his wicker chair and is just finishing off his scouse. Billy comes out.

BILLY. Hi Grandad.

GRANDAD. Where's me pudding?

Grandad watches Billy clank to his car. It is an old Volkswagen – in obvious danger of falling to bits.
Billy opens the door. It will only open about a foot – so Billy has to squeeze into it. He switches the engine on. A terrible noise is the result.
There is black smoke coming from the back – and a great shudder as he

moves off. After he has moved a few yards, he holds an old brass horn out of the window and squeezes it. It makes a ship's siren noise.

    Mrs Boswell comes out with a Police cone and places it in the vacant parking spot. She stands watching Billy as he hiccups along the road, pulling over and parking in front of Julie's house. She shakes her head, then takes Grandad's lunch tray from him.

MRS BOSWELL. Fresh raspberries, ice-cream and brandy sauce, Grandad.

GRANDAD. It'll have ter do, won't it.

She sighs and goes into the house.

Outside Julie's house Billy is trying to open the door of his car. He struggles but he can't open it. He tries to get out through the window but he can't. Finally he blows his horn again. The door opens and Julie appears. She is all dressed up and made-up. She looks at Billy.

JULIE. I thought the *Queen Mary* was back.

BILLY. (*Proudly.*) I bought a car.

JULIE. (*Offish.*) Is that what it is?

BILLY. You said – when we had the row – you said I'd be walking the streets twenty years from now with me—

JULIE. Flat feet and hands in yer pockets – yeah.

BILLY. So – I bought a car.

JULIE. (*Looking at the car, unimpressed.*) You'd better come in.

BILLY. I can't get out.

JULIE. I'm not surprised! I mean, you haven't ever bought anything yet that was *normal* – like – *normal* – have you!

BILLY. It's the door.

JULIE. It's not just the door Billy – it's everything. It's the scooter that would only turn left, the folding bike that wouldn't unfold. Even the skateboard you bought used to catapult you into the air whenever it felt like it. You don't need a *wife* Billy – you need a welder!

BILLY. I'll go to a garage on me way to work.

JULIE. Work! You call clanking around with a mouth organ in your gob and cymbals stuck to your ankles, work!

BILLY. (*Bluntly.*) At least I'm independent.

JULIE. How can you be independent when you're trapped in your car?

BILLY. It's only temporary.

JULIE. Yeah – it's only temporary – and when you do get out you won't be able to get back in. And when you *do* get back in, the brakes won't work, and when the brakes work the gear lever will fall off. And after spending a hundred quid on it, you'll sell it for twenty to someone who wants to use it as a greenhouse! I've seen it all before Billy.

She goes back into the house and slams the door.

BILLY. (*Shouting.*) There's no pleasing you is there! (*He chugs away.*)

A photographic studio

André is taking pictures of Aveline, who is posing on a high stool wearing rubber trousers and a rubber top. He snaps away, whilst she changes her position. She looks rather grave.

ANDRÉ. (*Stops – sighs.*) Oh come on love. I said, look sexy, as if you're about to indulge – not as if you've been doing it all night.

AVELINE. It's this rubber – it's like working in a microwave.

ANDRÉ. (*Taking more picture.*) Smile – come on – be a tigress – that's better – that's terrific.

We see Aveline's forced smile crumbling into a 'cry'.

(*To himself.*) Oh God. (*To Aveline.*) Keep the anguish *in* dear – be professional. You'll never be a model if you're going to let the entire world know when you're depressed.

AVELINE. (*Cries.*) I can't – I can't.

ANDRÉ. (*Taking pictures.*) Up a bit – up a bit.

Aveline wipes tears from her face.

Wonderful – fantastic – keep the chin down. I don't want to see your nostrils – you'll look like a horse dear.

Aveline goes into full, serious crying now.

All right, all right – we'll have a break.

He goes to pour coffee.

Watch your eyes – they'll go all red, and your face will swell up. I'm doing haute-couture, not a documentary on puffer fish.

André takes the sniffing Aveline a coffee.

ANDRÉ. There – get that down you – take your mind off your face – give your stomach something to worry about.

AVELINE. Ta.

ANDRÉ. Why don't you talk dear? Keep the circulation going. (*He pulls up a stool.*)

AVELINE. It's me dad. He left the house three years ago with his sandwich box, and he never came back – until the other day. (*Pause.*) Me mam got used to the situation, and she gathered us around her – me, our Jack, our Billy, our Adrian, our Joey – and she said, 'We're all on our own now, we either fight or we fall.'

ANDRÉ. Very poignant.

AVELINE. We gorra booklet from the Social Security office and we read it from cover to cover. It's amazing the things you can claim for. Then she said, 'We're a family – you must each go out and bring back a contribution. There are no jobs, no wage packets, so you do what the rats did – go secretly, and quietly, get what yer can, how yer can. Trust no one. (*Pause.*) We have this family pot – we put money in it – all of us – at the dinner table, before prayers. (*Reflectively.*) It always feels safe in our house. (*Pause.*) And then – he came. (*Pause.*) Me dad. (*Pause.*) He confused us – he reminded us of the good old days when he was a docker, and we played in the streets. He joked – and he – he sort of upset the table with the jigsaw on it – we were all in pieces again. (*Pause.*) After all me mam had done – and then – (*she sniffs again*) he pinched the money – (*pause*) from the family pot. He pinched it and left. (*Pause.*) And I don't know who to love any more.

ANDRÉ. You do what I do dear – you love yourself. There's nobody more reliable. (*Aveline looks at him.*) Oh yes, I had lots of people, a great entourage – friends, colleagues, lovers. They took me by the hand through golden fields, pointed to the world and told me it was mine, if I wanted it. (*Pause.*) All I want is love, I said, me loving you, you loving me. (*Pause.*) They left – one by one. Once the excitement wears off, people can't cope with the responsibility of love you see. So – (*pause*) – there was only me left. (*André looks at her and is embarrassed by his own soul-bearing now.*) Oh God – look at your face. You'll come out like a grilled tomato.

He takes her cup and goes to pour more coffee for her. As he pours he carries on talking.

ANDRÉ. We could do nude pictures – there's a market for them.

She is horrified. He continues without turning to face her.

Don't worry dear – it's purely business – and I never mix it. (*Pause.*) Tasteful ones of course. (*Turning to her.*) I thought you wanted money and fame, that's all.

In a transport cafe

A waitress is behind the counter. Mr Boswell is sitting at a table reading a paper – there are others eating in the cafe.

WAITRESS. One chips, black pudding, beans, sausage, tomatoes, egg, bacon, mushroom and fried bread.

Mr Boswell gets up and goes to the counter.

MR BOSWELL. Thank you, sweetheart. You're looking good, pink as a rose, pink as a rose.

WAITRESS. (*A little flirtatiously.*) Tea or coffee?

MR BOSWELL. Coffee my darling, make it black, black as a beetle's belly.

He takes his meal to the table, puts it down and goes back to the counter for his coffee.

WAITRESS. That'll be one pound sixty-four, but for you one pound twenty.

Mr Boswell puts some money down.

MR BOSWELL. Thank you my sweetheart and have a bread roll for yourself.

WAITRESS. (*Provocatively.*) Reckless, aren't you!

MR BOSWELL. You should know darling, you should know.

At this point Joey arrives by his dad's side.

JOEY. (*Quietly.*) Dad.

MR BOSWELL. Joey, what are you doing here son?

JOEY. I saw your cart outside.

MR BOSWELL. Oh yeah. (*To the waitress.*) My mobile emotional wardrobe.

JOEY. OK Dad, save the clever talk.

MR BOSWELL. (*To the waitress.*) You see what I do is I take off all me troubles, all me emotions, I shove them in me little cart, then I put on all my fantasies, all my dreams and (*pause*) . . . and I walk away.

JOEY. Walking away doesn't solve anything, Dad.

MR BOSWELL. That's not what I've found out son – you walk away from a fire, you don't get your arse singed. (*He sits at the table.*)

WAITRESS. (*To Mr Boswell.*) Eh, fluffy head, see you later.

JOEY. Not another one Dad, not another one.

MR BOSWELL. Don't be a silly bugger, it's just a frolic. She gets the flattery, I get extra beans.

JOEY. OK Dad, let's go for a little chat.

MR BOSWELL. What about me dinner?

JOEY. I'll buy you another when we get back.

MR BOSWELL. Can't we chat here?

JOEY. Of course we can. (*He pulls a chair out and sits opposite his dad.*) About the money, Dad.

MR BOSWELL. (*Looking around at the people and the tables.*) Should we er . . .

JOEY. Go for a little chat. Yes. (*They rise.*)

Mr Boswell sees a chap sitting by a table on his own. He puts his dinner down in front of him.

MR BOSWELL. Here you are mate, your luck's in, there's extra beans.

They both walk out.

The docks

Joey's car arrives. It pulls up by a wall near the water. Joey gets out immediately. He is angry. He goes to the wall and stares at the water. Silence from the car for a moment, then Mr Boswell's foot appears. He finally gets out. Pause.

MR BOSWELL. Have you got a fag?

JOEY. (*Turning on him.*) Why Dad – why?

Silence, Mr Boswell looks up at the cranes.

MR BOSWELL. There she is – the big crane – grey as a storm.

JOEY. It's not just the money – though it doesn't exactly land in the yard – it's doing it to *us* (*pause*) – family.

MR BOSWELL. It was there – that's all.

JOEY. Oh great – help yourself to the world, why don't you? (*Pause.*) Look, we don't have jobs – all we have is optimism. (*Pause.*) Well, there's nothing definite about optimism, is there? I mean, it's more what you *hope* will happen, not what *does* happen.

MR BOSWELL. I never have funny things like optimism myself – just a belly ache.

JOEY. *We* invited you into *our* house.

MR BOSWELL. It was my house once.

JOEY. (*Close to his face.*) But you weren't satisfied, were you? Oh, the food was good, the laundry was good – the service. (*Pause.*) But the maid began to look tired, didn't she?

MR BOSWELL. You're all on her side, aren't you? No chance for me.

JOEY. You didn't need us, did you? You had Lilo Lill. (*With disgust.*) How could you, Dad? She was half your age. I mean, she wasn't exactly subtle, was she? Every time she moved her knickers lit up.

MR BOSWELL. She was paradise.

JOEY. She was the town bike.

MR BOSWELL. She didn't cook like yer mam. Me socks were never dry – me shirts were never ironed. But she made a good cup of tea – and a man learns that a good cup of tea in a warm and friendly bed does more for his soul than a plate of scouse.

Joey looks at him – he understands.

JOEY. Where is she now?

MR BOSWELL. Oh – somewhere – bringing someone back to life, I suppose.

Joey gets his gold cigarette case out, opens it and holds it towards his father – who takes a long black cigarette out. He puts it in his mouth. Joey gets his gold lighter out and lights it for him. Mr Boswell puffs it and blows out the smoke, savouring it.

MR BOSWELL. When I'm brushing the streets, I don't get angry now. I feel sort of calm. (*Pause.*) Like a crippled man, who got to the top of Everest just before he fell and broke his leg.

Joey is moved now by his father – he tries to make up to him.

JOEY. (*With a playful punch.*) Hey – maybe she'll come back.

MR BOSWELL. (*Shaking his head.*) I hope not. I've had me fun – I'm knackered now.

JOEY. (*Bringing out his wallet.*) Listen – (*He takes two ten-pound notes out.*) I've done all right.

MR BOSWELL. (*Putting up his hand.*) Never son – never – I don't accept charity.

Joey puts his wallet back, but tries to hand the two notes to Mr Boswell. He declines.

MR BOSWELL. I have my pride.

JOEY. Come on – we're family – we share.

MR BOSWELL. (*Emphatically.*) No. (*He turns away.*)

JOEY. OK, OK. (*He puts the notes into his pocket.*) Come on – back to your cart.

Outside the dogs' home

Joey pulls up outside. He sits in his seat for a moment – obviously thoughtful. Then he gets out of the car and goes into the yard where all the dog cages are. He walks beside them in the usual way – showing nothing in particular – just the slow walk and the sad gaze.

 Finally he stops by a box which has written above it 'Donations'. He feels in his pocket for the two ten pound notes – they have gone. He turns his pocket out – and realises his father has pinched them. A moment of anger, then, calmly, he gets out his wallet, puts a five-pound note in the box and strolls out.

The Boswells' kitchen (after lunch)

Aveline is sitting at the table. She is idly playing with the teaspoon in her coffee. Joey is reading a paper. Adrian is finishing off his dessert. Mrs Boswell is mixing some cake mix in a bowl.

MRS BOSWELL. (*To Aveline.*) What are you doing home so early?

AVELINE. I've got the afternoon off. I'm working tonight instead.

JOEY. (*Looking up.*) Tonight?

AVELINE. Yeah – people *do* work at night you know. (*Looking at Joey.*) Some people work *all* night.

MRS BOSWELL. Don't be hard-faced.

AVELINE. Well, why is it such a big deal every time I do something different? Nobody asks *them*, do they?

MRS BOSWELL. I've told you – you're a girl. Girls are different.

JOEY. What kind of work are you doing tonight?

AVELINE. I'm modelling, aren't I?

MRS BOSWELL. Why can't you do it this afternoon?

AVELINE. He prefers to do it tonight. (*Pause.*) He does pay me you know – I pose when he says so.

ADRIAN. And *how* he says so.

AVELINE. And what's that supposed to mean?

MRS BOSWELL. (*Cutting in to stop the argument.*) You didn't eat your lunch.

AVELINE. I didn't *want* me lunch.

JOEY. Why?

AVELINE. I just didn't.

ADRIAN. So why did you come home for lunch?

AVELINE. I didn't come home for lunch – I came home because I've got the afternoon off. (*She stands up.*) I hate this house – I'm going to get a flat of me own as soon as I get enough money. (*She storms upstairs.*) And it won't be long now!!

> *She goes off.*

MRS BOSWELL. She's a worry to me, that girl. I wish I had one of those electrode things they put on migrating ducks to find out where they go – I could keep track of her.

JOEY. She's a good girl, Mam.

MRS BOSWELL. The bit of her that's me is a good girl – it's the bit that's her dad that worries me.

JOEY. (*Looking at Adrian.*) Leave it to us, we'll sort it out

> *Adrian acknowledges the look, and Jack comes racing in.*

JACK. There's someone here to buy my picture! Quick – someone – (*to Adrian*) – will you give us a hand to put it together?

ADRIAN. Can't you do it yourself?

JACK. I've got to be careful, the signature's still wet.

ADRIAN. Oh God – he's into fake art now. (*Adrian rises.*) If I've said it once, I've said it a thousand times, my job's hanging by a thread, hanging by a thread. (*He goes into the living room with Jack.*) OK.

JACK. (*In the living room, rubbing his hands together.*) A hundred quid. That's eighty quid profit – tax-free – not bad. And I get my Social tomorrow.

JOEY. (*Still reading, calling from the kitchen.*) Make sure they don't pay you in tomatoes or apples. (*He laughs to himself.*)

JACK. He won't let me forget, will he?

JOEY. (*Looks up from his paper.*) All right there Mam – you're doing a good job.

MRS BOSWELL. No thanks to your father.

JOEY. (*Nicely.*) We know Mam – we know what it's been like.

MRS BOSWELL. You don't, Joey, you can't. I was a young girl once – with dreams – the Belle of The Grafton I was. (*Pause.*) He was the first real boyfriend I had. Used to buy me Jacquard headscarves, and real silk stockings. We got married in St Jude's – the saint for hopeless causes. I knew, when I saw him trying to persuade the priest to sell the chalice off the altar, that he was up to no good. (*Pause.*) But there I was – stuck with him – until she came along. (*Pause.*) It's a lonely life Joey – you can't be part of yer children's lives – you can only watch. And although he always looked as if someone had emptied him out of the hoover bag – he was mine. (*Pause.*) Until she came along.

JOEY. He's on his own now.

MRS BOSWELL. Left him, has she?

JOEY. Moved on.

MRS BOSWELL. A tart.

JOEY. Yeah – a tart. (*Pause.*) I'll go and have a talk with Aveline. (*He rises and crosses.*) We'll sort it out, Mam.

Aveline's bedroom

Aveline is lying on her bed, staring at the ceiling. There is a little knock at the door.

AVELINE. Go away.

   Joey comes in – and looks at her.

Are you deaf, Joey?

JOEY. So, what's all this then?

AVELINE. All what?

JOEY. All this working late – all this bad temper – all this leaving home.

AVELINE. (*Suddenly.*) It's my body!

   Joey looks at her.

JOEY. So that's it – I thought so. (*He sits on Aveline's bed.*)

AVELINE. Not that it's in any danger, my body. I mean, the family will see to that, won't they? Apart from having to wear a whistle around me neck, if I'm two minutes late coming home, you all leap into your cars. I could have been engaged to Gavin Hughes now if you hadn't frightened him to death.

JOEY. He was no good for you Aveline – all he did was go round cutting people's hedges. He had no ambition – he declared everything!

AVELINE. He had his own hedge cutters.

JOEY. You know, princess, you don't *have* to do this job. I mean you're not exactly short of clothes – or 'things' – are you? We've got everything in our house – nobody goes short – we're family.

AVELINE. I'm sick of that word 'family'. I want to get me own things – I want Janet Reger underwear, a Gucci bag, a Cartier watch, I want to walk in the wind with all me Harrods labels showing.

JOEY. And what about your pride?

AVELINE. Pride! Where does pride get you? Me grandad's pride landed him in a wicker chair outside the same house he was born in. And me mam's reward for a lifetime of pride is to end her days having a very meaningful relationship with a microwave. (*Pause.*) No thanks.

JOEY. (*Stands up.*) OK – as you said, it's your life – your body. (*He strolls away.*) And let's face it – (*with emphasis*) – anybody can do it.

He goes. Aveline is not so sure of herself after that remark.

A busy street (*late afternoon*)

Billy is standing on the pavement playing his mouth organ and clanging his ankle cymbals. On the ground in front of him is a shoe box. He is not making a very good job of the 'sound', but people passing are putting money in and he has collected quite a lot.

A few yards away a very shy, very quiet girl arrives. she is dressed in long Indian-type clothes, lots of bangles, long plaits – a remnant from the 'flower power' days.

Billy notices her but he carries on with his 'music'. She places a small black cloth down, and on it she puts a straw hat upturned to collect money. She positions herself, with clasped hands and innocent upturned face. Then she suddenly opens her mouth and produces an amazingly loud and effective piece of soprano singing – Madame Butterfly in fact. The sheer suddenness and loudness of it completely drowns Billy's act out. He continues for a moment or two – but the crowds are moving to her now – and he stands there despondent.

After a moment Joey's Jaguar appears, followed by Jack's van, followed by Adrian on his motorbike. They all pull up behind Billy's old car. Joey gets out of his car and goes over to Billy.

JOEY. Come on, Billy, you're needed.

BILLY. What for?

JOEY. Family business.

Joey gathers up Billy's hat and hands it to him, then goes back to his car, with Billy dutifully following. Billy gets into his own car, Joey into his, and with Billy's car spluttering and jerking in the front, the family entourage moves off, slowly and menacingly.

André's photographic studio

André is arranging the set for Aveline's photographs. It consists of a chaise-longue and draped silk everywhere. He's just arranging some flowers when the studio door flies open. No one appears.

ANDRÉ. That you Aveline? (*Pause.*) Well, come on in dear – you're a model, not Kojak.

Joey enters, slowly.

JOEY. Mr André's?

ANDRÉ. And who might you be?

JOEY. I'm their brother.

Jack, Billy and Adrian now appear.

ANDRÉ. Oh my God – a herd of male models. Sorry – no vacancies.

The group stands silently.

Could you go please? I'm expecting a client.

JOEY. We know.

ANDRÉ. Know – know what?

JOEY. We know *who* you're expecting – and *why* you're expecting her.

Jack, Billy and Adrian group round Joey.

ANDRÉ. Listen – I'm not afraid of you, you know. I have nothing to hide. I'm a respectable business.

JACK. You mean persuading young girls to pose in the nude.

ANDRÉ. I do *not* persuade them – I merely put it to them – they do the rest. Anyway, what's wrong with the naked body? We've all got one.

JOEY. But some of us like to keep it private.

BILLY. Like our sister.

JOEY. Our little sister.

André stares at them.

ANDRÉ. Oh I see, it's 'Big Brother' is it, the 'Godfather', the scouse Mafia.

(*He waves them aside.*) Come to 'up' the fees have you? Well, if you expect me to pay her the same as the Social Security pay her, forget it dear. I'm on my arse like everybody else.

> *He gets on with the flowers. Joey jerks his head, as if to give a command. Billy and Jack move foward. Jack slowly undoes André's shirt.*

JACK. Excuse me.

ANDRÉ. I'll call the police – this is an invasion of privacy. Get off – stop it.

> *Adrian opens his briefcase and Joey takes out the bin liner, shakes it open and hands it to Adrian. Joey receives a shirt and trousers. A great shriek of protest from André. Then Joey receives a pair of boxer shorts – they are brightly coloured. Joey raises his eyes to heaven when he sees the shorts. He puts the clothes in the bin liner one at a time.*

JOEY. Oh yes – very nice dear.

> *He takes pictures throughout the dialogue.*

ANDRÉ. Indecent assault this is. You wait – you'll have to pay for this.

JOEY. Get him up Jack, keep him going. Chin up – down a bit – sexy smile – look at the lens. (*Angry tones.*) Sexy smile. (*Pause.*) Oh yes – very nice – now to the left – wet your lips – arms out – pretend you're running through a corn field dear. Wonderful, fantastic.

ANDRÉ. I'll get you – you bastard!!

JOEY. (*Clicks again.*) You look beautiful when you're angry.

A street

The entourage again, driving along. As they pass a builder's skip Jack's van stops. Jack gets out and throws the plastic bag containing André's clothes, on it. He gets back into the van. They drive on.

The Boswells' kitchen (*that evening*)

The entire family is seated around the table. The meal is served. Joey raises his glass.

JOEY. To a good day.

> *They all raise their glasses.*

ALL. A good day.

> *The phone rings and Mrs Boswell answers.*

MRS BOSWELL. Hello. Oh hello love. (*Pause.*) I haven't done apple sauce, Grandad. (*Pause.*) No – the red stuff is *cranberry* sauce. Of course you've heard of it. Now get it down you and shut up.

Mrs Boswell sits. She takes the lid off the pot. Joey puts something in immediately. Then Billy waves a five-pound note around.

BILLY. A fiver, look at that! A fiver! I'm putting a fiver in the pot.

MRS BOSWELL. (*Casually.*) Thank you Billy.

They look at Aveline.

AVELINE. I need some glitter blusher to highlight me cheekbones.

MRS BOSWELL. We need money to highlight the food cupboard.

BILLY. (*Whilst Aveline is getting her money out.*) I had to puff my way through six protest songs for that fiver. My throat . . .

JOEY. Billy!

BILLY. I'd have put more in but I've nearly worn me cymbals out.

JOEY. Billy.

They look at Adrian, who gets a pound out and literally throws it into the dish.

AVELINE. He'll break that pot one day.

ADRIAN. I do have my problems you know. It might not be wearing cymbals out or worrying about my cheekbones but I would quite like a new briefcase – after all it is my job.

BILLY. I'll put another fiver in tomorrow – they love me out there.

ADRIAN. Oh will somebody give him his money back?

The entire family stares at Jack now.

JACK. Do I have to?

MRS BOSWELL. I think I'm going deaf in this ear?

JACK. It's just I've never had a hundred quid of my own before. (*They continue to stare.*) It's all parcelled up by the bank. I don't like breaking into it. (*The stare continues.*) I'll put double in tomorrow. (*The stare forces him to get the money out of his pocket – he breaks the paper band.*) It's really spooky this house. The minute you make any money everybody stares at you. I've had better nightmares. (*He puts a five-pound note in the pot.*)

BILLY. Eh we're equal, me and Jack are equal.

JACK. All right, all right, save you mugging me.

Jack puts another five pounds in. Mrs Boswell is satisfied now. She puts her hands together for prayers.

MRS BOSWELL. We thank Thee, oh Lord, for blessing us with thy food, thy health, thy money and for giving our Jack the guts to part with his. Amen.

Billy makes a grab for some food.

ADRIAN. That's it, that's it, I can't sit next to him any longer.

JOEY. Don't snatch the food Billy!

JACK. He's been watching too many wildlife programmes about lizards.

ADRIAN. What with his elbows prodding my extremities and her perfume taking the lining off my throat, I leave the table in a worse condition than the leftovers. I'm going over there.

JACK. I wouldn't bother, it's worse sitting opposite than amongst it.

Mr Boswell suddenly appears. They all stare at him.

MR BOSWELL. The door was open.

BILLY. (*Apologetically to Mrs Boswell.*) I left it for the dog.

MR BOSWELL. Just thought I'd call – see how you are.

MRS BOSWELL. We don't want you here, Freddie Boswell.

MR BOSWELL. All safe and pink I see.

MRS BOSWELL. Timed it well, didn't you, Freddie Boswell.

Mr Boswell takes out a wallet and pulls out seven ten-pound notes. He puts the wallet back and takes the lid off the cockerel dish.

MR BOSWELL. It's seventy pounds I owe you, I believe. (*He looks at Joey.*)

JOEY. Oh – er – yes, yes.

MR BOSWELL. Right. Fifty for the pot and twenty from the pocket. (*He drops the money into the dish – and adds an extra tenner.*)

BILLY. Eh, that's a tenner.

MR BOSWELL. I've had a yellow day son, a yellow day.

BILLY. (*Suddenly.*) Would you like some dinner, Dad?

Mrs Boswell looks at Billy.

MR BOSWELL. No thanks son – it looks very nice – very green.

JOEY. Look Dad – we don't need the money.

MR BOSWELL. No – no – please. I bought a picture as a matter of fact, for a hundred quid. I'd been following it around, so to speak. Well, friends of mine bought it for me. (*Pause.*) Somebody ambitious had signed it Henry Moore. But he'll learn, he'll learn

Jack looks uncomfortable.

It was a Hughes Stanton.

They all stare.

JACK. A what!

MR BOSWELL. Sold it for seven hundred quid.

JOEY. Well done Dad, well done.

MRS BOSWELL. You always were a cunning bastard, Freddie Boswell – you'd sell the confessional box for a dog kennel if you had the chance.

MR BOSWELL. (*Going to her and speaking in a semi whisper.*) They're doing all right – our family. I wonder who they get it from. (*He goes.*)

Mrs Boswell and Freddie Boswell

Episode Five

The Boswells' kitchen (*morning*)

The entire family, with the exception of Aveline, around the table. They are all eating cereal hurriedly. Mrs Boswell comes into the room, draws her chair out, sits down and puts her hands together.

MRS BOSWELL. We thank Thee, Oh Lord

They all put their spoons down, and their hands together.

For keeping us safe through the night and for the food we're about to bolt.

Everybody picks up their spoons and begin to rush at the cereal again.

Amen.

They put their spoons down.

ALL. (*Quickly.*) Amen.

They then go back to eating their cereal. Adrian reaches for the coffee pot at the same time as Billy. Billy wins.

ADRIAN. Oh I've only got to be at work in twenty minutes, that's all.

JACK. You're not the only one that works. I work, (*about Joey*) he works, our Aveline works, our mam works, (*about Billy*) and he goes through the motions.

ADRIAN. I mean work, proper work, work that begins at nine o'clock, work that goes on until five o'clock. 'There are plenty more in the queue waiting for your job – get here on time or else', work.

Billy hands him the coffee pot, he snatches it from him.

ADRIAN. Left me some, have you?

Aveline comes rushing in.

AVELINE. Lemon juice please, Mam, for me skin. Is me bikini ready?

MRS BOSWELL. It's in the other room, love.

ADRIAN. (*To Aveline.*) What d'you want a bikini for?

AVELINE. I'm modelling, aren't I?

BILLY. She's modelling shelves.

JOEY. (*To Billy.*) Zip it Billy, OK!

JACK. Shelves. Can't they use books for that?

AVELINE. These are special shelves, you don't need brackets to keep them up. I have to sit on one to show how strong it is.

Billy giggles.

AVELINE. They don't just sit anybody on them you know. You have to look dead fantastic. Oh, I'll miss me bus.

She drinks her lemon juice.

JACK. Have you ever seen her run for the bus? Her skirt works its way up to her chin. When she gets on, she's all knickers and earrings.

AVELINE. Oh laugh. I nearly died.

ADRIAN. (*To Aveline.*) Hang on, I'l l give you a lift. (*He stands up and gulps down his coffee.*)

BILLY. I'm going busking today.

ADRIAN. Yeah, well don't agonise outside our office, again, OK? (*As he and Aveline leave.*) My job is hanging by a thread, hanging by a thread.

JACK. (*To Joey.*) I've got something good on today.

MRS BOSWELL. Don't talk about it Jack. Just buy it, check it, sell it, put the money in the pot and shut your gob.

JOEY. (*To Jack.*) Are you sure you know what you're doing, sunshine?

JACK. Of course I know what I'm doing – that chiffonier I bought yesterday made ninety quid.

JOEY. You found it, you bought it, polished it, sold it, delivered it, but all you got was a tenner. The people you sold it to made the ninety quid.

MRS BOSWELL. You live and learn, our Jack.

JACK. (*Getting up.*) The thing is, how do I live while I'm learning? (*He leaves shouting.*) Tarra, Mum!

Billy starts with his mouth organ, Joey goes off to the yard.

MRS BOSWELL. Off you go, Billy. I can't stand that row. Go on!

Joey comes back in with two Police cones.

JOEY. (*To Billy.*) Do something useful, put these in the gaps.

Billy goes out. Then Joey leaves.

MRS BOSWELL. (*Opening an envelope with the electricity bill in it.*) A hundred and forty-five pounds!

She gets the cordless phone and presses out the number. As she does so, Billy comes prancing in, doing his busking act. He plays the mouth organ for a moment, claps the cymbals, then stops and sings.

BILLY. Got no work, got no pay,
But I've got love to warm each day,

Got no future, got no bread,
But I've got dreams inside my head.

MRS BOSWELL. (*Shouting.*) Billy! I'm on the phone.

MRS BOSWELL. (*Into phone.*) Yes – hello – is that the Electricity Accounts
Department? Accounts – yes. Mrs Boswell here – Kelsall Street – reference
number 1487642. It's about the electricity bill. (*Pause.*) I know *how* to pay it
and where to pay it, and when to pay it. (*Pause.*) All I need is the money to
pay it. (*Pause.*) I haven't got a hundred and forty-five pounds – and anyway
how do you get it to that? Are we paying for the M62 to be lit or something?
(*Pause.*) I *know* we will have used that much – but *why* have we used that
much – we've only got to switch a night-light on and that wheel is going
round like a demented windmill. (*Pause.*) We have to eat, and keep warm,
don't we? What do you think we are, bloody polar bears? (*Pause.*) I'm not
writing any letters to anyone, or making any more phone calls. You can
spread the news love – yer not getting it! (*She puts the phone down.*)

*Joey comes into the room. He is in a black bath robe, with a gold 'J'
embroidered on the pocket.*

JOEY. Who were you on to? (*He sits.*)

MRS BOSWELL. The Electricity Department. (*She puts a letter on the table for
him.*) A hundred and forty-five pounds they want – they must think we grow
our own money. (*Joey opens the letter.*) 'We haven't got it,' I said, 'and that's
that – we're all unemployed here.'

JOEY. (*About the letter.*) It's my Gold American Express Card. (*He hands it
to her to look at.*)

MRS BOSWELL. It's not as nice as the Barclay one. (*She hands it back.*) 'Yer
not getting it,' I said.

*Billy comes in again and sits on his chair, doing his act. Mrs Boswell clears
the plates away. He goes through his song and cymbal act again.*

JOEY. OK – OK – yeah that's fine, that's great.

BILLY. I'm going to bring a new meaning to the art of busking, they love me
out there.

MRS BOSWELL. The feeling's not the same here.

The phone rings, Joey answers it.

JOEY. Hello – yes – it's Joey here. (*Pause.*) No – Freddie Boswell doesn't live
here any more – Mrs Boswell is here. Hang on please. (*He cups the phone.*)
It's for you Mam – the Sunset Lodge.

MRS BOSWELL. The Sunset Lodge!? (*She takes the phone.*) Hello – yes –

Uncle Cyril, yes he's ours. I've got his clean vest here. Oh – I'm sorry. Yes – well. (*Pause.*) How did it happen? (*Pause.*) Yes – I see – oh dear. (*Pause.*) No, no, it's all right – we'll call you back. I'll just have a word with the family. Yes. Thank you, thank you. Tarra. (*She puts the phone down, and sits.*) Uncle Cyril is dead.

JOEY. Oh God – no.

MRS BOSWELL. We'll have to let your dad know – he was his brother.

JOEY. I'll see to that.

MRS BOSWELL. Another excuse for him to come wheedling his way back into the family.

JOEY. One of the old school eh! Uncle Cyril – old sea dog.

MRS BOSWELL. We're going to have to bury him Joey – he's got nobody.

JOEY. I'll bet his ghost walks the docks every night.

MRS BOSWELL. It'll be too drunk to walk – it'll stagger.

JOEY. Remember how he used to bring us toffee apples from the *Brittanic*. And the parrot – remember the parrot?

MRS BOSWELL. I'll have to get in touch with Cravens – they did your granny. (*She gets up and goes to get the phone book.*)

JOEY. Unbelievable, that bird. I wonder where it got to?

MRS BOSWELL. I don't know, but wherever it was he'd get there pretty quick. He perched on the toaster.

   Pause.

JOEY. I think we should bring him home, Mam.

MRS BOSWELL. There isn't the space, Joey. When the whole family is at home, it's standing room only – we can hardly apply that to your Uncle Cyril can we?

JOEY. He'll be all right in the front room. We'll just have to put ourselves out.

MRS BOSWELL. I suppose you're right. (*She sits.*)

JOEY. He *is* family, Mam.

MRS BOSWELL. Yeah – he is family.

JOEY. His last voyage.

MRS BOSWELL. It comes to us all.

JOEY. OK?

Pause.

MRS BOSWELL. (*Nodding.*) I never did like him.

Outside the Boswells' house (*the following morning*)

All the Boswell cars and vans are parked outside the house, and Grandad is sitting in his wicker chair drinking a mug of tea.
A hearse comes slowly up the street with a coffin in it. A lady is sweeping her step. The hearse stops – the driver calls.

DRIVER. What number are you, love?

LADY. Forty-two. It's the kids – they took all the numbers.

DRIVER. Thank you, love.

He moves on. The lady makes the sign of the cross, then gets on with her sweeping.
Jack comes to the open door of the Boswell house, sees the hearse and calls into the house.

JACK. Joey – he's here.

Mrs Boswell comes to the door with Joey and Billy.

MRS BOSWELL. Get Grandad in.

Joey and Jack go to Grandad.

JOEY. Come on Grandad – up you get.

GRANDAD. I haven't finished me tea yet.

Joey takes his tea from him and then Jack and Joey each take an arm and literally carry him into his own house.

Gerroff!

JACK. (*As they go in.*) It won't be for long, Grandad. They're coming to clean the streets – we don't want you to get dusty do we?

MRS BOSWELL. (*To Billy.*) Shift your car Billy.

Billy, still wearing his cymbals, goes to his old car. The hearse is now waiting to pull in.
Aveline and Adrian now come to the door and watch, almost bored, as Billy's car splutters and bellows to make room for the hearse.

AVELINE. It's enough to wake him up.

MRS BOSWELL. (*Looking along the street.*) Here's Father Dooley.

Father Dooley is coming along on his bike.

Hello Father – lovely of you to come – he's a bit late.

Father Dooley gets off his bike and parks it behind Jack's van.

FATHER DOOLEY. (*Parking the bike.*) As long as the dear Lord transported him safely. (*He joins them on the step.*) And where is the departed's brother?

MRS BOSWELL. We couldn't find him Father – but we left a message at The Gun and Duck. All we have to do now is hope they gave it to him on the way in and not on the way out.

Joey and Jack come out of Grandad's house now. They each nod respectfully to Father Dooley – and all of them stand on the pavement now to watch the procedure in silence.
   Billy's car is still spluttering and banging – finally they park. Billy parks across the road.
   The men get out of the hearse and go to the back. The back opens outwards so there is no room to extend it because Jack's van is parked behind. The men look at the family, who look back, deadpan.

MRS BOSWELL. Move your van, Jack.

Jack gets in, revs up and reverses, knocking Father Dooley's bike over as he does so.

MRS BOSWELL. (*To Aveline.*) Pick the Father's bike up.

Aveline struts across in her tight clothes and picks up the Father's bike.
   Jack gets out of his van and joins the others on the steps. Now they all watch silently. The men ease the coffin out of the hearse – they carry it towards the house and when they are on the pavement the Father goes to address the coffin. The men stop.

FATHER. Welcome home, my son, welcome home.

He makes the sign of the cross. They all do the same. The Father closes his eyes and delivers a self-indulgent sermon.

Oh Lord, bless Thy sheep wherever they wander – bless the people whose hearts open up and call him to rest in the place he knew and loved.

Billy comes clanking back. The Father continues.

Give them courage and strength, oh Lord, to bear their grief, and deliver their loved one safely to Your keeping.

Billy clanks past and joins the others on the steps. The Father pauses whilst he does so.

Amen.

The two bearers look relieved. The Father goes to the others, and as the bearers make their next step towards the house we hear Mr Boswell shouting from the street.

MR BOSWELL. Cyril! Hang on there lad! I'm coming.

The two bearers stop again.
    Mr Boswell is charging along the street pushing his dust-cart. He stops outside the house, leaves the cart, dashes to the coffin, takes off his cap and stands looking at it. Everybody is silent – the bearers are becoming impatient.

MR BOSWELL. (*Quietly, to the coffin.*) I thought I hadn't seen you down at the Social Security lately. (*He looks at all the rest.*) A good man – liked a good laugh.

FIRST BEARER. If you don't mind, pal, we've got other people waiting to be delivered.

MR BOSWELL. OK mate, carry on.

The bearers take the coffin towards the front door. The family split up to make way and the coffin is carried inside.

MR BOSWELL. (*Looking at Mrs Boswell.*) It's very kind of you – taking him in like this. I know you never liked him.

MRS BOSWELL. (*Pointedly.*) I don't mind him now he's dead – it's people still alive that worry me. (*She goes inside.*)

Joey indicates that Mr Boswell should go next.

MR BOSWELL. (*Stops.*) Shouldn't someone tell Grandad?

JOEY. I'll do that.

Mr Boswell goes inside – the rest follow. Joey is last. He takes a look up and down the street. There is a figure at almost every door. They have all been watching. Some of them go inside – some are gossiping. Joey goes into the house and closes the door.

Grandad's parlour (*later that day*)

Grandad is putting a piece of lettuce in through the bars of the canary cage. Joey appears.

JOEY. All right, Grandad?

GRANDAD. Have you brought me lunch?

JOEY. Mam's doing it now.

GRANDAD. Me breakfast was late this morning. It was cold an' all. Late and cold, me breakfast was.

JOEY. Yes, well we've had a strange sort of day, Grandad. An upsetting day.

GRANDAD. She keeps putting sweetners in me tea.

JOEY. A very upsetting day.

GRANDAD. Newfangled they are – the world is full of people dying of newfangled things.

JOEY. I think I ought to tell you Grandad – about Uncle Cyril.

GRANDAD. (*Sitting down.*) Owes me four quid he does. (*He takes out a battered old wallet from his pocket.*) I've got it written down here. Look – Cyril – four quid – 3rd September 1964.

Pause. A long look from Joey.

JOEY. (*Sitting down.*) He's dead, Grandad.

Grandad is silent – he puts his wallet back.

JOEY. I know you never cared much for Dad's side of the family – but we thought you should know. (*Trying to joke.*) I think you've had your four quid, Grandad.

Silence.

GRANDAD. Them window boxes need painting out there.

JOEY. Just say the word, Grandad, just say the word.

GRANDAD. The kids have planted pot in them again – little bastards.

JOEY. It's a changing world, Grandad. Soon we won't be having cooked food, we'll take pills – steak pills, cabbage pills, rice pudding pills.

GRANDAD. Newfangled.

Joey is trying to get back to the subject of Uncle Cyril.

JOEY. I thought we'd have a burial at sea, being as he was a sailor.

GRANDAD. They get too much – the kids today. By the time they're five years old they don't want dolls and trains for Christmas – they want shares in British Telecom.

JOEY. It's the day after tomorrow.

GRANDAD. When I was a kid I had a hoop and a stick. That was it. I used to chase the bloody thing all round the neighbourhood – and when I got home, bread and syrup I got.

JOEY. You won't have to come, Grandad, to the funeral.

GRANDAD. You could get twelve chocolate caramels for a halfpenny in them days – no such thing as a bowl of fruit on the sideboard. We used to go into the greengrocer's for a ha'porth of fades. And off we'd go, happy as Harry, with our hoop and our stick and our knackered apples.

Joey just looks at his Grandad with affection.

JOEY. (*Getting up.*) No sense in mourning for the past Grandad – *now* is the important thing. (*Looking around and gesturing.*) You're doing all right, aren't you? Your own little house, meals on a tray, your family next door (*squatting next to Grandad*) – everybody rooting for you Grandad. It's not bad eh!

Long silence.

GRANDAD. He always wore white socks did Cyril – proper daft, they looked.

The Boswells' kitchen

The entire family – Adrian, Jack, Billy, Aveline and Joey – is seated around the table. The meal has been eaten and the table cleared. There is an enormous bowl of every kind of fruit in the centre of the table. Each person has a glass of wine. The bottles of wine are on a silver tray on the table. On the table there is a portable TV. A cartoon is showing and everybody is staring at it, except Joey. He is drinking his wine and studying some papers.

Mrs Boswell comes in, goes straight to the TV, switches it off and takes it away.

MRS BOSWELL. Have you no shame? With yer dead Uncle Cyril in the house.

AVELINE. Well, he can't hear it, can he?

MRS BOSWELL. Wash your mouth out, Aveline.

BILLY. It's weird having *him* here.

MRS BOSWELL. What's weird about it? It happens to us all. I'll be lying in there one day.

AVELINE. Oh don't Mam!

MRS BOSWELL. And don't think I won't hear everything you say – there's a lot out there we know nothing about.

JACK. Should have put him in a Chapel of Rest. He'd be amongst his own kind there.

MRS BOSWELL. The Chapel of Rest is not home is it – it's not family. I wouldn't put the dog in a Chapel of Rest.

AVELINE. Everybody else goes there.

MRS BOSWELL. I don't know what kind of a family I'm rearing – p'raps we should have put him in the yard with the bin bags.

JACK. It's a sort of racialism isn't it. Putting a dead person amongst live persons. You're just highlighting their difference.

MRS BOSWELL. What is he on about?

JACK. Well, you're making a statement aren't you? You're not actually saying it but you're showing that we're alive and well and he's dead and not well.

They all stare at Jack.

ADRIAN. (*To Jack.*) Why must you always complicate things? You just open your mouth long before your brain's ready for it.

JOEY. We are all entitled to say what we think Adrian, and Jack had a good thought there. (*To Jack.*) Work on it, son, come back to us when you're ready.

ADRIAN. It's just that he spreads gloom and doom around. (*To Jack.*) We didn't kill him, you know.

AVELINE. The other thing is that with Uncle Cyril here, we've got nowhere to sit.

MRS BOSWELL. You can sit in there (*indicating*) any time – his sitting days are over.

ADRIAN. I don't think we need to discuss Uncle Cyril's physical setbacks – death should be dignified. We had enough bother getting him into the house – what with runaway vehicles, hysterical relatives, pontificating priests, and him (*looking at Billy*) clanging about with his singing knees. Let him be, now he's here.

AVELINE. I hardly knew Uncle Cyril anyway.

MRS BOSWELL. He gave you pocket money when you were a kid.

AVELINE. I don't remember getting pocket money from him.

MRS BOSWELL. That's because he gave it to your dad to give to you – and you never got it. But he gave it just the same.

ADRIAN. He used to take me on his ship.

MRS BOSWELL. Chief chef he was – that's an honourable position.

ADRIAN. He used to force me to walk out the doors, past the gate policemen, with a side of beef in me school satchel. Sometimes it was tins of ham. I would have been taller but for him. Still he's dead now.

JOEY. (*Suddenly looking up from the papers.*) I think a man should die as he lived. (*Indicating the papers.*) It's no good putting a man like Uncle Cyril in a plot of land. He was a wanderer, a seafarer, a man of substance. You can't put a free spirit in a plot and stick a stone on him. You do that to budgies and hamsters.

MRS BOSWELL. Your dad would never allow cremation – you know what he's like. He always said he wouldn't like to end up with someone gravelling their path with him.

JOEY. A seaman's burial – that's what he should have. We'll scatter his ashes in the sea.

BILLY. Isn't death cruel? First you die, then you're cremated, then you're chucked in the water.

JACK. (*To Joey.*) Which sea?

JOEY. The Mersey.

JACK. That's not 'sea'.

JOEY. It's river isn't it? It goes to the sea.

JACK. Yes, but it does have a habit of coming back again.

JOEY. All right – so Uncle Cyril spends his afterlife going to Blackpool and back. It's better than being stranded ashore isn't it!

ADRIAN. How will you do it?

JACK. (*To Joey.*) I'm not rowing out in that river – it's polluted. Have you seen it – have you seen that water?! It'd burn the bum off a seagull.

JOEY. I'll try and get the *Edith May*. She's moored in the docks.

AVELINE. I modelled anoraks on her.

MRS BOSWELL. He'd be at home on a sailing ship – especially one from his own city. He loved his own city. 'There's no thrill,' he used to say, 'like the sight of the pilot boats waiting at the Bar, and the *Royal Daffodil* with her cargo of lovers, and the sound of a good scouse voice selling her "luverly white celery".'

JOEY. I'll arrange it all.

The phone rings, Mrs Boswell answers it.

MRS BOSWELL. (*She gets up.*) Hello. (*Pause.*) Hello Grandad – you've had your lunch. (*Pause.*) I don't think you should love – no. (*Pause.*) Why don't you remember him as he was? (*Pause.*) He's nice and comfortable and he's got the radio. (*Pause.*) All right, love, all right – if that's what you want – all right – yes – come in later, love. Yes. Tarra. (*She puts the phone down.*) Grandad wants to come round and see him.

JACK. That won't do him much good, will it? We could end up with two of them in there.

They all giggle except Joey.

MRS BOSWELL. (*Angrily.*) It's funny, is it? There's someone sleeping their final sleep in the next room and you lot find it funny.

JOEY. (*To Jack.*) OK – so watch the words, will you. (*Billy can't stop giggling.*) Billy!!!

Mrs Boswell sits at the table.

BILLY. (*Apologetically.*) Sorry.

JOEY. Dying is not funny – OK?

BILLY. OK – sorry.

JOEY. Specially in Sunset Lodge.

BILLY. Yeah, especially in Sunset Lodge.

JACK. We're just embarrassed, that's all. Well, people look silly lying down don't they? And there's no conversation – all you can do is stare at them. I mean, if they said, 'Who do you think you're looking at?' you'd have something to go on wouldn't you – something natural.

AVELINE. If he said that to me I'd run non-stop to Africa.

All but Joey begin to giggle. A stare from Mrs Boswell stops them.

JOEY. (*Getting up.*) I'll go and sort the funeral out. (*To Billy.*) You go down to the Social and sort the electricity bill out.

BILLY. What?

JOEY. (*Putting the envelope on the table and going up close to Billy.*) The electricity – we can't afford it. Go and sort it out.

ADRIAN. But we can afford it!

JOEY. But we can't afford to let them see that we can afford it.

BILLY. I don't know how to sort things out – you do that.

JOEY. It's time you learnt then, isn't it?

The phone rings and Mrs Boswell answers it.

MRS BOSWELL. Hello, hello, Grandad. What? Now? I don't think you should, love. . . . (*She puts the phone down and speaks to the rest of the family.*) He's coming round now to see Uncle Cyril. Jack, help your Grandad to pay his last respects.

JACK. Not me, you must be joking. I haven't got the right temperament for it.

MRS BOSWELL. Billy's too young. Joey's got to sort the funeral out. Adrian will be sick and Aveline's a girl. (*There's a knock at the door.*) There he is, go on. (*Jack leaves very reluctantly.*)

Inside the DHSS building

There are a number of people waiting. Billy is amongst them. He sits uncomfortably, waiting for his number to be called. A man starts to shout at one of the girls behind the glass.

MAN. Listen, love, don't look at me like that! If it wasn't for the misfortunes of people like me you wouldn't have a bloody job. *I* am a fully paid-up member of the 'Inner City Catastrophe'. And when there's no strikes or riots to take me mind off things, I have to fill me time in, don't I? So, what's buying and selling the odd car, cleaning the odd window, digging the odd garden, earning the odd quid? What's it got to do with you?

DHSS GIRL (MARTINA). Sorry, Mr Wilson, we'll have to review your case. Next!

MAN. (*Mimicking her.*) Next.

   It is Billy's turn. He gets up and crosses to the booth.

MAN. (*Putting his face up to the panel.*) You think you're God Almighty sitting there in yer life-proof plastic box, don't you? (*To Billy, as he arrives at the desk.*) She thinks she's God Almighty, mate.

MARTINA. (*To Billy, sharply.*) Yes.

BILLY. (*Sitting down.*) It's – it's the electricity bill – we can't afford it.

MAN. (*Through the window.*) They can't afford their electricity bill.

MARTINA. (*Ignoring the man.*) Name?

BILLY. Billy.

MARTINA. (*Sighing.*) Surname.

MAN. Just give them yer number son – they understand numbers better here.

BILLY. Boswell.

MARTINA. Oh – Boswell.

   Billy hands her the bill, she looks through a card file. The man begins to sing.

MAN. Land of Dope and Tory,
Mother of the poor,
Marching on our arses
Through the final door

He begins to wander out, stops at the exit, turns, looks around and shouts.

I'll be back! You load of twonks! (*As he goes.*) Taxi!!

Martina looks at Billy.

MARTINA. I don't know you, do I?

BILLY. No – our Joey usually sees to things. He's arranging to bury our Uncle Cyril – (*proudly*) so I'm the head of the family today.

MARTINA. I see.

Pause.

BILLY. (*Handing bill to girl.*) We can't pay.

MARTINA. I see.

BILLY. We're all out of work.

MARTINA. I see.

BILLY. Except our Adrian – but it doesn't go round – one wage packet.

MARTINA. No.

Pause.

BILLY. We look after our Grandad an' all.

MARTINA. I heard – yes.

BILLY. We're a family you see – we help each other. (*Pause.*) We don't mind being hungry and without, and without jobs, without clothes, and degraded – but we're not keen on hypothermia.

MARTINA. It must be very hard for you.

BILLY. (*Casually.*) So – could you see to that then?

MARTINA. Would you like us to pay by cheque or cash?! (*Billy looks at her.*) Mr Boswell – (*pause*) *Junior* – the day your family suffers from lack of food, lack of jobs, lack of money – lack of *anything* – those Liver Birds will clack with astonishment and lay an involuntary egg. There's more money going into your house than goes through Tesco's till. And as for hypothermia, I shudder to think what you'll claim for next. With a bill like that it'll probably be for treatment of first degree burns.

Pause.

BILLY. So you won't help?

MARTINA. No.

BILLY. We'll just have to fade away then.

MARTINA. You won't fade away – with all that heat you'll melt. (*She plonks the bill in front of him and calls out.*) Next!

The Boswells' living room

Jack and Grandad are standing silently by the coffin. Jack is staring everywhere but at the coffin. Grandad, on the other hand, is closely examining Uncle Cyril.

JACK. OK, Grandad, you've seen him now. (*He looks at his watch.*) Twenty minutes we've been here, Grandad. I'm getting depressed now.

GRANDAD. He looks old.

JACK. Yeah, well he hasn't got any thoughts in his head, has he? It's thoughts you see on a face, Grandad, it's just a blob otherwise.

GRANDAD. He owes me four quid.

JACK. He probably forgot. I mean, you do don't you, when you're having a heart attack.

GRANDAD. (*Looking into the coffin.*) We'll all be like that one day. You could be walking along the street, riding on a bus, sitting in your own little garden. It comes to us all.

JACK. It does, Grandad, yeah. (*He makes a nervous noise.*)

GRANDAD. And don't think, because you're young, it won't happen to you, 'cos it can.

JACK. I know, Grandad, I know.

GRANDAD. (*Pointing upwards.*) One wrong word, one wrong move, he's only got to lose his rag with you and wallop, up you go. (*He peers into the coffin again.*) Always wore white socks did Cyril. They won't look so daft where he is.

JACK. (*Fearfully.*) Could we go now, Grandad? Only I'd quite like to go to Mass.

Albert Dock (*two days later*)

The Edith May *is moored in the enclosed dock. She is in full sail – the crew are just about to free the rope.*

SKIPPER. (*Shouting to man on quay.*) OK – let her go!

The rope is thrown. On the deck Mr Boswell, Mrs Boswell, Billy, Jack, Adrian, Aveline, Grandad and Father Dooley sit in a row on a wooden bench. They are all muffled up against the cold, and each one, except the Father, holds a wreath. Joey is by the rail. He gazes out across the water.

GRANDAD. How long are they going to be? It's time for me lunch.

Pause.

MR BOSWELL. He'd be ever so proud would Cyril – proud and as pink as a pig on a postcard.

FATHER DOOLEY. Oh lucky man indeed, indeed.

GRANDAD. Aye – well when I go I don't want to be buried at sea, not with my arthritis.

AVELINE. We'll scatter your ashes in a bowl of soup, Grandad.

MRS BOSWELL. Wash your mouth out, Aveline.

BILLY. I feel sick.

JACK. So do I.

MRS BOSWELL. Oh God listen to them – going private to Rodney Street doesn't make them any stronger does it.

MR BOSWELL. He was a good man, a good man. Everybody loved our Cyril.

MRS BOSWELL. I didn't.

FATHER DOOLEY. Father forgive her – grief makes her tongue incompatible with her mind.

AVELINE. I like him better now – now that I know he used to give me pocket money. (*To Mr Boswell.*) Well, he used to give it to *someone* to give to me.

MR BOSWELL. And what does that mean?

MRS BOSWELL. You know very well what it means.

FATHER DOOLEY. Let us pray as we speed across the water to cast our brother to his final resting place.

MR BOSWELL. I don't know what you're talking about. (*To Aveline.*) I don't know what she's talking about.

MRS BOSWELL. You were always a liar, Freddie Boswell. You've got a calculator in your gob you have, it converts everything into lies.

Billy is holding his stomach, Jack is looking terrible and clutching at his wreath.

Jack, give over – yer crushing the flowers.

MR BOSWELL. (*Leaping up.*) Trust you, trust you Nellie Boswell – unbending, unforgiving, unrelenting.

MRS BOSWELL. At least I'm not unconcerned Freddie Boswell – unconcerned, unmoved, undeniably unreliable.

ADRIAN. Oh God it sounds like a television quiz.

MRS BOSWELL. (*Standing up and shouting.*) And unconscious. That's what you've been – unconscious. The kids came and yer never even noticed. When our Jack was born you were playing darts in Blackpool. When our Adrian was born you were marching through the city protesting because they were pulling The Blue Bell pub down. When our Aveline was born you wandered into the hospital with a book of boys' names. And when our Billy was born you were running barefoot through Sefton Park with Lilo Lil.

MR BOSWELL. I was there when Joey was born though, wasn't I? I was there then – for the first-born.

MRS BOSWELL. You were so pissed you sat at the next bed for twenty minutes gazing at the wrong baby.

MR BOSWELL. Fine thing – I can't even bury me own brother in peace.

JOEY. (*Calling.*) Quiet now – this is a funeral – OK?

FATHER DOOLEY. (*Praying.*) We ask Thee, oh Father, to guide this loving family safely through the angry waters.

MR BOSWELL. Yer a bitter woman, Nellie Boswell, a bitter woman, – standing there – (*pause, then as an afterthought*) – with the bag I bought you.

MRS BOSWELL. Oh bring up the bag now – the one you bought me thirty years ago. The *only* one you ever bought me. Bringing it up, are you?

MR BOSWELL. I loved you when I bought you that bag.

FATHER DOOLEY. And we ask Thee, Father, to bless the bag—

MRS BOSWELL. I hope so – it was our wedding day.

FATHER DOOLEY. And bless the precious contents thereof, as we Thy humble servants . . .

MRS BOSWELL. See if I care about the bag. (*She throws it overboard.*) Now I've nothing belonging to you, Freddie Boswell – nothing. And when the funeral is over, you can go back to yer dust-cart and leave us alone. We don't need you, Freddie Boswell.

She stops, and puts her hand over her mouth. Then she goes to the rail. The bag is drifting away. She calls, anguished.)

Uncle Cyril!

The whole family look helplessly at each other. Silently they stand and, taking their wreaths with them, they go to the rail, led by Father Dooley. He closes his eyes and lifts his head.

FATHER DOOLEY. We ask Thee, oh Father, to forgive the somewhat premature departure of our loved one. And we ask that in Thy loving compassion You will guide his mortal remains to the great sea where his soul and his spirit wander. And in Thy mercy, oh Lord, we plead that You deliver these Thy servants united in their grief, across the turbulent waters (*getting carried away*), through the great storms of Thy universe . . .

Mr Boswell is dabbing his eyes, Mrs Boswell is looking blank, Jack and Billy are feeling sick and shivering. Grandad is eating a mars bar, Aveline is arranging her neckline and generally preening. Joey just stands gazing out to sea, dramatically.

. . . across the cruel waves of Thy creation. And safely to the tranquility and peace of a loving home.

He indicates for Mr Boswell to cast his wreath. He does so. It lands upside down on the water. Father Dooley raises his eyes to heaven, and as the rest throw their wreaths he continues.

We commit our loved one's remains to the waters and may he rest in eternal peace. Amen.

Father Dooley then starts the hymn 'For those in peril on the sea'. One by one the family join in.

Outside the Boswells' house

It is dark except for the street lighting, and there is a lighted window as we travel slowly up the outer wall of the house – following an electric wire. We hear this dialogue, and the sound of general eating and clinking of glasses.

FIRST LADY'S VOICE. A lovely man was Cyril – yer did him proud.

MAN'S VOICE. Cheers Cyril.

MORE VOICES. Cheers!

SECOND LADY'S VOICE. Life has to go on, doesn't it?

FIRST LADY. Lovely fruitcake.

SECOND LADY. I said to our Tony, death is not like a strike – one out, all out. We have to carry on – we have to find a way.

We see now that the electric wire is draped across to the nearest street light and plugged in.

MRS BOSWELL. Oh yeah, we have to find a way.

Julie and Billy

Episode Six

The Boswells' kitchen (*morning*)

The entire family are at breakfast. The table is laden as usual – several packets of cereal, coffee, tea, fruit, a tray with marmalade and an assortment of jars on it, a dish of boiled eggs. Billy is pouring the last of the orange juice. Mrs Boswell sits silently with her hands together, waiting for him to finish. Then – silence. She closes her eyes, so does he.

MRS BOSWELL. We thank Thee, oh Lord, for the food on the table, the clothes on our back, the blood in our veins and the DHSS. We ask Thee to send us out into the faithless world with our spirits high and our bellies full – and to bring us safely back to Thy table, with our pockets in a similar condition. Amen.

ALL. Amen.

Everybody grabs at the toast, except Joey who waits until they have all taken what they want. There is none left. Joey sits quietly. One by one they each put a piece back.

MRS BOSWELL. I hope you all washed yer hands. Our Joey is a human being, not a steriliser. (*The phone rings.*) Oh God – there's Grandad. (*To Jack.*) Did you put sugar in his tea, Jack? (*She gets up.*)

JACK. Three. I put three in.

MRS BOSWELL. (*On the phone.*) Hello – oh hello, love. (*Pause.*) Jack put sugar in yer tea, Grandad. Yes – why don't you stir it?

AVELINE. (*Sighing.*) Honestly – all he ever thinks about is food. Why don't we just put him on a drip?

MRS BOSWELL. (*Cupping the phone.*) Aveline! (*Nicely.*) Just a minute, Grandad. (*To Aveline.*) How dare you? (*Pointing.*) That is a man of great age, that is a man who fought for our country. *That* is your Grandad – and after a lifetime of working to feed everybody else, he is now worried about feeding himself. Respect please!

AVELINE. Sorry!

MRS BOSWELL. (*Going back to the call.*) Sorry love – what were you saying? (*Pause.*) I did put a spoon on your tray – yes – (*getting angry*) – and salt – and sauce – and your breakfast was delivered to you *before* everybody else got a look in – as usual. And anything not placed on your tray can be found in your cupboard – which is restocked every week – by me – and which (*a real shriek*) is only two yards away.

She puts the phone down and stands there – upset. Joey goes to her.

JOEY. Hey come on, Mam. Don't worry about it.

He steers her back to her chair.

You worry too much about all of us. (*He sits.*)

ADRIAN. Especially him Mom – he's as tough as a butcher's block.

BILLY. We spoil him – that's the trouble. He's only got to cough and we book him into Lourdes.

JOEY. (*To Billy.*) Hey – who gave you the go ahead?!

BILLY. Well I am a member of this family, aren't I?

JOEY. Only just sunshine – you're still in rompers – so shut it.

ADRIAN. Look after yourself, Mom. (*To the others.*) She could, of course, if you lot did more for yourself. You know, little things like putting your own sugar in your tea and breathing. You look after yourself Mom.

Joey picks up Mrs Boswell's coffee and hands it to her.

MRS BOSWELL. You're right – I'm letting things get on top of me.

JOEY. How would you like a little holiday? The Seychelles – Barbados . . .

JACK. Or Rome – she didn't see the Pope last time because she was jammed behind a pillar.

MRS BOSWELL. I'll be all right – eat your breakfast all of you.

They all eat. Then suddenly she turns to Joey.

How's the money situation, son?

JOEY. It's fine – the family accounts are fine. There's three hundred in Brian Cartwright's – two hundred in Kevin Waring's.

JACK. I've got more than two hundred in.

JOEY. You're not Kevin Waring, are you? You're Joan Hepworth.

JACK. Joan Hepworth – great – why couldn't I be Brian Cartwright?

AVELINE. Because I'm Brian Cartwright.

JACK. Oh great. What happens if I want to draw something out?

JOEY. You ask Aveline, don't you? And if she wants to draw something, she asks you. It's called role reversal.

JACK. There's no privacy in this family. We're like apes – you can't pinch a banana without the whole jungle knowing about it.

ADRIAN. I don't get this – I'm the only one actually *working* and I don't have a bank account.

JACK. You're straight, aren't you? You can't have everything, (*emphatically*) Adrian. (*He laughs.*)

ADRIAN. All right, so I prefer the name Adrian. Is there anything wrong with that?

AVELINE. You were christened Jimmy.

ADRIAN. I didn't have any say in the matter then, did I? It was 'Dip your head in the font, shut yer gob, yer name's Jimmy.'

AVELINE. Snob.

JOEY. (*To Jack.*) OK – cut it out. There's no crime against having style. (*To Mrs Boswell.*) We've got enough money, Mam, so don't worry.

BILLY. When am I going to have a bank account?

MRS BOSWELL. When you earn money.

BILLY. I need capital.

JOEY. You've had capital – six times. First it was a ring for Julie – then it was a car. You've got to make money, *make* money.

BILLY. I'll hire it out as a getaway car.

JACK. They'd have more chance with a milk float.

MRS BOSWELL. (*Getting up suddenly.*) I'd better go and make it up with Grandad.

JOEY. (*Restraining her.*) There's no need. (*She sits down again.*) He'll be fine – finish your meal.

BILLY. Yeah, have your coffee – and then go to Barbados.

AVELINE. (*Brightly.*) Why don't you take Dad with you? (*A glare from Mrs Boswell to the rest.*) Well, you must have loved him once. (*To Jack.*)

MRS BOSWELL. I don't remember.

AVELINE. I thought love was something you never . . .

ADRIAN. Will somebody push the mute button on her mouth?

JOEY. Right – you're all going to do the washing-up.

Mrs Boswell is open-mouthed. He looks at the others – they are horrified.

Aren't we?

ALL. (*An assortment of agreements.*) Yes – oh yes – we will – yes . . .

The phone rings, Mrs Boswell jumps up.

JOEY. Take it easy. (*He gets her to sit down.*)

Mrs Boswell answers the phone. They continue breakfast.

MRS BOSWELL. Hello. (*Pause.*) All right, love, all right. (*She puts the phone down calmly.*) He doesn't feel well.

JOEY. OK, OK – probably something he ate.

JACK. It's not what he ate, it's how he eats it. You know how people eat oysters – he can down a whole dinner like that.

BILLY. We'll have to watch him, you know. The other day he picked up the Vim instead of the salt and put it all over his poached egg.

JOEY. (*Quietly.*) I'll just go and see if the post has come. (*He gets up in a leisurely way.*) Er – any more coffee there, Jack? (*He goes out of the room.*)

Outside the Boswells' house

Joey comes out of the house quietly but hurriedly. He closes the door without a sound, then goes to Grandad's front door. He knocks, then puts a key in. Just as he is opening the door the rest of the family come charging out of the Boswells' house and straight into Grandad's, pushing Joey against the door as they pass.

Grandad's parlour

Grandad is sitting in his chair staring into the fire – a lonely figure.
    The family suddenly burst in. They stand in a group by the door, Mrs Boswell in front.

MRS BOSWELL. Are you all right, love?

Grandad is silent. She goes to him and gets down on her knees.

Where are you not well, love? Can you point to it?

Grandad looks at her, then points silently to his head. Mrs Boswell looks fearfully at the rest.

You've got a headache, love, is that it?

Grandad shakes his head.

What then?

AVELINE. He's lost his plank!

ADRIAN. (*Reprimanding her.*) Aveline! God she's about as subtle as a ton of gravel.

MRS BOSWELL. (*To Grandad.*) Say something Grandad. Tell us what's wrong, love.

Joey comes in and strolls over to Grandad. The others knit together in a worried bunch.

He can't speak, Joey.

JOEY. (*Casually.*) Now then Grandad – what's this, what's this?

Mrs Boswell sits. Joey stands in front of Grandad – then kneels down.

Come on son – talk it out.

Long pause.

GRANDAD. I'm fed up.

MRS BOSWELL. (*Getting up.*) Fed up – is that all?

Joey puts his hand out behind him to curb her, and she sits down again.

JOEY. Why are you fed up, Grandad?

Pause.

GRANDAD. I'm fed up being – being – nobody.

AVELINE. A nobody! Me mam never stops running around after you – it's like an intensive care unit in here.

JACK. We've left our breakfast to come and see to you, Grandad.

BILLY. And another thing, Grandad . . .

JOEY. (*Shouting, for the first time ever.*) Shut it!!

They all look amazed. He turns to Grandad again – quietly.

Go on son – you were saying.

Pause.

GRANDAD. I feel – (*pause*) – like a toy – that's been put back in its box. (*Pause.*) Me winder's stuck – all it needs is a touch – and off I'd go. But nobody opens the box. (*Pause.*) I'm useless – old and useless. Was a time I could put me hand in me wallet and say – there you go, lad, there you go. But I'm – (*pause*) I'm just a parasite now.

Joey gets up.

JOEY. (*Walking round the chair.*) Oh – I see – you're a parasite now, are you? Listen, Grandad, why do you think you're in this house – *our* house? (*He squats down.*)

GRANDAD. I don't know.

JOEY. Because we're in your house.

GRANDAD. Means nothing.

JOEY. Oh yes it does. You charge us rent – we charge you rent.

GRANDAD. Means nothing.

JOEY. It means we both claim rent off the DHSS.

GRANDAD. Oh.

BILLY. (*Bluntly.*) And there's your incontinence Grandad – we get thirty quid for that.

GRANDAD. I'm not incontinent.

JOEY. (*Looking at Billy.*) Of course you're not incontinent Grandad. Who would suggest such a thing? But you've got your little window boxes out there Grandad – so we get an allowance for gardening equipment, and your deaf aid, in case you go deaf.

JACK. And remember when you started drinking a lot of water Grandad, and Dr Bennet said he'd have you tested for diabetes? We claimed for a fridge to keep your insulin in.

GRANDAD. I haven't got diabetes.

JOEY. Of course you haven't, Grandad. But there are lots of other little items, little nameless things, which all help to drive the engine that moves the ship, that takes us all to better shores. (*Pause.*) And you're part of it Grandad – you're the skipper. The only difference between you and us is that we go out every day to beat the bastards, and all you have to do is be here and keep (*pause*) your eyes to sea.

GRANDAD. You mean – I'm – not a parasite.

JOEY. You're pulling your weight, Grandad, you're the caviar.

MRS BOSWELL. We need you Grandad.

AVELINE. And we love you.

GRANDAD. I'm thinking of putting me rent up.

JOEY. So are we, skipper, so are we.

The grounds of a Catholic church

We hear the following dialogue. Then we see Jack digging a small hole in the soil of a grave. The name on the gravestone is 'Emily Boswell – Dear Mother of Nellie Boswell, and Much-Loved Grandmother of Joey, Jack, Adrian, Aveline and Billy'.

MRS BOSWELL. I'm a lucky woman, Father, I know that.

FATHER DOOLEY. Indeed my child, indeed.

MRS BOSWELL. I have a lovely family and in spite of the struggle and the hardship, Father, we pull together, all on the same end of the rope, all with each other in mind

FATHER DOOLEY. A just reward, my child, for a good, kind and true follower of the faith.

MRS BOSWELL. My only sin is this feeling in me heart towards the father of me children. I can't feel love for him, Father, I can't feel tolerance. All I can feel is the desire to punch his gob right through the back of his thoughtless, selfish head and to . . .

Jack is burying a golden candelabra in the grave.

FATHER DOOLEY. Oh Lord, we ask Thee to comfort Thy loving servant, and to show her the way to peace and tranquility. Teach her to set aside her feelings of resentment, and to find solace in the knowledge that she is surrounded by (*he doesn't believe this particular statement*) honest and upright children who will bring her joy and a proud heart. Amen.

MRS BOSWELL. Thank you, Father.

Jack is filling in the hole. He hastily puts back a vase of flowers, smooths the soil and stands up.

JACK. Thanks, Gran.

He runs off to his van which is parked nearby, and drives away.

The living room in Julie's parents' house

Julie is standing gazing out of the window. Billy is sitting on the settee staring at her. The atmosphere is very tense.

BILLY. (*Eventually.*) It can't be true – someone's made a mistake.

JULIE. (*Turning to him.*) What do you mean Billy, 'It can't be true'? Girls *do* get pregnant you know – the universe depends on it. And of *course* someone's made a mistake – you have!

BILLY. (*Scared.*) Me! Why me?

JULIE. Because, Billy, you are the cause – you are the father. You did it. (*Precisely.*) You – were – there – at – the – *time*!

BILLY. Oh God.

JULIE. (*To the window.*) I'll bet he's laughing his head off an' all.

BILLY. (*Pathetically.*) I haven't any money Julie. I haven't any job. Me last five quid went yesterday on seat covers for me car.

JULIE. (*Sighing.*) You know something Billy – you amaze me. That car doesn't even go – and if it does manage to leap about for a minute, the wings fall off. And while you're nailing them back on again, the vibration causes the radiator to empty itself. Buying seat covers for that car, Billy, is like buying carpets for a house that hasn't got a roof. And yet, you sit there, talking about it, boasting about it, *loving it*. And I'm standing here (*pause*) with our baby. (*She almost cries.*)

He goes to touch her.

JULIE. Don't touch me Billy Boswell – you've done enough damage.

He sits down again.

BILLY. (*Tenderly.*) Julie – we'll work it out.

JULIE. How?

BILLY. Something will happen.

JULIE. (*Sitting down.*) I know *something* will happen Billy – I'll get fat – me mam will come home sober one night and she'll tell me dad, and they'll send a helicopter to his ship and he'll come home on compassionate leave to throw me out and hang bits of you from every lamp post in the street. (*Pause.*) And I don't have to tell you with bits he'll see to first. (*Pause – dramatically.*) I could get rid of it of course.

Billy stares at her horrified.

JULIE. I could go to the hospital in me lunch hour – a bit of inconvenience, the odd twinge, a cup of tea, and that's it, over and done with. (*She suddenly shouts.*) And failing that I could go for a ride in your bloody car. It'd all be over by the time we reached Sefton Park!!!

BILLY. (*Shivering.*) I'm not cut out for all this – nobody warned me about all this . . . I thought life was a laugh – I thought . . .

JULIE. You know what thought did Billy – it followed a muck cart and thought it was a wedding.

BILLY. I'm too young for all this. I haven't been abroad yet – or worn a suit. (*Pause.*) I haven't been allowed to go and see an 'X' rated film yet.

Julie gazes at him.

JULIE. (*Going to him, compassionately.*) Oh Billy – here I am worrying about having a baby. I've got two, haven't I? I've got two babies.

BILLY. Me mam'll go mad. She's in and out of the confessional box by the minute – she'll have to move in now.

JULIE. It's not a sin – having babies. She had dozens.

BILLY. Five she had – five.

JULIE. Well it's more than us, isn't it?

Pause.

BILLY. (*Suddenly.*) We'll put our name down on the housing list.

JULIE. What for?

BILLY. A house.

JULIE. Have you any idea how long the house list is?! By the time it gets to us (*pointing to her tummy*) he'll be wanting a house himself.

BILLY. Maybe we could move in with me Dad.

JULIE. What! In a high-rise block. I'm having a baby, not a bloody albatross!

BILLY. (*Shouting fearfully.*) *Where* then, *where*?

Pause.

JULIE. (*Quietly.*) Nowhere, Billy. (*Pause.*) Nowhere – nothing – no one – describes the likes of us perfectly.

A back street

Joey's car is moving along smoothly. Joey is at the wheel, and one feels that, although he is acting calmly, he is restless and anxious.

Another car comes up behind him. Joey looks in the mirror, and almost immediately another car enters the other end of the street. The two cars block Joey between them. All three cars stop.

The man in the car behind Joey gets out. He is dressed in a smart suit, hat and camel coat. He leans against his car and lights a cigarette. The man in the front car gets out – he also leans against his car and lights a cigarette. Silence.

Then Joey gets out of his car – and lights a cigarette with his gold lighter. He looks at each of the men.

JOEY. (*Giving a charming tut-tut to the man in front.*) One-way street – well I never.

The two men close in on Joey who stands unmoved and unafraid. They position themselves either side of him.

FIRST MAN. We had an interesting game of poker the other night, didn't we Yizzel?

YIZZEL. Yeah – we did.

FIRST MAN. Won quite a bit of money, didn't we Yizzel?

YIZZEL. Yeah – quite a bit.

FIRST MAN. Only trouble was – the man we played with didn't have the readies, did he Yizzel?

YIZZEL. Sort of ran out.

FIRST MAN. (*Taking hold of Joey's lapel.*) Yeah – sort of ran out.

Joey looks at the man squarely. He lets go.

FIRST MAN. The thing is – and not to emphasise the point too much – or put an unwarranted importance on it – or indeed to impart to you the feeling that it has some significance – it was your father.

Joey is undaunted.

(*To Yizzel.*) See that – not a flicker – not a wince – not a swallow. We're dealing with an iron man, Yizzel.

YIZZEL. (*Peering at Joey.*) Maybe he's saving it all for the bad news.

FIRST MAN. Oh yeah – the bad news. (*He peers at Joey.*) I'm a compassionate man. I have a son and daughter, a cat, a canary – (*through gritted teeth*) and a bastard dog that goes for me every time I walk into a room. (*Nicely again.*) Now – your father is a dustman. (*Pause.*) Nice, sociable people, dustmen. They go out with their little carts and they clean up after us. (*Pause.*) Like our mothers. Now, I wouldn't harass a harmless dustman, would I? (*Through gritted teeth again.*) But dustmen's sons are different.

YIZZEL. Five hundred quid – three o'clock – Wednesday. (*Pointing to the ground.*) Here!

FIRST MAN. In readies.

YIZZEL. No tricks.

FIRST MAN. No pigs. (*Pause.*) I knew a man who turned up with the pigs. (*To Yizzel.*) It wasn't nice, was it Yizzel?

YIZZEL. (*Clutching his crotch.*) Ooooooh.

FIRST MAN. (*Pushing Joey.*) Move.

YIZZEL. (*Giving him another push.*) Yeah – move.

Joey gets into his car.

FIRST MAN. (*Through the window.*) A real carver – Yizzel. Top of his trade.

YIZZEL. (*Through the window.*) If you don't cough up – Yizzel find out.

They each go to their cars. Joey waits quietly. The first man deliberately reverses into Joey's car before he moves off. Yizzel deliberately bangs into the back of Joey's car before he is able to move forward. Joey just sits there, his face set. The three finally move away.

The estate agent's office

Adrian is practising what to say to his boss.

ADRIAN. I do realise that this is a remendous step forward Mr Hayworth. (*Pause.*) Oh thank you (*pause*) Graham. And I'm aware of the honour and indeed the responsibility. I have always felt that my job was hanging by a thread, hanging by a thread. (*Mr Hayworth comes in.*) But obviously you have insight and perception and drive.

MR HAYWORTH. Well now, Mr Boswell.

ADRIAN. Sorry, I was just . . .

MR HAYWORTH. I like to see a man rehearsing life. It shows – what were you saying? Insight, perception, drive. You'll need those things out there. (*He crosses to window.*)

ADRIAN. Out there?

MR HAYWORTH. In the street dear fellow – in the city – in the world. Out there where we all have to tread at some time or another.

ADRIAN. Oh – yes.

MR HAYWORTH. Especially those who are made redundant. (*Turning to Adrian.*)

  Adrian stares at him.

Business is not good, old man, not good. (*He sits down.*) It was a hard choice – sorting out the winners from the wimps. But a man only reaches my position in life by observing the rules, and the rules are that one must respect the hierarchy, honour the pecking order – each man on his own particular platform, with his own particular power, each man ready to serve his betters. So you will appreciate that when someone of reasonable status suggests that the meek shall inherit the earth, I am in a quandary, I am in a dilemma. After all, who am I to question the man at the top? The decision is obvious – you are strong – so you are out.

ADRIAN. (*Sitting down, and speaking in a doomed tone.*) May I point out to you, (*pause*) sir, that I come from a large family, and that I am the only one in our crowded, humble house that has a job (*pause*), sir. (*Pause.*) But for my salary, my brothers and my sister and my deserted mother would have no clothes – (*pause*) – sir. No food – there would be no heat, no light, no hope. And may I point out, sir, my old and fragile grandad would be the first to suffer – sir – the first to dwindle away – in his little corner, on his piece of off-cut Vet bed – (*pause*) sir.

MR HAYWORTH. (*Saying the final word on the subject.*) Yes – you *may* point it out to me, Mr Boswell.

A street

Aveline is clip-clopping along past some shops in her tight skirt, high heels, etc. A couple of young boys pass. They make loud appreciative noises.

FIRST BOY. How about it, sweetheart?

AVELINE. Isn't it time you went home and got your gripe water?

A little further on there are two more youths.

YOUTHS. Whoaaah!

Aveline seizes her whistle, which is round her neck, and blows.

YOUTH. OK, OK – forget it.

She goes on and sees a book stall. There are lots of magazines displayed outside. Aveline's eye catches the cover of one of them. The picture is of a topless girl, posing sexily. It is in fact Aveline. She stops open-mouthed.

AVELINE. Oh no – me Mam'll kill me.

She gets some dark glasses out and puts them on, then slinks away.

The Boswells' kitchen

The entire family are seated at the kitchen table. There is a huge ornate dish in the centre, with a ladle in it. This contains scouse. The cockerel dish is also evident. Mrs Boswell is saying prayers. The rest of them look worried.

MRS BOSWELL. We thank Thee, oh Lord, for this family meal and our table of plenty. And for keeping us safe through a safe and prosperous day.

She opens her eyes and looks around at the others, who are sitting silently, eyes closed. She closes hers again and says emphatically.

We thank Thee particularly, oh Father, for the good and *prosperous* day.

She looks at them again, their eyes are open. Joey is the first to reach for his wallet. He takes out a ten-pound note and puts it in the cockerel dish. Jack takes out five pounds from his pocket. Adrian takes two pounds from his wallet, Billy takes fifty pence from a little tin in his pocket. Aveline takes a pound coin out of her purse. They drop all this money into the cockerel dish.

MRS BOSWELL. Amen!

THE OTHERS. Amen!

Mrs Boswell starts to serve scouse out of the big dish. The family are all somewhat subdued.

JOEY. You shouldn't be doing all this, Mam, we'll get a woman in.

MRS BOSWELL. I don't want a woman in – I had one once who came to help when your dad was ill. (*Pause.*) You know the rest.

BILLY. (*Without thinking.*) Lilo Lil!

JOEY. Billy!

MRS BOSWELL. That's her. A perfectionist she was, everything shining, everything right. She starched your dad's pillow cases, bleached his sheets, ironed his pyjamas and then she made up his bed. All smooth and professional, like a hospital bed it was, even the covers had to be folded over. Straight and proper. (*Pause.*) I suppose, being a perfectionist, the only thing left to do was to get in with him.

JOEY. (*Sympathetically.*) Mam . . .

MRS BOSWELL. You can't trust them outside. Our dog knows better – you won't catch him trusting them. He pinches from their bins, chases their cats, pees on their steps, then comes home with a smile on his face.

She has finished serving them all now.

I'm taking Grandad's tray round – you start.

She picks up Grandad's tray and looks at the family, all of whom are either gazing at or playing with their meal.

MRS BOSWELL. What's the matter with it?

JACK. (*Quickly.*) Nothing, it's great.

AVELINE. (*Tasting.*) Mmm. Lovely.

ADRIAN. Smashing.

BILLY. Wow, spectacular.

MRS BOSWELL. There are times – especially when you're being devious – you all sit there looking like a group photograph of your dad. (*She goes out.*)

Aveline appeals hastily to Joey.

AVELINE. Joey, I'm dead worried, I've got something to tell you before me mam comes back.

ADRIAN. (*Quickly.*) So have I.

BILLY. Me too.

There's only Jack left, they all look at him.

JACK. Yes, count me in on the grief.

JOEY. OK OK, one at a time – no embellishments.

AVELINE. I saw a picture on a magazine cover, of a topless girl, that looks like me.

JOEY. So, what's the problem if she only looks like you?

AVELINE. It *is* me. I did it ages ago, when I was new at the job and daft.

JACK. Now she's old and daft.

JOEY. OK. We'll come back to it. (*He looks at Adrian.*)

ADRIAN. I lost my job today. I'm redundant.

JOEY. That's no sweat. We can take care of that. (*He looks at Billy.*)

BILLY. It's Julie – she's pregnant.

JOEY. Oh God it's getting worse.

BILLY. She says I did it.

JOEY. What do you mean she says you did it?

BILLY. She's right, I did.

AVELINE. Eh – isn't he clever?

Joey is harassed, he sighs and looks at Jack.

JOEY. All right, go ahead.

JACK. Mine's more complicated. I was down Lark Lane – you know, looking out for the odd chance to make some readies, and I saw two guys by my van. One of them reached inside, then they both turfed off down the street, and when I got there, there was this candelabra on the front seat. Silver it was, anyhow I didn't think too much about it. (*Joking.*) I mean, a candelabra on the seat – it happens all the time doesn't it?

JOEY. No embellishments.

JACK. So I switch my radio on and there's this guy describing some things that have been stolen.

JOEY. (*Impatiently.*) So, what did you do?

JACK. Well, I suppose I should have gone to the police, but they would never have believed me. And I didn't want them round here worrying me mam.

JOEY. So, what did you do?

JACK. I buried it on our granny's grave.

AVELINE. I think that's disgusting. She was very honest, our granny. When someone dropped a cigarette behind one of her cushions she only claimed for half a chair. Now she's got to share her grave with a nicked candlestick.

JOEY. Jesus what a mess.

Mr Boswell suddenly appears in the doorway, they all look surprised.

MR BOSWELL. The door was open – just passing.

Joey in particular looks at him.

Everything all right? Everything red as a rose?

JOEY. (*Calmly.*) Everything's fine Dad . . . how about you?

MR BOSWELL. Oh good and bad. Bright and dull, up and down, the usual.

AVELINE. Mam's next door with Grandad.

MR BOSWELL. All right is he?

JACK. He's fine.

MR BOSWELL. And yer mam?

JOEY. We're all fine.

BILLY. Do you want some scouse, Dad?

MR BOSWELL. No ta, I've got a sandwich on me cart (*pause*) I er . . . I won't be seeing you much.

AVELINE. (*Concerned.*) Why?

MR BOSWELL. Oh I thought I would move on.

JACK. Move on, where to?

MR BOSWELL. Another place.

BILLY. What about yer job, Dad? You must be the only one in this city with a job.

ADRIAN. And this city is yer home – I mean it's where you live.

MR BOSWELL. All streets are the same when yer sweeping them.

JOEY. (*Looking at him directly.*) Being drummed out are you, Dad?

Mr Boswell just nods his head at Joey, Joey mutters to himself.

JOEY. *Bastards!*

MR BOSWELL. Well, better go before your mam gets back. No use the canary hanging around, when the cat's on the loose. Ciao.

AVELINE. (*Calls.*) Dad.

Mr Boswell just goes out.

JOEY. It's all right, I'll see to him. Now listen, you tell Mam nothing. We'll talk about things later. Make plans. If we're going to give her a load of worry, we'll give it to her when it's cleaned up, OK?

They all agree.

JACK. I'll get those dippers.

JOEY. Forget it.

JACK. One of 'em wore a big fur coat, I don't know what kind of animal it was but after that coat they must be extinct.

JOEY. (*Looking at him.*) Was it full length?

JACK. Yes.

JOEY. Light-coloured?

JACK. Yes, sort of pet rabbit coloured.

Joey sits back with a smile, and dabs his mouth with a napkin.

JOEY. I think we've sorted three problems out.

JACK. Three?

JOEY. Yours, mine and Dad's.

They all look at him.

A back street

The street is deserted, except for the first man's car, which is parked halfway along, blocking the way. The first man and Yizzel are leaning against it, smoking. Suddenly the first man nudges Yizzel. They both look.

Joey is walking along the centre of the street, a lone figure walking gracefully as usual. The two men are alerted and straighten up as he comes towards them.

FIRST MAN. No tricks.

JOEY. Good day to you, gentlemen. (*He looks at his watch.*) On time, I believe.

The first man thrusts out his hand for the money.

FIRST MAN. You can cut out the Starsky and Hutch bit. Five hundred pounds – readies – now.

JOEY. Ah yes. (*He puts his hand in his coat.*)

The two men tense up and clench their fists.

JOEY. How much did you say – five hundred pounds? (*He brings out the candelabra.*) I think this will cover it.

The men look startled.

YIZZEL. (*To first man.*) Now? (*Meaning, Shall I clober him?*)

JOEY. You were seen putting it into a van. (*At this point Jack's van comes slowly into the street and stops facing the car.*) A relative of mine. (*Pause.*) We're a big family (*pause*) a big – strong – united —

YIZZEL. (*To first man.*) They might have told the pigs.

JOEY. . . . . honourable family.

All three glare for a moment, then the first man snatches the candelabra.

JOEY. (*Withdrawing it and holding out his other hand.*) Change.

FIRST MAN. Change?

JOEY. I'd say it's worth six hundred quid, wouldn't you?

FIRST MAN. He must be . . .

JOEY. Or seven hundred even? The longer it takes, the more it will go up.

At this point Billy's old car comes crunching into the street.

FIRST MAN. What the hell's that?

JOEY. Family runabout.

The first man looks at Joey for a long time. Joey stands his ground with his hand out.

JOEY. I forgot to mention, we're not known for our patience.

The first man finally gets out his wallet and slams the money, note by note, into Joey's hand. He snatches the candelabra.
Joey puts the money in his pocket and then opens their car door for them. He then closes the door and calls to Jack.

OK. Let them through.

Jack reverses slowly and just as the first man's car starts to follow, he suddenly goes into gear and slams into the front of their car.

JOEY. (*Charmingly.*) Oh dearie dearie me.

At this point Billy revs up and slams into the back of their car. Billy's car just shudders and more or less just falls to pieces. Joey raises his eyes to heaven.

The dogs' home

Joey is walking past the cages as usual, silently, sadly. The attendant is sweeping around.

ATTENDANT. Afternoon Mr Boswell.

Joey walks on. The attendant follows, he points to a dog.

He's the chap.

Joey stops and looks at the dog. Whilst doing this he takes out his wallet and hands the attendant a hundred pounds. Then he puts his wallet back and walks away.

The Boswells' kitchen (evening)

All the family (except Mrs Boswell and Joey) are sitting around the table drinking coffee. Jack is counting his ten-pound notes (change from the candelabra), Billy is sitting with his head in his hands, Aveline is playing with the sugar and Adrian is just staring. Joey comes into the kitchen and throws a pile of magazines on to the table.

JOEY. At least there's none left in the shop our mam goes into.

AVELINE. Oh thanks, Joey.

ADRIAN. My job was always hanging by a thread, hanging by a thread.

JOEY. (*To Aveline.*) Clear them away.

AVELINE. (*Getting up.*) I'll put them in a bin bag. (*She goes out.*)

JACK. A hundred quid. Not bad, not bad.

ADRIAN. Considering Joey did all the work, had all the worry.

JACK. All the worry?! I haven't slept since I buried that candelabra and if you don't believe me you can check. There are 3,796 rose buds on that wallpaper up there, the house opposite has 400 tiles on its roof and the chap next door goes for a pee at one o'clock, three o'clock and quarter past six.

JOEY. (*Indicating the money.*) How about sharing it with Adrian?

Jack makes his nervous noise.

He won't be collecting a wage packet after this week.

JACK. Why is it that every time I make any money I have to give some away? He never gave me any of his wages when I was on a down, did he?

JOEY. You only have down days – he's got to face down weeks. (*Pause.*) He's family, Jack.

Jack reluctantly hands Adrian two ten-pound notes. Aveline comes back into the kitchen and sees this.

AVELINE. Oh – are we collecting for our Adrian? (*She puts two pounds down in front of Adrian.*) There you are. (*She crosses round the table and sits.*)

Billy gives Adrian fifty pence.

ADRIAN. I'm very moved, very touched, I'll pay you all back.

JACK. Oh, it's all right.

ADRIAN. I've always wanted to be a Buddhist – this moment could tip the scales.

JACK. A Buddhist! They don't eat meat.

ADRIAN. I know, I quite like a salad existence.

JACK. And they shave their heads, you'll look like an old baby.

JOEY. The thing is, what're we going to do about *him*?

They all look at Billy.

Haven't you heard about contraceptives, sunshine?

BILLY. She said I had nothing to worry about.

JACK. They all say that at the time, but what they mean is, you have nothing to worry about yet.

BILLY. She said she was on the pill.

JOEY. They forget to take it, Billy. You should check.

JACK. Never get under starter's orders until you see the empty packet.

BILLY. I'm too young for all this.

ADRIAN. You should have thought about that.

BILLY. I've got my busking to think about. They love me out there.

ADRIAN. I can't believe it. A baby is going to be born and waiting for him is his dad with a mouth organ in his gob and cymbals strapped to his knees.

BILLY. (*Standing up and shouting.*) Oh you're all very clever, aren't you? You've got it all worked out. What I want to know is – why is it that you've all been at it longer than me and I end up pregnant?

Mrs Boswell enters with two bags of groceries.

AVELINE. Oh hello, Mam.

JOEY. (*Taking the bags.*) Give me those. (*He puts them on the draining board.*)

ADRIAN. (*To Mrs Boswell.*) Coffee, Mum?

MRS BOSWELL. Thanks.

Joey comes back to the table and Adrian pours the coffee.

Everything all right?

JOEY. Everything's fine, Mam, everything's fine.

MRS BOSWELL. Right, I'd like you all to go about your business. I've got things to do in here, like a dinner to cook.

All except Billy get up to go.

AVELINE. D'you want any help, Mam?

JACK. Yeah, we could peel the . . .

MRS BOSWELL. (*Cutting in.*) No thank you – I just want you all to go.

Billy starts to get up.

Except our Billy, I'd like a word with Billy.

Series Two

Jack

Episode One

A city street (*morning*)

Billy is busking. Beside him sits the family dog, and in front of him is a cardboard notice which reads: 'Loving Relationship – Baby and dog to support'. People are watching and a couple of them throw money into Billy's box.

Julie comes along – she reads the cardboard notice, then picks it up, tears it up and throws it away. Billy's busking goes off-key as this is done – then he stops.

BILLY. Eh Julie – what did you do that for?

JULIE. Because it's a lie – that's why.

BILLY. No it's not. It's just another version of the truth, that's all.

JULIE. I haven't had me baby yet, have I? And as for him (*indicating the dog*), he's the only dog I know that has a choice of pudding after every meal!

BILLY. I have to earn my living Julie – you're always saying we have nothing, and yet when I try to get something . . .

JULIE. And as for supporting *our* loving relationship – I don't want supporting thank you. I'll support myself – you're not going to drag me into the family keep net – I don't want your mam standing over my baby's pram waving the book of Boswell rules.

BILLY. (*Muttering.*) What pram?

JULIE. The pram *I'm* going to work for.

BILLY. That's what I'm trying to do.

JULIE. This isn't *work* Billy – clanging your knees together to keep people's mind off your voice isn't work! What kind of future is that for my baby?

BILLY. Last time we spoke it was all *my* fault – now suddenly it's your baby.

JULIE. (*Going up close to him.*) *I'm* making this baby, not you, Billy. It's in *my* body – I'm feeding it, building it, I'm going to give birth to it. All you did was fumble your way through some biological frenzy.

She walks away, trotting in her high heels. Billy composes himself and starts to busk again. Then he stops.

BILLY. Fumble!?

The Boswells' kitchen (*morning*)

The rest of the family are finishing their breakfast. Mrs Boswell is folding washed clothes and placing them in a neat pile.

ADRIAN. I see Billy's out early these days – taking approaching fatherhood seriously.

JOEY. It'll do him good – responsibility – reality – he'll have to rely on his brain now, instead of other parts of him.

JACK. He won't have any other parts of him, the way he's going on. All that banging and blowing – you've seen what happens to the hoover bag.

JOEY. He's young – he can take it.

ADRIAN. Young! He's never been young – he was born old. He . . .

MRS BOSWELL. I hope you're not going to criticise too strongly, Adrian. You know the family motto – 'Us and Ours'.

ADRIAN. Sorry. (*Pause.*) I have lost my job.

MRS BOSWELL. We know love, we know.

JOEY. You're part of the plan now son – you must get out there with the rest of us and bring in the pennies.

ADRIAN. Oh God.

MRS BOSWELL. Oh, another thing, Joey. While we're on family business, we must order the pram, and book Julie into Sandfield Park. Best to get it done now.

AVELINE. She doesn't want to go to Sandfield Park – she wants to go ordinary.

MRS BOSWELL. Yeah – well she's having a Boswell baby and the motto is 'Extraordinary yes – ordinary never'.

ADRIAN. How many mottos have we got?

JACK. Hundreds – one for every cock-up.

AVELINE. I wish I was having a baby.

MRS BOSWELL. Aveline!

AVELINE. I'd have a little green lawn with a cream pram on it – and me washing all white and see-through.

JACK. I thought you wanted to be a top model.

AVELINE. I do – and I will be – but now and then I have fantasies about being normal.

MRS BOSWELL. It's a pity we can't get close to Julie – I've asked her to tea, but she won't come.

AVELINE. She hates us, that's why.

MRS BOSWELL. Perhaps she's embarrassed about her mother – let's face it she hasn't been sober for years. Talk about the sailor's friend – she can sing 'Nellie Dean' in four different languages now.

JACK. I don't think we should push it Mam. I think we should wait until nearer the time, she'll need people more then.

MRS BOSWELL. It's funny, I used to lie in bed at night after your father had left, and I used to wonder how you'd all turn out. I had visions of failing to guide you properly – I was convinced that because there was no dad in the house I'd end up with a prostitute, a gangster, a kleptomaniac, an alcoholic and a poof. (*Pause.*) But you're all good – every one of you. (*She crosses herself.*) Thanks be to God.

JACK. Hey, I'm on to something today.

ADRIAN. What?

JACK. I'm going to make my fortune today.

AVELINE. What will they pay you with this time – apples, tomatoes, or your actual money?

JACK. No – this is the business. I got tipped off.

JOEY. Don't blow it – OK?

JACK. What do you think I am?

Joey gives him a look. At this point Billy comes in. He is upset – he is still wearing his cymbals. He draws out a chair, sits down and buries his head in his arms. The family look at each other.

JOEY. How about some breakfast, son?

No response.

MRS BOSWELL. What is it, love?

JACK. You'd better check – see he hasn't cut his throat on his mouth organ.

BILLY. (*Raising his head.*) Oh funny!

JACK. There yer go.

JOEY. What's happened?

BILLY. Julie tore my card up – she said it was lies.

JOEY. Then you write another one out – you don't let a woman run your life.

BILLY. But I love her. (*Pause.*) She's got shiny hair, and a little body – and smooth skin – and she walks behind me like a little sparrow. (*Pause.*) Twittering.

JACK. That's the problem with being in love, you start talking through your hormones.

BILLY. Yeah – well you've no need to pass comment – you cried when Marjorie Wainwright left you.

JOEY. Billy.

JACK. OK, OK – so I cried through my hormones.

AVELINE. (*Compassionately.*) Ah – isn't he human!

Billy is about to speak.

JOEY. Billy! (*Pause.*) You know, son, before you learn how to cope with everything else in life, you're going to have to take a few lessons in diplomacy – your mouth is permanently plugged in, isn't it? (*Pause.*) That was a very traumatic time for our Jack – maybe he'd like to forget about it – maybe it's his own private memory – maybe just mentioning it makes him anguished and despondent.

BILLY. Sorry.

JACK. It's all right – it was bad at the time.

JOEY. (*To Billy.*) You see.

JACK. But I realise now – she's just a big, fat slob.

A sigh from Joey.

MRS BOSWELL. When is Julie going to come to tea, that's what I want to know?

BILLY. I don't know.

JOEY. It's up to you sunshine – train them early.

MRS BOSWELL. (*To Billy.*) After all, the child might be the *only* extra Boswell we'll get. Our Jack's too disillusioned, our Joey is too wise, our Adrian is too depressed – and Aveline doesn't want to spoil her body. You're the only one thick enough to wade in there.

ADRIAN. (*Suddenly.*) I've met someone – actually – a girl.

They all look at him.

MRS BOSWELL. We must be grateful for that.

ADRIAN. Carmen. (*Pause.*) That's her name.

AVELINE. Is she Spanish? I can't stand Spaniards – they smell of olive oil and they're cruel to bulls.

ADRIAN. No – she isn't Spanish – she's English.

JOEY. That's great Adrian – you must bring her round – let's have a look at her.

ADRIAN. Not yet – it's in the early stages.

JOEY. When you're ready, son, when you're ready.

The cordless phone rings. Mrs Boswell takes it out of her apron pocket.

MRS BOSWELL. Your breakfast's on its way, Grandad. By the time you open your front door it'll be there. (*Pause.*) Oh – sorry. (*She hands the phone to Adrian.*) It's for you – Carmen.

Adrian takes the phone.

ADRIAN. (*Sloppily.*) Hello Carmen—

The rest finish eating, making a definite effort not to seem to be listening.

Yes, yes, it's me. It was – yes – wonderful.

JACK. It's in the early stages!

Adrian eases himself out of room.

ADRIAN. Tonight? Er, I think I've got something on. (*Pause.*) Er, just a moment, I'll check my diary and cross it out. (*To the family.*) She wants me to take her out for a meal, what should I say?

They all stare at him. Joey is the first to dip into his wallet, then Jack, then Aveline – finally Billy. They put the money in the centre of the table, silently.

I'm very moved. (*He goes back to talking into the phone.*) I've done it – I've crossed it out. So I'll see you tonight. (*Pause.*) It will be wonderful. (*Pause.*) I'll wear my brown cords again. Bye. (*Kiss*).

Mrs Boswell reaches for the phone; he gives it to her. He continues awkwardly.

She likes that sort of thing.

They all look at him.

Outside the Boswells' house (*later that day*)

Mr Boswell is sweeping the street; his cart is parked nearby and his radio is playing. He is whistling to the music.
A taxi pulls up outside; Mrs Boswell gets out. She is loaded with groceries. She takes the bags out first, then pays the driver.

MRS BOSWELL. (*To the driver.*) It wouldn't harm you to get off your arse and help, would it?

TAXI DRIVER. The last time I got out to help someone, darlin', somebody nicked me taxi – OK?

He drives away. Mr Boswell goes to Mrs Boswell as she is picking up the groceries. He picks up two bags.

MRS BOSWELL. What are you doing sweeping round here, Freddie Boswell?

MR BOSWELL. I'm just meandering – bringing back the colour to the cheeks of me childhood street.

MRS BOSWELL. Always play-acting, always talking poetic. (*They reach the door.*) You can put them down.

MR BOSWELL. I believe I'm going to be a grandfather.

MRS BOSWELL. Who told *you* that?

MR BOSWELL. (*Playfully.*) Mother Nature – 'Oh look,' she said, 'There's Julie, your Billy's girl – isn't she getting fat?'

MRS BOSWELL. You left us – it's nothing to do with you now – nothing that happens in this family has anything to do with you.

MR BOSWELL. Billy's one of my lads, whether he becomes a tramp or a king. He's my lad, and it's no good rushing to the church and sitting in that sinners' advice box either because nothing can change it.

MRS BOSWELL. What do you want from us?

MR BOSWELL. Just the odd pink word – the occasional white smile – the glad blue eye. (*He walks to his cart.*) Just something to keep me company when I'm brushing up the chip papers and the contraceptives.

MRS BOSWELL. (*Calling after him.*) It won't be enough though, will it? Give you a crust of bread and you'd take over the bakery.

He goes off down the road whistling. She calls after him.

We don't want you to come through the door of this house any more, Freddie Boswell!

Then she takes a box of chocolates out of one of the bags and knocks on Grandad's front door. After a moment the door opens.

I brought you some . . .

Grandad's hand snatches the chocolates and the door slams shut. Mrs Boswell raises her eyes to Heaven, unlocks the door of her own house and begins to take the groceries in.

The living room in Julie's parents' house

Billy is on the telephone. Julie is sitting on the sofa knitting.

BILLY. Oh – hello – I'm applying for the job at the garage please – yeah. (*Pause.*) Billy. (*Pause.*) I'm seventeen years, four months next week. (*Pause. An 'Oh God' look from Julie.*) Boswell. (*Pause. He then cups the phone and turns to Julie.*) He wants to know if I'm collecting Social Security.

JULIE. (*Drily.*) Tell him you need the job to buy a wheelbarrow to collect it in.

BILLY. I am – yes – just a bit you know – now and then – occasionally – when I think on. (*Pause.*) I see – yeah – OK – I'll ring you then. Thanks. Tarra. (*He puts the phone down.*) They've got enough on now – I've got to ring back next week.

JULIE. It's not much of a status job is it – car-washing. I'd rather you stuck to busking – at least you're self-employed.

BILLY. You're a snob, Julie.

JULIE. I don't want the father of my baby plodding about in wet wellies and wearing an anorak with 'Wonder Wash' written all over it.

BILLY. It's good money.

JULIE. Money is not everything Billy – pride is more important.

BILLY. All right then – we'll go down to the estate agent's and say, 'We want a house please – we haven't got any money, but we've got a lot of pride.'

JULIE. We don't need a house, we can stay the way we are.

BILLY. You mean you don't want us to get married now?

JULIE. The thing I dreaded, Billy, was being found out – being pregnant and not married – slowly running out of excuses for turning into an Easter egg. But it doesn't matter now – everybody knows.

BILLY. And what about me? How do you think I feel?

JULIE. Relieved. (*Billy looks at her.*) Oh come on Billy – you've looked like an old man this past four months. I only told you that we needn't get married two sentences ago, and already your acne's coming back.

BILLY. I want to do the proper thing, Julie.

JULIE. Of course you want to do the proper thing – but what are you going to do it with?!

BILLY. When my mam and dad first got married they had *nothing* – no house, no money, no job.

JULIE. Oh I know – and look how they've progressed. Yer mam still lives in the house her mother was born in. She comes home from the supermarket every day like a knackered packhorse. And yer dad pushes a little yellow cart around with a council brush in it!

BILLY. I don't like the way you talk about my mam and dad, Julie. They're good people.

JULIE. All that – and they don't even live together.

BILLY. They fell out, that's why. That can happen to anyone.

JULIE. Yeah – your mam fell out with the world, and you dad fell out of her bed, straight into Lilo Lil's.

BILLY. You hate my family, don't you?

JULIE. Yeah – I do. And my own no better. My dad's got a woman in every port, and my mam's got a fella in every pub. I want to be different Billy – different from all of them.

BILLY. I'll always love you, Julie. (*Pause.*) Even when you're married to someone else.

She looks at him. They kiss.

JULIE. Oh Billy – I wish you didn't have a way with you.

BILLY. Will you come to our house?

JULIE. No Billy.

BILLY. One day – any day – just try us out Julie – just – walk in.

JULIE. No.

A posh road with expensive houses

Jack's van is parked outside one of the houses, and Jack is carrying a very large picture down the drive. He calls to a couple who are standing at the front door.

JACK. Tarra – thanks! I suppose I'll get rid of it some time.

He manoeuvres it through the gate and takes it to his van, then props it up against the van whilst he opens the back. He carefully places the picture inside, pauses, looks at it and throws it a kiss.

JACK. (*To the picture – a tasteful nude.*) OK darlin' – it's you and me and the bank.

He hastily gets into the van and zooms away.

Inside the DHSS building

There are quite a few people waiting. Joey is sitting by the window – and a girl is just finishing putting some papers away. She finally looks up at Joey and is immediately struck by him.

GIRL. (*All soft.*) Yes?

JOEY. I am Joey – Joey Boswell. You're new here, aren't you?

GIRL. Yes.

JOEY. Ah – then you won't know about the spectacular relationship I have with the staff here.

The usual girl, Martina, appears.

MARTINA. I'll do this one.

FIRST GIRL. (*Starry-eyed.*) What did you want?

MARTINA. Anything he can get.

She moves the first girl out of the way and sits down opposite Joey.

Afternoon, Mr Boswell.

JOEY. You are a very possessive woman.

MARTINA. I'm waiting, Mr Boswell.

JOEY. Right – yes – it's about our rent – it's gone up.

MARTINA. (*Staring at him.*) Go on.

JOEY. That's it – it's gone up – so our little present from you needs to be reassessed, doesn't it?

MARTINA. You mean – there's no complications, nothing devious – just a straightforward 'The rent's gone up'?

JOEY. Right.

She gets a form and begins to write.

Oh – and our grandad's has gone up as well.

She puts her pen down.

Only, I have explained, he can't come himself as he has several problems, apart from being old.

MARTINA. I know – he's deaf, daft and dithery – and he's claiming for all three of them.

JOEY. I just thought we'd get the two done together – save you time and me walking all this way twice.

MARTINA. In your Jaguar.

JOEY. Ah yes – loaned to me by a dear old lady so that I may do her shopping and take her to the seaside.

MARTINA. I'd start the violins up but they can't play for laughing.

JOEY. (*A sigh.*) Cynical lady – so cynical.

MARTINA. Now, your rent's gone up, and your grandad's rent's gone up, which means that you've put his up and he's put yours up.

JOEY. That is correct, yes.

MARTINA. You know Mr Boswell, in this life we are supposed to live and *learn*, and I already know the answer but I will ask this question – why do you live in his house, and he live in yours? Why can't you each live in your own?

JOEY. Well it's a long story – when our mam was sadly deserted by our somewhat . . .

MARTINA. (*Interrupting.*) All right, all right – it's breaking me up. How much?!

JOEY. He's put ours up three pounds, we've put his up three pounds, so we need an extra six pounds per week.

MARTINA. I see, you're in each other's houses so you can charge each other rent and claim it from us.

JOEY. (*Tut-tutting.*) Dear, oh dear, where do you get this bitterness?

She pushes two forms towards him. He gets out his gold pen and pushes the top – a little musical box plays 'Rule Britannia' as he signs with a flourish. The girl raises her eyes to heaven. He pushes the form towards her.

MARTINA. We'll get you one day Mr Boswell. You'll walk in here with a story as watertight as a colander, and I'll be waiting Mr Boswell, I'll be waiting.

A city street

Jack's van is coming along – a dog runs out from the pavement. Jack has to stop quickly. As he jerks to a halt there is a bang in the back of the van. He gets out, rushes to the back and opens the doors. The picture has fallen and the gold frame is broken.

JACK. Oh shit! (*He turns and looks down the street after the dog.*) I'll get you next time! I won't stop next time – they'll have to shovel you up mate!! Go on with you!!

He turns to go back to his van just in time to see two youths trying to remove the picture.

Hey you!

They let go and run.

You little bastards!

Jack runs to the picture. The rest of the frame is broken now, and he examines a scratch running across the canvas.

JACK. (*Sighing, then to the picture.*) It's all right sweetheart – just a scratch. No one will notice it when you get your clothes on.

He painstakingly loads it into the van again, slams the doors, gets in and drives off.

Grandad's living room

Adrian is sitting in the chair and Grandad has a tray on his knee, with a cup of coffee and a piece of cake on a plate.

ADRIAN. It's nice and cosy in here Grandad – I've never really noticed it before.

GRANDAD. Is this me proper tea? Or just a snack between me lunch and me tea?

ADRIAN. (*Looking around.*) Now that I'm redundant I know what it's like 'to stand and stare'.

GRANDAD. 'Cos if it's me proper tea – I have two cakes.

ADRIAN. Do you remember Grandad – when you were a young lad, courting my granny – do you remember what it was like?

GRANDAD. It was a pain.

ADRIAN. A sort of – (*pause*) – exquisite pain?

GRANDAD. No just a pain – like you get when someone kicks you in your goolies.

ADRIAN. I've met someone.

GRANDAD. Stay clear – that's what I say – stay clear.

ADRIAN. Her name's Carmen.

GRANDAD. Is she Spanish?

ADRIAN. No – she's . . .

GRANDAD. Noisy women, the Spanish – they're all tits and tambourines.

ADRIAN. I've never felt like this, Grandad.

GRANDAD. Stay clear.

ADRIAN. The thing is – we wondered – *I* wondered, if we could use your front parlour – you know – just once or twice, until we get to know each other properly. Only she lives with her parents, and you know what our house is like – we haven't anywhere to go, you see, Grandad.

GRANDAD. What's wrong with a shop doorway?

ADRIAN. It's not very romantic is it, Grandad, a shop doorway? I mean, you've only got to lean against it and the alarm goes off.

GRANDAD. You get everything too easy, you kids. I used to court your granny in the grounds of the Co-Operative Rest Home. (*Reflecting.*) It was nice and quiet there.

ADRIAN. So, we were thinking of tonight, Grandad, after dinner. (*Grandad looks at him.*) Your parlour.

GRANDAD. How long will you be? I go to bed after *Question Time*.

ADRIAN. You can go to bed Grandad – we won't disturb you.

GRANDAD. I'm not having hanky-panky going on in my parlour. There's been enough of that over the road – see where it's got our Billy.

ADRIAN. He's only young Grandad – I'm older and more experienced. I've – er – I've done it all, shall we say.

GRANDAD. Mother Nature is like a spider – and when you get caught in her web she's not bothered whether or not you've done it all. She's just glad that you're stuck there, suspended, tangled and helpless. (*Emphatically.*) Doomed.

A back street

Jack is driving his van. He is whistling with joy. Suddenly two men run out in front of the van and wave frantically. One of the men gets into the passenger seat and pulls out a gun. He presses it in Jack's side.

FIRST MAN. OK pal – we need a ride.

The other man goes round to the back of the van and gets in.

Right – get moving.

Jack is terrified. He revs up and drives off. The second man appears menacingly behind him.

SECOND MAN. And don't stop until we tell you.

JACK. Where to?

FIRST MAN. Manchester.

JACK. Manchester! I'm on my way home – me dinner's ready.

FIRST MAN. (*To second man.*) Oh goodness me – his dinner's ready. (*Fiercely, to Jack.*) Move!

SECOND MAN. Nice picture you've got here.

JACK. Oh yeah – it's rubbish really – I was taking it to the tip.

FIRST MAN. Oh yeah.

JACK. I er – stole it.

The two men glance at each other.

SECOND MAN. Why did you steal it if it's rubbish?

JACK. (*With a casual shrug.*) Well, you don't have much chance to get your eye-glass out when the alarm bell's going and there's an Alsatian hanging on to your arse, do you?

The men laugh at this. The first man puts the heavy hand of friendship on Jack's shoulder. Jack winces.

Can I make a phone call?

FIRST MAN. (*To second man, nicely.*) Can he make a phone call?

SECOND MAN. (*Sweetly.*) Of course he can – and give him a whistle to blow while he's out there.

FIRST MAN. (*A change of tone, pushing the gun in Jack's side.*) If I pull this trigger, mate, your guts will get to Manchester before we do.

Outside the Boswells' house (*evening*)

Joey comes out of the door holding a tray laden with food, fruit, etc. He carries it to Grandad's house next door and knocks. He deliberately holds the tray high so that when Grandad opens the door and goes to grab it the tray isn't there.

GRANDAD. Give over!

JOEY. Dinner is served, Grandad. (*He lowers the tray.*)

GRANDAD. I hope it isn't chicken again – I had chicken yesterday. I'm sick of chickens – the world must be full of bloody chickens.

He grabs the tray and closes the door. Joey smiles to himself and strolls back to the house. Grandad opens the door again.

GRANDAD. *And* I only had one cake for me tea!

A country road (evening)

Jack's van is parked. The two men are pinning Jack to the side of the van. The first man has him by his jacket. Jack has a black eye.

FIRST MAN. That wasn't a very nice thing to do, now was it?

JACK. I'm sorry – only I suddenly remembered – about my problem – and it made me panic.

FIRST MAN. Problem?

SECOND MAN. (*Tightening his grip.*) What problem?

JACK. Oh it's nothing – I've learned to accept it now.

FIRST MAN. (*Close to him, threatening.*) *What* problem?

JACK. (*Dramatically.*) I haven't long to live.

The men glance at each other uneasily.

It's er – my heart – it's clapped out. Instead of the valves going (*using his fingers to indicate the rhythmic movement*) de da, de da, de da, de da, it goes (*quicker movement of fingers*) da, da, da, da, da, da.

The two men look at each other fearfully.

It's all right – I took a tablet just before you punched my face in – opens up the arteries – keeps me going.

Pause.

FIRST MAN. (*Backing down, now, letting go of Jack.*) Yeah – well.

SECOND MAN. Just watch it.

FIRST MAN. Yeah – watch it.

They begin to back away.

SECOND MAN. You'd better watch it, mate.

FIRST MAN. Yeah.

Suddenly they run off into a field. Jack loosens his clothes, gives a sigh of relief, then rushes to his van and gets into the driver's seat.
He tears off. After a moment of high speed the back door of the van flaps open and the picture spills out. Jack pulls up with a screech, runs back for

*the picture, drags it to the van, puts it in again, rushes to the drivers seat
and zooms off again.*

JACK. (*Calling to picture as he drives.*) OK darlin' – we're going home.

The Boswells' kitchen (*evening*)

The family are still eating.

ADRIAN. (*Suddenly.*) I bumped into Carmen today and we talked.

Silence – they all think about this.

AVELINE. Ooh – you're breaking down all the barriers aren't you – colliding
and talking.

ADRIAN. Anyway, we're going out for a meal later, and then we're going to sit
in Grandad's parlour – (*pause*) – to talk.

MRS BOSWELL. Yes, well see you behave yourself.

JOEY. (*To Mrs Boswell.*) He's no chance with Grandad – I've tried it – he
comes in every two minutes to water his aspidistra.

ADRIAN. And the good news is – she's coming to tea – tomorrow.

MRS BOSWELL. Oh – isn't she lovely? (*To Billy.*) You see!

BILLY. I can't get Julie to come – I've tried.

ADRIAN. You're not masterful enough, that why.

BILLY. Masterful! You can't be masterful with Julie – she's like one of those
jungle frogs you read about – when she's annoyed she trebles her weight and
goes a funny colour.

JOEY. You've got to be tough with them Billy – start the way you mean to go
on.

AVELINE. I love tough fellas – they're like big dogs – they look twice as
helpless when they're offering you their paw.

ADRIAN. I just said to Carmen – my family want to meet you – tomorrow for
tea – prompt – no arguing. Now, what's next on the agenda? (*Pause.*) She
leaned over and kissed me – (*pause*) – on the mouth.

Billy stares at him thoughtfully. They eat. The dog barks.

MRS BOSWELL. Oh God – there's the dog now – he'll be worn out, he's
courting somewhere in the Truebrook.

BILLY. I'll let him in. (*He gets up and goes out.*)

MRS BOSWELL. I'm worried about our Jack.

AVELINE. He'll be all right Mam – don't worry.

Outside the Boswells' house

Billy opens the door and lets the dog in. Then he looks over towards Julie's house. He braces himself, then strides purposefully across the road, and knocks loudly on her door.

BILLY. (*Calling.*) Julie!

   The top window opens – Julie pops her head out.

JULIE. What do you want, Billy?

BILLY. (*Tough attitude.*) I want *you*, Julie.

JULIE. You'll have to wait, I'm not dressed.

   She closes the window. Billy stands with his arms folded, waiting.
   Jack's van is coming along the street. He pulls up outside – he is dishevelled, and has a black eye. He beeps his horn.
   Aveline comes trotting out and moves the Police cone for him. She goes back into the house. He pulls in and gets out of his van, rushes to the back, opens the door and smiles through his pain at the sight of the picture. He moves the piece of broken frame and very carefully begins to ease the canvas out of the van.
   Meanwhile Julie's door opens – Julie is there. Billy just grabs her wrist.

BILLY. You're coming with me, Julie.

JULIE. Billy – let go of me.

BILLY. Me mam's cooked dinner and you're coming – now – prompt – and no arguing.

JULIE. (*Trotting behind him as he keeps hold of her hand.*) I'm not coming – I'm not. Get off me, Billy Boswell.

BILLY. Shut up! (*Pause.*) Woman.

JULIE. I'm warning you, Billy.

BILLY. And watch that baby!

   Jack is picking up the picture and he begins to carry it towards the house. Julie breaks free from Billy just as they near Jack.

BILLY. Julie – I've told you.

JULIE. (*Standing and yelling at him.*) You're not my boss Billy Boswell – you don't own me – I hate your family!

JACK. (*Lowering the picture.*) Oh – hi Julie.

JULIE. And that includes you, Jack Boswell.

She punches a hole right through the picture and walks back to her own house. Jack just stands there with a doomed look, holding his precious picture.

BILLY. (*Calling.*) Will you come to tea tomorrow then?

The Boswells' kitchen (teatime, the next day)

The whole family are sitting around the table – but now Carmen is sitting next to Adrian. They are gazing at each other. Julie is sitting next to Billy. Mrs Boswell is busy in the background arranging cakes on a plate. Joey is pouring and handing each person a glass of wine.

JULIE. (*To Jack.*) I'm sorry about your picture.

JACK. It's all right – I'll get a tenner for the frame when I knock it back together.

JOEY. (*To Jack.*) Don't worry sunshine. We'll get them – you'll see.

BILLY. (*To Julie.*) They held him up with a water pistol!

JOEY. Billy! Shut it – OK.

MRS BOSWELL. (*Going to the table.*) Right – that's it – you can all start.

They all do.

After prayers.

They all stop. Mrs Boswell puts her hands together – so do the family. The two girls just sit watching.

We thank Thee, oh Lord, for another day, for our Jack's safety, for the company of new friends, and may they bring joy to their loved ones and *enrich* our family.

She opens her eyes and looks at the two girls.

Eventually. Amen.

THE REST. Amen.

They all start to eat now. Adrian puts a cake on Carmen's plate, all the time gazing at her. Billy grabs two cakes for himself, puts them on his plate – then becomes aware of Joey's gaze. He swaps plates with Julie, giving her the one with the cake.

AVELINE. (*To Carmen, who is gazing at Adrian.*) I love your earrings – where did you get them?

No reply from Carmen.

I was only being nice – I don't like them at all – they're dead common. (*She reaches for some food.*) Excuse me.

CARMEN. (*Tremendously posh.*) Oh – I'm so sorry.

Aveline looks open-mouthed. The rest all glance at each other. Billy stares – he is about to pass comment.

JOEY. Billy.

They all eat silently. Mr Boswell wanders in. They all look but say nothing. Mrs Boswell glares at him.

MR BOSWELL. All the colours of the rainbow hey – all the colours of the rainbow. (*Pause. Then, to Mrs Boswell.*) You said, don't come through that door again, so I came through the window.

The rest giggle. Mrs Boswell stops them with a glare. Then she and Joey look at each other – Mrs Boswell nods.

JOEY. Sit down, Dad, and have your tea.

Mr Boswell does this, as Joey pulls out a chair.

MR BOSWELL. Like old times. (*Pause.*) Except that I used to sit in *that* chair.

He looks at Mrs Boswell. She stares back at him, then moves as if to stand.

JOEY. Stay there, Mam, stay there. (*To Mr Boswell.*) Fruit cake or cream cake, Dad?

Grandad and Aveline

Episode Two

Outside the Boswells' house (*morning*)

Aveline comes out of the house. The milkman is placing milk on the step next door (not Grandad's). He stays in the stooped position as Aveline's high boots and legs appear – and he fixes his gaze on them. Aveline knocks on Grandad's door – and whilst she is waiting she looks at the milkman.

AVELINE. Could you leave some yoghurt at ours, please?

MILKMAN. (*Composing himself.*) Yoghurt sweetheart – what kind? Apricot – strawberry – pear – raspberry – black cherry – orange – pineapple – banana – goat – Jersey cow – Greek – French – English – high-fat – low-fat – live . . .

AVELINE. Some with no preservatives in it.

MILKMAN. Sorry love – you'll have to go to the cranks' shops for that – we only sell the poisonous stuff.

AVELINE. OK. (*Knocking on the door again.*)

> *The door opens immediately. Grandad appears in his dressing-gown – he has a bib tucked in around his neck.*

GRANDAD. I've been up all night waiting for my breakfast – you'd need a magnifying glass to see that supper last night.

AVELINE. It's me, Grandad. I'm going to Manchester to do my modelling test.

GRANDAD. Modelling test?

AVELINE. It's a big job Grandad – all the top models are after it. If I get it I'll pay for a Jacuzzi to be fitted in your back yard.

GRANDAD. A young girl like you shouldn't be going to foreign parts on her own.

AVELINE. Manchester isn't foreign Grandad – come on now, give us a good luck kiss. (*He does so.*) See you later love. Tarra.

> *She wiggles off down the road. Grandad watches.*

GRANDAD. All that wiggling – she'll wear her bones out.

> *Aveline is still walking down the road. A woman is taking her milk in.*

WOMAN. Hello Aveline – going modelling?

AVELINE. Yeah – it's me big chance.

WOMAN. You look lovely, queen.

AVELINE. Thanks.

> *Aveline goes forth towards fame.*

The Boswells' kitchen

The radio is on. Mrs Boswell picks up the coffee jug and puts it on the table.

RADIO VOICE. I hope the music is helping you stay bright and sunny, because with the time now at 8.21 the weather certainly won't. We expect a cloudy day with low temperatures . . .

Mrs Boswell turns the radio off. Then she goes to the hall and shouts.

MRS BOSWELL. Joey – Jack – Billy – Adrian – it's ten o'clock!

She goes back to the table. Adrian arrives in a great flurry. He is wearing his shirt and a pair of underpants – and carrying his trousers.

ADRIAN. I've got to be down at the Social Security by 10.30. I'll never make it. (*He starts climbing into his trousers.*) To think I should come to this. My pride is hanging by a thread – hanging by a thread.

MRS BOSWELL. We've all come to this, Adrian. (*He is struggling with the trousers.*) And take it easy before your thread snaps altogether.

Joey comes strolling in.

JOEY. Greetings. (*He sits down. To Mrs Boswell.*) OK, Mam?

MRS BOSWELL. Fine love, fine. Had a good night?

JOEY. Not bad – not bad.

Jack comes into the room.

JACK. Who's been using my electric razor?

JOEY. Not me sunshine – I have my own. (*Smiling.*) The one with the gold letter J on it – remember!

Jack and Joey sit.

ADRIAN. I keep *my* razor under my pillow – along with my toothbrush and my back brush – you daren't put your soul down in this house.

Billy comes strolling in.

JACK. (*To Billy.*) Have you had my electric razor?

BILLY. I haven't got anything to shave, have I?!

Billy sits.

JACK. It's Aveline – she's been stripping her legs again. Have you seen the gear she's got up there? Body scrub, body rinse, body revitaliser, body loofa, body oil – the average body grows a new skin every seven days, hers has to get one out every half-hour.

MRS BOSWELL. I hope she gets the job today – it's her big chance, her dream day.

JOEY. We'll soon know – we'll soon know. (*He looks at the blinking Billy.*) All right there, son? Having trouble opening your eyes, are you?

BILLY. I didn't leave Julie's until three o'clock this morning – she keeps thinking the baby's coming.

MRS BOSWELL. She's got two weeks to go yet.

BILLY. I keep telling her that. 'What do you know about it?' she says. 'Well, I know that pregnancies last nine months,' I said. 'So where were you on Monday, 25th January, between ten o'clock and the rest of the night?' she said. 'What's that got to do with it?' I said. 'You see,' she said, 'you think you know everything about the game of life and you can't even remember the kick-off!'

JACK. It brings it all back to me – the kind of conversational trap you fall into with women. They take every sentence you utter and string them together until they're long enough to strangle you with.

ADRIAN. Carmen isn't like that – she responds to human communication. She has a sense of intellectual skill if you like – she enters the verbal arena, sniffs out your weaker statements and returns them to you, without biting your individuality.

A long family silence.

JACK. She'd do well at Crufts.

MRS BOSWELL. Jack!

JACK. Well – what garbage! If that's what A-levels do for you, I'm glad I had to have my tonsils out.

JOEY. OK, OK, let's have a peaceful breakfast shall we – the world is waiting for us out there.

BILLY. It isn't waiting for me – it couldn't care less about me. I busked all day yesterday – by five o'clock my knees were knackered and my cymbals were bent. Two quid I got – two quid!

JOEY. It's no good busking outside the big shops where people have just spent their money, you should do it outside the DHSS where they've just collected it!

MRS BOSWELL. Let us pray.

They all put their hands together.

We thank Thee, oh Lord, for the fruits of thy earth. We ask Thee to watch over Julie with her baby – and Aveline with her modelling – and we ask Thee to go with each one of us through our day of searching, and may we return joyfully with a goodly share of bread – the kind you eat, and the kind you spend. Amen.

ALL. Amen.

MRS BOSWELL. (*To Billy.*) It's your turn to take Grandad's tray round, Billy.

BILLY. Why can't he come and get his own tray?

MRS BOSWELL. (*Muttering.*) If God could hear him now.

BILLY. I thought he could hear everything.

MRS BOSWELL. (*To Joey.*) It's no use Joey – he's becoming unmanageable.

ADRIAN. (*Muttering.*) *He's* going to be a father – him! A father! Oh God.

JOEY. (*To Billy.*) Grandad could come and get his own tray – but *we* don't want him to, because he is old, and you are not. He has earned a rest, and you have not. And he is our grandad – and in spite of the way you look, you are not. Now go on – move.

BILLY. Why can't we put a hole in the wall, then we can pass things through to him?

JOEY. You've seen what happens to things when you put holes in them Billy – you had a reasonable head on you until Mother Nature put a gob in it.

Outside the Boswells' house

Billy comes out with the tray for Grandad. He puts the tray down on the step, then knocks on Grandad's door. He strolls off back to the house. Grandad's door opens – Grandad looks at the tray.

GRANDAD. (*Calling to Billy.*) Hey!

   Billy stops and looks. Grandad indicates the tray. Billy goes back reluctantly. He picks up the tray and hands it to Grandad who snatches it.

This is a street you know, not a bloody prison block.

   He slams the door.

Inside the DHSS building (*later the same day*)

Adrian is sitting amongst some others waiting. He is very nervous, and out of place. He has his briefcase on his knee. The three DHSS girls are occupied.

VOICE. Next!

ADRIAN. (*To chap sitting next to him.*) I'm redundant.

CHAP. Oh yeah.

ADRIAN. I've never been here before.

CHAP. Oh.

ADRIAN. I've paid my taxes of course – so I'm entitled to be here.

CHAP. Yeah.

ADRIAN. That's the only reason I am here.

CHAP. Yeah.

ADRIAN. It's not the money.

CHAP. No.

USUAL GIRL (MARTINA). Next!

Adrian looks around.

CHAP. It's for you – your tea and toast is ready.

Adrian gets up and goes to the chair in front of the desk. He sits down.

MARTINA. Name?

ADRIAN. Boswell – Adrian.

MARTINA. Address?

ADRIAN. My actual place of residence is—

Martina is writing it all down on her form. Then something dawns on her.

MARTINA. Boswell? Oh no – not another one? There can't be another one – only rabbits and bacteria multiply that fast.

An irate man comes into the office. He is dressed very shabbily and has a small, red flag tucked into some string which is tied around his coat like a belt. He wears a red rosette in his hat, and a pair of bright red leg warmers. He goes straight to the counter, takes Adrian by the shoulder and holds him while he bellows at Martina.

MAN. OK little bright flower – where's me money?!

MARTINA. (*Casually – she's seen it all before.*) Would you wait your turn please, Mr Wilson?

MR WILSON. Now listen, little child of joy, little flame in the dark, little rainfall in the desert, I've been waiting 'my turn' for long enough. My mam sat in here before I was born waiting *her* turn.

MARTINA. (*Sighing.*) I know, Mr Wilson, you've played us that one before.

MR WILSON. I spent my entire gestation period on one of those chairs. I came into this world clutching an application form, and when I began to talk, the first word I uttered was not Mamma or Dadda – it was 'Next'! (*He looks finally at the cringing Adrian.*) I'm going to kill you shortly! (*Then, to the girl again.*) So just you find me my money, my little singing bird, my little buttercup of the fields. You'll find my form at the bottom of the shit pile on your apathy tray. (*To Adrian, tightening his grip.*) There are too many of us – some of us have to go!

Adrian is terrified. Then, in strolls Joey.

JOEY. Greetings.

MARTINA. Oh God!

JOEY. (*To Mr Wilson.*) Well, well, if it isn't Devious Dick. I'm glad I've seen you. (*He lowers his voice.*) Only our meter wants fixing, and rumour has it that you're undercutting Screwdriver Lil by a third.

The two stare at each other.

Would you unhand my brother please?

The man does so.

Thank you.

MR WILSON. You're a lucky man, Boswell. If I didn't have a taxi waiting – (*walking to exit*) I'll be back – you load of twonks.

JOEY. (*Turning and smiling charmingly at Martina.*) Ah! Good morning – just calling in to help my somewhat inexperienced brother through the labyrinths of humiliation. (*To Adrian, who is devastated.*) Pull yourself together Adrian – this is England. (*To Martina.*) Oh, and when you've branded hin, tabulated him, put a ring on his leg, a metal tab in his ear and wired him up to your computer, could I have a word with you please? Only I've just finished reading a little government booklet called *Are You Getting Enough?* (*Pause.*) You may proceed. (*With a smile.*)

Joey goes and sits down. Martina glares at Joey, then stares at Adrian savagely.

MARTINA. You were saying . . . ?

ADRIAN. My actual place of residence is . . .

MARTINA. I know where you live Mr Boswell – The Palace of Kelsall Street – we've got it marked on our map with a big black cross. We organise coach tours for the Heads of Department to go and look at it. It saves us explaining where all the money goes, you see. (*She pushes a form towards him.*) Fill this in.

Adrian is gobsmacked.

Outside an Anglican cathedral

There are some huge blocks of sandstone near the entrance, from which there is a complete view of the city. Jack and another, younger man are sitting on the stones. Jack is staring thoughtfully at a gold bangle. The young man stares out at the view, then speaks.

MAN. (*Impatiently.*) Oh come on – it's a dead bargain.

JACK. How do I know it's gold?

MAN. It's hallmarked, isn't it?

JACK. You could have done that.

MAN. Forget it. (*He snatches it back.*)

JACK. Let's see it again.

The man sighs and gives it back to Jack. Jack gets out a little eye-glass and looks at it.

MAN. (*Pointing to an engraving on the bracelet.*) That says 'Mother'.

JACK. In know what it says – I *can* read you know.

MAN. That's a genuine gold bangle, that is – early Victorian. The engraving would cost a packet.

JACK. It's the engraving that devalues it. I mean, you can't give your girlfriend a bangle with 'Mother' on it, can you?

MAN. Give it to your mother then.

JACK. I don't want to give it to my mother. She's got dozens of them – all up one arm and down the next.

MAN. You can get the engraving rubbed off.

JACK. That'll cost me, won't it?

MAN. Well, take off the little piece of gold with the engraving on it.

JACK. The bangle will fall to bits then.

MAN. Change the word then from 'Mother' to 'Martha'.

JACK. I don't know anyone called Martha.

MAN. Sell it then to someone who either wants to give it to their mother, or who knows someone called Martha.

JACK. How can I sell it – I haven't bought it yet?

MAN. Make me an offer.

JACK. (*Thoughtfully.*) Well . . .

MAN. Bearing in mind that it's gold – and it's Victorian.

JACK. And it's got 'Mother' engraved on it.

MAN. Oh Jesus!

JACK. Two quid.

MAN. Two quid! It's worth more than that melted down.

JACK. Melt it down then.

MAN. It wouldn't be a bangle then, would it?

JACK. At least it wouldn't have 'Mother' engraved on it.

The young man sighs.

It isn't easy is it, buying and selling things.

MAN. Dead right.

JACK. I've been doing it for three years – I still haven't got it sorted. (*Pause.*) I bought a dozen radios – when I opened the box there were three on top – the rest was filled with apples. (*Pause.*) I even tried to sell a bike to the priest. It was only *his* wasn't it – they'd only pinched it from him in the first place. (*He looks at the young man.*) Stealing's no good – stolen things are no good – at least I've found that out.

MAN. I didn't steal that – I found it.

JACK. You'll never go to heaven when you die.

MAN. I did – honest – in the precinct.

JACK. Two quid, did you say?

MAN. Go on then.

Jack gives the young man two pounds and takes the bracelet. He looks at it. Then, with great deliberation, he hurls it far away. The young man looks amazed. Pause.

JACK. Save either of us getting into trouble – OK? (*He gets up.*)

MAN. I've told you – I didn't steal it – I found it.

JACK. Yeah, yeah, I know. That's the trouble with life – everywhere you look – gold bangles.

He walks away.

Outside the Boswells' house

Jack is waiting to park his van. He gives a little beep, waits, another beep. Adrian comes out. He is wearing a towel around him, and he has shaving soap all over his face.

ADRIAN. All right, all right.

JACK. What's the matter with your arse – have you got Blue-Tack on it or something?

ADRIAN. I'm having a bath, aren't I?

He takes the police cone and goes inside the house, muttering as he goes. Jack parks his van. Just as he gets out, Joey's Jaguar comes along. Jack picks up the police cone for his car, Joey parks and gets out. As Jack is going into the house, Joey calls him.

JOEY. Hey, Jack!

JACK. What?

JOEY. Have you seen Aveline?

JACK. I've only just come home.

JOEY. She's not back yet – she hasn't telephoned either.

JACK. It's only 6.30.

JOEY. She left the house at half-eight this morning.

JACK. She can look after herself – she's got her whistle, and her handbag is so full of jars and bottles she could lay King Kong out with it.

JOEY. (*As they go in.*) All the same – it's a long time. Mam's panicking, so watch it.

They go inside.

The living room in Julie's parents' house

Julie is lying on the settee holding her tummy. Billy is sitting on the chair looking anxiously at her.

BILLY. Where's the pain, Julie?

JULIE. In me armpits – where do you think?

BILLY. Well I don't know, do I? It says in the medical book that pain is often felt away from the site of the trouble.

JULIE. So it is. The pain's over here where I am – the trouble's over there where you are.

BILLY. Oh come on Julie, don't be like that – we're going to have a baby.

JULIE. *I'm* going to have a baby, Billy.

BILLY. I can't help it if Mother Nature's arranged it that way, can I? (*Julie winces.*) I'd better call our mam and our Joey.

Billy gets up to go to the phone.

JULIE. I don't want your mam and your Joey – I just want the ambulance.

BILLY. They've booked you in Sandfield Park, Julie.

JULIE. I'm not going to Sandfield Park – I'm going to the hospital.

BILLY. But Sandfield's better for you.

JULIE. It's not better. It's just posher, that's all. And just because I went to tea at your house once doesn't mean they own me. (*She clutches her tummy.*)

BILLY. (*Knowledgeably.*) How often are the contracts coming?

JULIE. (*Looking at him.*) You mean the contractions.

BILLY. Yeah – how often are they coming?

JULIE. Listen to him – the busking gynaecologist.

BILLY. (*Standing and putting on a bossy attitude.*) Now listen to me Julie – I've put up with a lot from you. I've let you walk all over me because – well, you were pregnant – but from now on, I'm the boss Julie. I'm the father, so I'm the boss, all right.

Julie gives a little cry of pain. Billy hides his fright.

Right. I have a plan, Julie, and we're going to stick to it – OK. (*He puts the phone down.*) They're engaged, so I'll go over and get them, right? That's what I'll do. They're just opposite – it's no problem, it's no problem. (*He looks at her anxiously.*)

JULIE. I don't want a fuss, Billy.

BILLY. My family don't fuss, Julie. I am not fussing, we are not fussers. (*She yelps in pain.*) Would you like me to bring you something from the chippy?

Julie turns away. Billy goes to the doorway.

BILLY. I'm not ready for all this.

The Boswells' street

Billy comes out of the house and walks slowly across the road. He is almost crying – the whole experience is too much for him. He reaches the door, hammers loudly on it and calls out fearfully.

Joey!

After a moment Joey comes to the door.

JOEY. Hello son – lost your key?

BILLY. It's Julie – the baby.

JOEY. OK sunshine – don't panic. I'll get her to the nursing home – you come and have a coffee with Mam.

They go in.

BILLY. (*Tearfully.*) I'm frightened, Joey.

JOEY. There's nothing to be frightened of, son. Mam's done it five times, hasn't she?

The Boswells' kitchen

Mrs Boswell is sitting by the table. Joey ushers Billy in.

JOEY. It's Julie, Mam. I'll have to go.

MRS BOSWELL. Oh God bless us and save us.

JOEY. Look after our Billy, will you? (*To Billy.*) And you look after Mam.

He rushes out.

MRS BOSWELL. (*To Billy.*) Sit down love – this calls for a little drink.

She sits, then goes to get the drinks.

Jack come down – Julie's baby's coming!

Mrs Boswell pours the drinks out.

BILLY. She looks bad, Mam.

MRS BOSWELL. Of course she does – you'd look bad if you'd got to do what she's got to do. She has got to transport that huge lump into the big world, hasn't she? Only women can do that – a man couldn't give birth to a jelly baby.

BILLY. It would be much easier if we laid eggs – like the birds.

MRS BOSWELL. (*Sitting down again.*) People aren't trustworthy enough for that, Billy. They'd go round nicking each other's eggs, wouldn't they? God knew what he was doing.

Jack comes in.

JACK. Hey – what's this then?

MRS BOSWELL. It's Julie.

Jack picks up a glass. So does Billy. So does Mrs Boswell.

JACK. Congratulations.

They clink glasses. Then the phone rings. Mrs Boswell quickly answers it. The two boys drink their whisky.

MRS BOSWELL. Hello, yes. (*Pause.*) Aveline! I'm worried sick about you – where are you?

AVELINE. (*On the phone.*) I'm in Manchester.

MRS BOSWELL. How did it go, love?

AVELINE. (*Nearly crying now.*) I didn't get the job, Mam.

Jack continues pouring more drinks.

MRS BOSWELL. Oh well never mind – come on home now – you'll have plenty more chances. I've made your favourite pudding.

AVELINE. I can't.

MRS BOSWELL. What do you mean – you can't?

AVELINE. I feel ashamed.

MRS BOSWELL. Ashamed! What of?!

AVELINE. I didn't get the job, Mam.

MRS BOSWELL. I know love, I know – it doesn't matter.

AVELINE. I can't come home – the whole street will be laughing at me. (*She puts the phone down.*)

MRS BOSWELL. (*On phone.*) Aveline! (*Pause.*) Aveline!

She puts the phone down and looks at Billy.

She didn't get the job – she won't come home.

Jack pours another drink for Billy and himself. Mrs Boswell begins to cry.

Where will she go – my little girl?!

She quickly picks up the phone again and dials three numbers. The other two drink their drinks.

Hello – Police please. (*Pause.*)

BILLY. She looks really bad . . .

MRS BOSWELL. Hello – I want to report a missing person please. It's my daughter – she's been abducted.

BILLY. . . . really bad.

The Boswells' street

Joey's Jaguar is parked outside Julie's house, and the nearside door is open. Joey is knocking on Julie's door.

JOEY. Julie, Julie – open the door love – it's Joey.

JULIE. (*Behind the door.*) Go away.

JOEY. Come on Julie – you don't want your baby to be born on the hall floor, now do you – he'll go through his life feeling inadequate.

JULIE. I'm having *my* baby *my* way, Joey Boswell.

> *An ambulance comes up the street – light flashing, siren going. It comes to a halt outside Julie's house. Two men rush out and open the back doors. They pull down some steps. Then one of them gets a blanket from inside the ambulance, and the two go to the door.*

FIRST MAN. (*To Joey.*) Excuse me, pal. (*He knocks on the door.*) Ambulance love!

JULIE. Coming!

JOEY. I was just going to give her a lift – still, you're here now.

SECOND MAN. Yeah.

JOEY. You know where it is do you – the nursing home.

FIRST MAN. We've got instructions to go to Mill Road – Maternity.

JOEY. (*Charmingly.*) Ah well – there's been a slight change – she's going to Sandfield Park Nursing Home now – shortage of beds – cutbacks – you know. I've just been in contact with them – it's all arranged.

FIRST MAN. Are you the father?

JOEY. No, I'm the brother of the father. The father's a bit over-wrought – he's having a cup of coffee with his mother.

> *The two men glance at each other. Joey holds out his hand to them.*

Joey Boswell.

At this point Billy comes running out of the Boswells' house.

BILLY. Joey – Aveline's phoned – she won't come home – she's missing in Manchester. Me mam's going spare. (*He runs back into the house again.*)

JOEY. (*To the ambulance men.*) Excuse me.

Now a police car comes hastily up the street – its lights flashing. It shrieks to a halt outside the Boswells' house. Joey smiles charmingly at the ambulance men.

We're having a few family problems.

Julie comes out of the house and the two ambulance men go to her.

SECOND MAN. OK, love, take it easy.

The first man puts the blanket around her.

FIRST MAN. Can you walk, sweetheart?

JULIE. I'm fine – I'm fine.

Joey goes to take Julie's case: she snatches it away. One of the ambulance men goes inside the ambulance with Julie, the other closes the door. Joey goes to him.

JOEY. Sandfield Park – OK?

SECOND MAN. OK mate – if you say so.

The ambulance drives off. Joey goes to the policemen.

JOEY. (*Charmingly.*) May I help you gentlemen? We seem to be having a variety of little setbacks involving the family.

Billy and Jack come out of the house, both tipsy. They get into the cars making a great deal of noise, backfiring, gear changing, slamming doors. Grandad's door opens. He comes out.

GRANDAD. (*Yelling.*) Stop this bloody racket – go on – piss off the lot of you. (*He closes his door.*)

JOEY. (*Charm again.*) That was our grandad – loved and respected by all.

Mrs Boswell comes out of her house.

MRS BOSWELL. Joey! Go after those two – they're drunk.

JOEY. (*Nicely.*) Excuse me.

He smiles and goes calmly to his car, gets in and then zooms away. The two policemen look blankly at each other, then with one accord they race to their car and zoom after the others.

A city street

A cavalcade zooms past: first the ambulance, then Billy's car, then Jack's van, then Joey's car, then the police car. They are all speeding through the city. The ambulance's lights are flashing, and the siren is going. Billy is honking his terrible fog horn. The police siren is going. Passers-by watch in amazement.

Another city street

The chase continues: all the vehicles speed through another street.

A tranquil cornfield (evening)

The birds are singing. Adrian and Carmen are lying on their backs, gazing up at the sky. Adrian's lips are covered with smudged red lipstick.

CARMEN. I've never done it in a cornfield before.

ADRIAN. (*With authority.*) Nature's place.

CARMEN. Have you?

ADRIAN. (*Boastfully.*) Most men have – haven't they?

CARMEN. Have they?

ADRIAN. Ye–e–s.

CARMEN. I don't know any girls who have done it.

ADRIAN. Well, girls aren't as inventive, are they?

    Pause.

CARMEN. So, if none of my friends do it, who do your friends do it with?

ADRIAN. Well – you're a girl – you've done it.

CARMEN. Yes – but only with you. I haven't done it with all the others. Who do *they* do it with?

ADRIAN. Maybe I was wrong – maybe most men *don't* do it. Maybe – *nobody* does it. Maybe you and I are the only people in the entire world who *have* done it. (*He kisses her.*) Aren't we lucky?

    Pause.

CARMEN. The place I enjoyed doing it most was in that wood in Wales.

ADRIAN. Pennyth – by the stream.

CARMEN. And Formby.

ADRIAN. The sandhills.

CARMEN. Yes. (*Pause.*) When we're married we'll be able to do it all the time.

ADRIAN. Like now – yes.

CARMEN. I'm glad I'm physical.

ADRIAN. I'm glad you're physical too.

CARMEN. When you're physical with someone, you can overcome arguments and quarrels by just – doing it.

ADRIAN. Was Alan Wentworth physical?

CARMEN. No.

ADRIAN. Didn't you do it with him then?

CARMEN. Nearly. (*Pause.*) Did you do it with Helen Pope?

ADRIAN. No. (*Pause.*) Well, not in a cornfield.

CARMEN. Where then?

ADRIAN. It's not important. (*Pause.*) Where did you nearly do it with Alan Wentworth?

CARMEN. I forget.

Pause.

ADRIAN. He can't have been much good at it.

CARMEN. No.

Pause. Adrian sighs. Carmen reaches out and touches his arm.

It'll be better next time – you'll see. Lots of fellas . . .

ADRIAN. (*Broken.*) You keep saying that. (*Pause, quietly.*) You keep saying that.

Sandfield Park Hospital, a private waiting room

Joey is sitting reading a paper. Jack walks over to join him.

JACK. (*Thoughtfully.*) You know, I think God was a scientist. He made a nice little world – all green and harmonious – and then, like all scientists, he wanted to progress. So he shoved in a few bothers like women, and love, and sex. Then he hyped it up a bit by giving men minds and women bodies – and oh boy what a mess.

JOEY. What brought that speech on?

JACK. Birth – it's a profound thing, birth – we can't live without it.

JOEY. What's all this about our Aveline?

JACK. She didn't get the job – she said she's too ashamed to come home.

JOEY. (*Wearily.*) Oh God, it never rains, does it?

The door opens. The sister (an Irish nun) comes in with Billy. He is dressed in a green operating apron. He still has a mask on, showing only his eyes, wide open.

SISTER. He has a daughter – all is well.

JOEY. (*Giving the shocked Billy a playful punch.*) Hey – a girl – isn't that fantastic?

JACK. We'll have to get her kitted up with a whistle.

JOEY. Thank you, sister.

SISTER. Room 54 – she'll be ready in a few minutes. You can come along when the father has had time to get over it.

JOEY. Great!

She goes. Joey looks at Billy.

Well done son – you got this one right. Sit down – take the weight off your mind.

Billy slowly pulls the mask down – he looks elated.

BILLY. It was amazing – it was a miracle. I've never – it was – it . . . (*He can't finish – his face crumples from elation to tears.*)

JOEY. Hey – come on now. If you're going to go through life performing miracles, you've got to be tough. Hasn't he?

Jack is whimpering too.

BILLY. I'm not ready for all this.

The Boswells' kitchen (*later that evening*)

Jack, Billy, Joey and Adrian sit round the table chatting. Mrs Boswell is just putting the final dish down. She sits down and puts her hands together.

MRS BOSWELL. Prayers! (*They put their hands together.*) We are grateful, oh Father, for the new and perfect child – and the safety of her mother – and we pray for the father. (*Pause. She is upset now.*) We ask Thee, dear Lord, to bring our Aveline home. (*She can't continue.*)

BILLY. (*Outburst.*) She has no right to do this – no right.

JOEY. Billy!

BILLY. Walking out like that.

ADRIAN. (*Suddenly coming to the rescue.*) And we ask Thee, oh Father, to help our mam through this grief and worry.

The others look at him in amazement.

Well, it is an emergency.

ALL. Amen.

They each reach for some food. Mrs Boswell takes the lid off the family pot.

MRS BOSWELL. I know you all had a messed up day – but things have to be paid for.

Joey puts money in. He looks at Billy.

BILLY. I haven't busked today.

Joey puts money in for him.

ADRIAN. (*Feeling in his jacket pocket.*) I can give you a cheque – there's still a morsel left in my redundant account.

Joey puts money in the pot.

JACK. (*Feeling in his trousers' pocket.*) I know there's fifty pence stuck in the lining somewhere.

JOEY. All right – cut the fumbling. (*He puts another ten pounds in.*) Now eat your dinner.

JACK. Thanks.

ADRIAN. Thanks.

BILLY. Thanks. (*Pause.*) Where does he . . .

MRS BOSWELL. Billy – we only ask where money has *gone* to, not where it comes from. All right?

They eat.

BILLY. It's funny not having Aveline sitting here saying (*he mimicks*) 'I'm a model, aren't I? I'm going modelling.'

MRS BOSWELL. If she was here, it could have been a happy, lovely day – with the new baby. She's never been away from this house – never.

JACK. She'll appreciate it more when she comes back then, won't she? I know I did that night I was in trouble.

BILLY. Oh yeah – I remember that – it was foggy, wasn't it? You went camping.

JOEY. All right, all right – enough.

JACK. You won't stop him now.

BILLY. You ended up at the airport.

JOEY. Who are you telling this story to Billy? We've all heard it.

JACK. Leave him – he likes the end bit.

BILLY. You and your mate had pitched your tent and when daylight came you noticed you were on the main runway.

Billy laughs out loud at this – the rest are deadpan and silent. His laughter trails away.

MRS BOSWELL. (*Deliberately ignoring Billy.*) How is Carmen, Adrian?

ADRIAN. Oh – great. It's really good. She can't get enough of me.

There is a call from the hall – it is Mr Boswell.

MR BOSWELL. Anyone home?

MRS BOSWELL. It's your dad.

JOEY. (*Calls.*) Come in, Dad!

MRS BOSWELL. I wish you'd all shut that door when you come in – we might as well have a cat flap.

Mr Boswell wanders in.

MR BOSWELL. (*To all.*) Don't stop – just calling – just seeing how things are on this bright pink evening.

ALL TOGETHER. (*But not in unison.*) They're fine Dad – fine – great.

MRS BOSWELL. You're a grandad by the way – a girl – all is well.

MR BOSWELL. I know. (*Mrs Boswell glares at him.*) The thing about living in a high-rise is you can check on the storks as they fly past!

All except Joey giggle a bit.

MRS BOSWELL. (*Coldly.*) You don't make *me* laugh, Freddie Boswell.

JOEY. Sit down, Dad.

MR BOSWELL. No – it's all right. I only came to tell you – Aveline is with me.

MRS BOSWELL. With you!

JOEY. It's all right, Mam. (*To Mr Boswell.*) Is she all right?

MR BOSWELL. All the colours of an apple, son, all the colours of an October apple.

MRS BOSWELL. How could she – how *could* she? This is her home.

MR BOSWELL. She was embarrassed. She's OK now though – we've had a little talk. She's ready to come home.

Silence.

(To Billy.) So long – Dad.

He leaves.

MRS BOSWELL. He frightens me.

ADRIAN. He's your husband – how can he frighten you?

BILLY. Julie frightens me.

MRS BOSWELL. He's like a quietly soaring bird of prey – all feathers and eyes – doing nothing in particular, but planning, planning.

JACK. He's probably lonely – I mean things will seem pretty quiet after Lilo Lil, won't they? Imagine waking up to an inflated dinghy every morning.

ADRIAN. I feel sorry for him.

BILLY. *(Laughing.)* An inflatable dinghy.

ADRIAN. Oh God, will somebody shut him up? It's like having a meal with a talking primate.

JOEY. *(To Billy.)* Hey – shut it – OK. *(To Jack.)* You'd better go and pick our Aveline up. I'll stay here. *(He indicates that he is worried about Mrs Boswell.)*

JACK. Oh – right.

MRS BOSWELL. *(Looking round the table.)* I suppose you'll all leave – one day.

A street

Jack is driving Aveline home in his van. The radio is on and music is playing.

AVELINE. Is my mam all right?

JACK. She's all right – she was dead worried though.

AVELINE. I keep telling her – I'm a grown person.

JACK. Nobody's safe these days – not even grown persons.

AVELINE. I should have come home.

Silence. The music stops on the radio.

RADIO ANNOUNCER. Now, with the last record coming up, let me first remind you of the announcement I made at the beginning of the show.

AVELINE. Still – we do daft things, don't we?

ANNOUNCER. Mabel of Strathmore Road is offering a hundred pounds reward for the return of a gold bangle with the word 'Mother' engraved on it. It was lost somewhere between Lord Street and Kelsall Street and, says Mabel, it's of special sentimental value, so here we go.

Music.

JACK. Yeah – we do – we all do daft things.

Mrs Boswell

Episode Three

The Boswell's kitchen (*morning*)

It is breakfast time. The entire family are around the table. Mrs Boswell is preparing Grandad's tray. A huge packet of cornflakes is being passed around the table. When each member of the family has filled their dish, the milk is passed around.

MRS BOSWELL. Who's going to take Grandad's tray?

EVERYBODY BUT JACK. Jack!

MRS BOSWELL. Come on Jack – it's unanimous.

She turns and sees that they have all started to eat.

MRS BOSWELL. Spoons down – all of you. (*She sits in her chair.*) I suppose you think that if you do it often enough I just won't bother about prayers.

JACK. We say them at lunch – and dinner. We talk to God more often than we talk to our dad.

BILLY. And let's face it, he doesn't *do* anything.

MRS BOSWELL. He gives you health – and strength – and a mind, and a body. You can see and hear, can't you? You can walk.

JACK. They're standard items though, aren't they?

MRS BOSWELL. They are not standard items – some people haven't got all of them. In fact, when I hear you talk this way, I begin to think he left a few things out when he was planning you.

BILLY. Why doesn't he . . .

JOEY. Billy.

BILLY. Why am I only allowed half a sentence in this house?

ADRIAN. Because we all know what the other half is going to be – so we prevent ourselves from having to listen to it.

MRS BOSWELL. (*Putting her hands together – so do they all.*) We thank Thee, oh Lord, for the dawning of a new day. Take us through it safely and – unlike the breakfast conversation – may we reap benefit from consulting our brains before using our gobs. (*Pause.*) And please bring our Aveline back again.

JOEY. Don't upset yourself, Mam. She's got to stretch some time.

MRS BOSWELL. But she came home. She said she was glad she was back, and now she's gone again.

JACK. Girls are like that. They leave everything. Houses, husbands, the washing up. The world's in a mess because of girls.

BILLY. The world's in a mess because of Julie.

ADRIAN. Carmen's not like that.

JACK. That's just because she's not tired of you yet. You wait, you'll look out through your little lovesick window one day and she'll be marching down the street with her bum wiggling and your heart trapped in her handbag.

BILLY. And she'll empty it out somewhere, with all the other rubbish she carries around with her.

ADRIAN. (*To Billy.*) Oh, you're experienced, are you? You know all about women.

BILLY. Listen, I've been going with Julie for two years now. She's a right bag of tricks, she is. I was sixteen when I met her. A year later I had my fortieth birthday.

MRS BOSWELL. The tray's ready now, Jack. (*Jack gets up and takes the tray.*) And tell him the eggs are not free range, but the hens that lay them run around in a shed.

Jack goes out.

Outside the Boswells' house

Jack comes out with the tray. He goes to Grandad's door and knocks. It opens. Grandad's hands appear, they grab the tray. The door is shut. Jack knocks on the door. Grandad opens it.

GRANDAD. What?!

JACK. (*Taking a second boiled egg out of his pocket and holding it up.*) Don't you want your extra egg, Grandad?

GRANDAD. (*Snatching at it.*) You do it on purpose, don't you? You all come round – doing your little 'tricks'. Scientists do it to monkeys to see how long it takes to turn them daft. You won't turn me daft. (*He slams the door.*)

Jack stands there with the egg. The door opens again. Grandad snatches it.

Piss off!

He slams the door. Jack smiles and goes back into the house.

The Boswells' street (*later the same day*)

Mrs Boswell is walking along towards the house. She is carrying some groceries. There is an old lady brushing the pavement outside her own house. (This is Mrs Stevenson. She is very slow – and stops to catch her breath.)

MRS BOSWELL. (*As she passes.*) Are you all right, love?

MRS STEVENSON. Fair to middling, Mrs Boswell, fair to middling.

MRS BOSWELL. Isn't there anybody to do that for you?

MRS STEVENSON. No. There's no one, I've out-lived them all – it's the ginseng.

MRS BOSWELL. I'll have to try this ginseng.

MRS STEVENSON. Goes straight to yer faculties. How's your Aveline?

MRS BOSWELL. Oh she's fine. She rings home every day in between modelling.

MRS STEVENSON. I never see our Graham now. He went to Palma for a fornight. Next thing I know he'd become a full-time hippy. I got a rose and a joss stick through the post in 1969 and that was it. (*She gives a sigh.*) Still, we struggle on, don't we love, we struggle on.

MRS BOSWELL. (*As she leaves.*) We'll live in hope if we don't die of despair.

MRS STEVENSON. Aye.

There is the sound of the cordless phone.

MRS BOSWELL. Excuse me, love, there's the phone.

She puts her shopping bag down and gets the phone out of her handbag.

Hello, yes. (*She picks up her bag and walks as she speaks.*) Oh it's you, Grandad. (*Pause.*) I've got fish for your lunch. (*Pause.*) I don't know where it was caught, do I? They don't have labels saying 'Not caught in polluted water', do they? (*Pause.*) You can have baked potato then with cheese and cream. (*Pause.*) I know the world is radioactive, love. And you can take your pick – polluted fish, insecticide potato or radioactive salad. (*She puts the phone back.*)

The dog is sitting outside the front door. He has a frozen chicken in his mouth.

MRS BOSWELL. (*Muttering to herself.*) Oh God – he's been into the takeaway again.

She unlocks the door and the dog goes in. At this point, Billy's old car comes along the street. Mrs Boswell puts the shopping inside the house, then goes and moves the Police cones for Billy to park. She takes them inside.
Billy gets out of his car – he is wearing his cymbals on his knees. He slams the car door and the window slides down with a thump. He pulls a fed-up face and clanks into the house.

In the Boswells' house

Mrs Boswell is unloading her groceries. Billy comes into the living room. He sits down – fed up.

MRS BOSWELL. (*Calling.*) What's the matter, Billy?

BILLY. I've been singing all morning – my throat's sore and my knees have got brain damage. (*He indicates his mouth organ.*) Look – I've worn the maker's name off my mouth organ.

MRS BOSWELL. It's a hard life son – at least you're not alone.

BILLY. That's not how it feels. (*Pause.*) They used to love me out there.

Mrs Boswell goes to Billy in the living room.

MRS BOSWELL. Yes – well – there are too many of you now, Billy. It's like *Saturday Night at the London Palladium* in town – you can't move for buskers and performers. That chap that breaks stones on his chest will kill himself one day.

BILLY. I should have gone to acting school.

MRS BOSWELL. Oh my God – what do you want to be an actor for?

BILLY. I want to act, don't I?

MRS BOSWELL. You'd have to learn Shakespeare – you can't even remember what you go to the shops for.

BILLY. That's different, isn't it?

MRS BOSWELL. The only difference is you can ring home and ask what you're down at the shops for. You can't make a phone call from *Hamlet.* Get your dirty feet off my silver tray.

BILLY. I'll go over and see Julie and the baby.

MRS BOSWELL. Give her a kiss from her nan.

BILLY. (*As he goes.*) OK.

Outside the Boswells' house

Billy comes out of the front door. He is just in time to pick up a Police cone for Joey as he cruises to a halt outside. He puts the cone in the hall, then clanks across the road to Julie's. Joey gets out of his car, watches Billy, then calls him back.

JOEY. Hey – Billy!

Billy turns.

Come here son.

Billy trudges back.

What's the matter?

BILLY. I'm fed up – all I made was four quid this morning. (*Pause – brokenly.*) I'm a father.

JOEY. Come on, lad, pull yourself together.

BILLY. Everything's building up.

JOEY. Then you must do something about it, sunshine.

BILLY. What! Do what?

JOEY. Sit down – and *think*.

BILLY. I can't think – my head's too crowded.

JOEY. It's confused Billy – your head's confused because it has to listen to those things clanging all the time it thinks you're a herd of cows.

BILLY. What else can I do?

JOEY. Try using your head – give your knees a rest.

BILLY. I want to take Julie presents – and flowers. I want to be – (*pause*) – exciting. I want to drive her to town and take her to lunch. I want her to be proud of me. You need money for all that.

JOEY. I'll tell you what – if you promise me that you'll think something out for yourself, and follow it through, I'll lend you the Jag to take Julie out.

Billy just gazes at him open-mouthed.

You can take her to town and buy her lunch.

BILLY. When?

JOEY. Tomorrow – I've got nothing on tomorrow.

BILLY. You mean in the Jag – (*pointing*) – that Jag?

JOEY. That very Jag.

Billy smiles happily. He starts to run to Julie's.

BILLY. (*Shouting.*) Julie! Julie!

Joey smiles, then wanders back to his car. He touches it lovingly, and is clearly having grave doubts about the wisdom of his generosity. He goes into the house.

Another street

Jack's van is parked by a phone box. Jack is looking towards the phone box impatiently. Adrian is in there using the phone.

ADRIAN. (*Waiting for the pips, then speaking.*) Hello – Carmen?

Phone box/the shop where Carmen works

ADRIAN. (*In the phone box.*) Hello Carmen?

CARMEN. (*On the phone, in the shop.*) Hello Adrian?

ADRIAN. How are you?

CARMEN. I'm fine. And you?

ADRIAN. I'm fine.

CARMEN. Wasn't it wonderful last night?

ADRIAN. (*Not convinced.*) Yes – yes it was – wonderful.

CARMEN. I've never done it at the back of the shop before.

ADRIAN. I hope your boss doesn't find out. (*Pause.*) I'm sorry – it's not the most inspiring place for making the universe move.

CARMEN. It's a beautiful place. (*She looks around dreamily.*) The best place on earth.

ADRIAN. P'raps if we tidy it up a bit.

CARMEN. You were wonderful.

ADRIAN. Yes. (*Pause.*) I'm with Jack – we're going on a job together.

CARMEN. I've never had such a fantastic lover.

ADRIAN. Well. (*He gives a nervous laugh.*) I don't know about that.

CARMEN. Tiger!

Jack is impatient. He beeps the horn.

ADRIAN. I'd better go – Jack's waiting.

CARMEN. Adrian?

ADRIAN. Yes?

CARMEN. It doesn't matter you know. I love *you* – as a personk, the way you look, the way you think. After all, it's not the Olympics, is it? I mean, nobody's standing around giving you marks out of ten, are they?

ADRIAN. Carmen – if you didn't keep mentioning . . .

CARMEN. It'll be even *more* wonderful next time – you'll see. (*She throws a little kiss and puts the phone down.*)

> Adrian does the same. Jack beeps. Adrian comes out of the phone box clutching his briefcase. He gets into the van, it drives off.

Julie's living room

Julie is ironing. Billy is kneeling by the side of the crib holding a great big toy up for the baby to see.

BILLY. (*Making various train noises.*) All aboard please!

JULIE. Take that away, Billy. She'll be afraid to travel when she grows up.

> *Billy puts it down.*

BILLY. Can I pick it up?

JULIE. 'It' is she – and no.

BILLY. I *am* her father.

JULIE. You keep telling me that Billy – millions of other men have managed it you know. Mother Nature didn't put any extra time in on you.

BILLY. It says in the book that babies like contact.

JULIE. They do – but not with the floor. You've only got to start dreaming and you'll forget she's there. (*Pause.*) I'd rather go on the bus tomorrow.

BILLY. Oh Julie – don't come that. What's wrong with going to town in our Joey's car?

JULIE. It's not *ours*, is it? It's not yours – so it's a lie isn't it – it's fancy dress.

BILLY. It's a favour.

JULIE. I don't like that word either – 'favour'.

BILLY. He loves that car – sometimes I don't think you understand about a man and his car.

JULIE. Oh yes I do. You love that thing you've got – the one that falls to pieces every time you switch on. It's got me thinking that you'd love me better if my arm dropped off every time you touched me.

> *Billy goes to her.*

BILLY. I do love you Julie – I don't look at anyone else.

JULIE. It's that family you love – all of you – clamped together like stale wine gums.

BILLY. If you're going to talk about my mam, Julie . . .

JULIE. Now, would I talk about your mam – or anybody else at No. 30? Would I take that risk?! (*Pause – under her breath.*) No wonder Aveline left.

BILLY. She hasn't left. She's trying out the world that's all. She rings me mam every day – every single day.

JULIE. I know, you're always phoning your mam – all of you. 'I'm just around the corner Mam,' 'I won't be long Mam,' 'I might be late Mam,' 'D'you mind if I breathe Mam?' If anything happened to her, British Telecom would go bankrupt.

BILLY. Yes – well I hope when *she* (*meaning the baby*) grows up – she's as loyal to you and me as we are to each other – that's proper family that is. (*Pause.*) I love you, Julie. (*He kisses her hair.*)

JULIE. I'm calling her Francesca.

BILLY. (*Thinks.*) Good. I like that – it's a good name.

JULIE. I'm glad – 'cos I'm calling her it anyway. (*She puts down the iron and looks at Billy.*) All right – I'll go to town in your Joey's Jag. Anything to take the daft look off your face.

BILLY. Oh great! We'll have one of our own one day.

JULIE. When your ship comes in?

BILLY. Yeah – when my ship comes in. It's on it's way up the river, you'll see.

JULIE. It's a long time coming. Has it got an engine this ship of yours?

They kiss.

A street

The houses are the larger, more desirable ones, but a bit in need of care. Jack and Adrian are travelling in the van.

JACK. Now, what it is, this chap has got a load of hats, about a hundred.

ADRIAN. You told me, you told me.

JACK. But they're not any old hat – they're 1920s. Hats – genuine 1920s. (*Pause.*) Fifteen quid he wants.

ADRIAN. They'll be worth a fortune.

JACK. He doesn't know that.

ADRIAN. Didn't you tell him?

JACK. I'm buying them, aren't I? I'm buying them to sell again.

ADRIAN. Oh. Yes – yes.

JACK. So when you see them – don't go hysterical all right – save it until we're on the road.

They pull up outside the house.

ADRIAN. Right.

They get out of the van and go up the small drive to the house.

JACK. We'll just give him the money, collect his hats, and go. All right – no hysterics.

ADRIAN. Right.

They get to the front door and find it slightly open. They glance at each other. Then Jack pushes the door slightly and calls. Adrian clutches his briefcase close to him.

JACK. Anyone there?!

There is the sound of footsteps. Adrian moves behind Jack. A man of about forty-five appears, a rather swarthy character.

ROBBER. What do you want?

JACK. Er – I spoke to someone – it must be your father – a mature gentleman.

ROBBER. Yeah – so what?

JACK. He's got some old hats – I arranged to collect and pay for them.

ROBBER. Wait there. (*He goes inside.*)

ADRIAN. I wouldn't like to get on the wrong side of him.

JACK. (*Calling.*) Er – two big boxes they were – under the stairs. (*Calling again.*) Do you need any help, mate?

The man appears carrying a heavy box with hats stacked in it. He silently plonks it in Jack's arms. Then he goes away again.

ADRIAN. Hey – they're fantastic – real felt – real straw.

JACK. (*From behind the box.*) No hysterics – OK.

Jack takes the box to the van. Adrian is now presented with the second box – he still keeps his briefcase in one hand.

ADRIAN. (*To man, from behind the box.*) We'll bring you the money – my brother has got it. He's buying the hats – I'm redundant from real-estate.

Adrian plods to the van. Jack takes the box from him and puts it in the back with the other one.

JACK. I'll go and pay.

ADRIAN. (*Clutching his arm.*) Listen, Jack—

JACK. What?

ADRIAN. Fifteen quid – oh come on – you can't—

JACK. That's what the old guy said – fifteen quid. He chose the asking price, not me.

ADRIAN. But they're worth that each.

JACK. All the more profit then.

He walks away.

ADRIAN. (*Shouting.*) It's cheating!

Jack stops, then Adrian says more quietly.

It's not playing fair.

Jack comes slowly back and stares into Adrian's face.

JACK. The thing about playing fair Adrian is – it only works if everyone does it, and the sad fact is – *nobody* does.

ADRIAN. He doesn't know their value – you do.

JACK. Do you know why surgeons make more money than us, Adrian? Because they know how to take people's guts out, we don't.

ADRIAN. But he's old, you said.

JACK. He's lucky – with all this tension I won't have the privilege of getting old.

ADRIAN. Twenty-five – make it twenty-five. (*Dramatically.*) 'He that giveth more receiveth more.'

JACK. Who composed that crap?

ADRIAN. I did.

Jack sighs.

JACK. OK – twenty-five.

Adrian, fairly pleased, gets a big picture hat out of the box and puts it on.

Jack goes back to the house. Adrian closes the van doors. As Jack is coming back through the gate, an old man comes shuffling along – he is carrying a walking stick. Jack sees him and smiles.

OLD MAN. Oh, you've come for the hats, have you?

JACK. It's all right, Grandad, we've seen to it.

OLD MAN. Had them years, you know. They came from me grandfather's shop – never wanted to part with them. Still, times is hard now.

JACK. We've seen your son.

ADRIAN. And there's a little surprise for you.

OLD MAN. Son? I haven't got a son. I live alone.

A car screeches past them. The two look at each other and race into the road to see the car disappear.

Inside the DHSS building

The usual DHSS girl has her head down, absorbed in some paperwork. Joey wanders in. He goes to the chair in front of the girl and sits down. She carries on writing for a moment, then becomes aware of something. She stops writing and lifts her head, eyes closed.

THE USUAL GIRL (MARTINA). The smell of expensive aftershave, the jingle of gold, the rustle of leather – *real* leather. Could it be Mr Boswell – eldest brother of all the other little Boswells?

JOEY. Greetings – a good day to you.

MARTINA. It has been – up till now.

JOEY. I'll get to the point. It's about our Billy.

MARTINA. That's the young one, isn't it? The one who approaches any problem in life with a completely open mouth.

JOEY. The same.

MARTINA. Why can't he come in himself?

JOEY. Well, he's shy – vulnerable – doesn't quite know how to jump from the nest.

MARTINA. Busy sharpening his beak on his mouth organ, is he? (*Pause.*) I saw him Mr Boswell – busking.

Pause.

JOEY. Oh that – yes. Not very lucrative – people just won't part with their money, will they? *Not* that we're complaining – it isn't easy to come by, is it? (*With extra charm.*) You'll see to that.

MARTINA. I threw ten pence in myself – I thought he was retarded.

JOEY. The thing is, I'm encouraging him to start a business, a sandwich delivery business. He'll need a little van of course – and some containers, some bread, the odd bottle of mayonnaise – and what immediately sprang to mind was . . .

BOTH TOGETHER. The Enterprise Allowance Scheme.

MARTINA. Yes. I thought it would.

JOEY. I understand that for a new business venture he can claim forty pounds a week for the first year. (*Pause.*) I read a lot you know – and I have this retentive memory.

MARTINA. Then you will also remember that it only applies to people who can prove that they are investing a thousand pounds in the venture – ten hundred pounds Mr Boswell. Now, where would your little brother get that from, I wonder!

JOEY. Well – we'd . . .

MARTINA. Club together.

JOEY. Yes.

MARTINA. As a family.

JOEY. Correct. It would be hard—

MARTINA. But you'd manage.

JOEY. Yes.

MARTINA. Because that's how you are in your house.

JOEY. United – yes. That's our strength you see – we stick together. We're the great white whales in the sea of society.

Martina pushes a form towards him.

MARTINA. Tell him to fill this in.

JOEY. I will – thank you.

MARTINA. And tell him I'll be here – waiting.

JOEY. Wonderful.

MARTINA. With my harpoon.

Joey laughs.

A country road

Jack and Adrian are driving home in Jack's van.

JACK. I'll have to pull up somewhere and break my heart. (*He pulls up, sighs and puts his head down on his arms.*)

ADRIAN. I'm sorry. (*Pause.*) I'll get the hang of it all one day.

JACK. (*Head up – mimicking the old man.*) 'He's taken me radio, twenty quid in cash.' (*He mimicks Adrian.*) 'That's all right. We'll cover that, Grandad.' (*He mimicks the old man.*) 'And me chess set, and me carriage clock.' (*He mimicks Adrian.*) 'Don't worry – it was our fault, we'll cover it. (*Pause.*) No, we won't call the police if it upsets you.' (*To Adrian.*) Twenty-five quid for the hats and forty quid for the robbery – sixty-five quid that's cost us.

ADRIAN. I had to – I thought he was going to have a heart attack.

JACK. You didn't even notice the three I had, I suppose.

ADRIAN. I kept thinking – it could have been our grandad.

JACK. How is it that every time I do a job I come out with less money than I went in with?

ADRIAN. You're kind, that's why – you've got a soul.

Jack looks at him – he quite likes that remark.

JACK. Our Joey's kind – *he* always comes out winning.

Pause.

ADRIAN. Ah – but he's clever as well.

Jack glares at him and starts the van.

A street next to a park

Mr Boswell is sweeping leaves along the street. He remembers the following conversation.

MR BOSWELL. I don't see what you're worrying about – a lovely girl like you should be thinking about marriage and kids, not modelling. Modelling is unreliable – one pimple on your face and you've had it.

AVELINE. Well, marriage isn't all that reliable either, is it? Look at you and Mam.

MR BOSWELL. It was all on the cards, love, all on the cards. Your mother has a practical head on her. She needed a man who was solid – a man who would put his key in the door every night and save her from the pot-holes of life. I used to go home all right but I could never find the keyhole.

AVELINE. I'm like you Dad – a free spirit.

MR BOSWELL. I'm not a free spirit. I'd love to be tied – tied and tethered like an old brown donkey to an old brown barn.

AVELINE. Go on – I remember you – like a monkey on elastic you were.

MR BOSWELL. They were the days of the ships and the cranes – and the tug boats. The days when sailors used to walk down the gangplanks like penguins, straight up the street and into the Ocean Club. (*Pause.*) The days of the docker.

AVELINE. It makes me sad to see you brush the streets – you're too good for that – other people's rubbish.

MR BOSWELL. There's no better way of studying the human race than studying their rubbish.

AVELINE. And talking of rubbish – what about Lilo Lil?

MR BOSWELL. (*Eyes shut, ecstatic.*) Paradise. Pink as a petal.

AVELINE. She was like a tarantula – a fella couldn't walk along Lime Street without walking into *her* parlour. She didn't just have a red light, she had arrows painted on the pavement! How could you, Dad?!

MR BOSWELL. (*Mimicking her.*) 'How could you, Dad?' – that's what you all said. But I'd rather lie on my deathbed thinking 'How could you?' than 'Why didn't I?'

AVELINE. Will you ever come back Dad – home?

MR BOSWELL. Now and then sweetheart – now and then.

A pub (lunchtime, the next day)

Jack is sitting by a table. Adrian is at the counter – he has ordered two beers. He takes the first one to Jack and puts it down on the table.

JACK. Cheers! Not that I can afford it.

ADRIAN. I'll get them. I really am sorry about yesterday.

JACK. Forget it.

> *Adrian goes back to the counter to get his own beer and has to wait to pay.*
> *While Jack is sitting there he suddenly finds himself face to face with the robber. They exchange a quiet stare. Jack makes a little nervous noise and the robber glances at the fellows near him. Slowly and deliberately they get up and go and sit on either side of Jack. He is rigid with fear, but manages to force a smile.*

JACK. (*Looking at the robber.*) You're not from round here, are you? Only, I thought I hadn't seen him before.

ROBBER. Ho – ho. (*Pause.*) When we move, you move – OK?

JACK. Oh – yeah.

ROBBER. After all, I don't want people going around pointing me out now, do I?

JACK. Why would I point you out? I've never seen you before.

SECOND MAN. He's a liar Dino – never trust a liar.

ROBBER. I mean it's very inconvenient – bumping into a witness all the time – very nerve-wracking.

JACK. Witness? What witness?

SECOND MAN. Adamant, Dino.

ROBBER. Yeah – adamant.

SECOND MAN. As well as a liar.

The two men each take a drink, then put their glasses down in unison.

ROBBER. Should we be off then?

SECOND MAN. Yeah – let's be off – (*emphatically*) all three of us.

ROBBER. Nice and friendly like.

The two men get up – Jack rises with them. Adrian looks in horror as the three go out, and he sees that the two men have got Jack by his arms. Adrian thinks for a moment, then goes out to the door of the pub.

Outside the pub

Adrian appears at the door of the pub. He stares after the three who are walking away, Jack squashed between them. They turn into a little alleyway with a dead end. Adrian rushes to a phone.

The Boswells' kitchen

Joey is drinking coffee and reading the paper. Mrs Boswell is making the dinner. Joey puts the paper down, runs his hand through his hair and sighs.

MRS BOSWELL. Don't worry, Joey. He won't crash your Jag, not with Julie and the baby in it.

JOEY. I'm not worried Mam – it's only a car.

MRS BOSWELL. Set the table for me, love.

JOEY. I hope if the baby's sick they hold it over the ashtray.

The phone rings, Mrs Boswell takes it from her apron pocket.

MRS BOSWELL. Hello. Oh it's you Adrian – hang on love – he's here. (*She hands the phone to Joey.*)

JOEY. Hello – yes.

We hear Adrian's voice in a panic.

Where? Button Street. I'll be there.

He puts the phone down on the table and puts his jacket on.

MRS BOSWELL. What is it, Joey?

JOEY. (*Nice and calm.*) Nothing Mam. The van's broken down – Adrian and Jack want a lift home and I'm going to pick them up – OK?

He wanders out and pauses at the door.

Get the old scouse on – all right.

Mrs Boswell smiles and Joey leaves.

Outside the Boswells' house

Joey comes out, he is in a hurry this time. He stops for a moment, remembering that his Jag is not there. He goes to Billy's car and tries to open the door. It has to be prised open and Joey has to squeeze into the car. For a second, while he is sitting in the driver's seat, one leg is still hanging out. He has to help it in by pulling on his trousers. He shuts the door, switches on and off he goes with a bang. Mrs Boswell comes out and puts a Police cone in the space. She watches Joey go.

A street near the alleyway

Adrian is looking at his watch anxiously, and peering down the alley at the parked car.

In the robbers' car

The car is parked in the alley with its back towards Adrian. Jack is sitting on the back seat, with the second man clutching him menacingly. The robber is sitting at the steering wheel.

ROBBER. So what should we do with him, Jacko?

JACK. (*Friendly.*) Oh, Jacko, that's *my* name.

The men stare at him.

Without the 'o'.

The second man gives him an extra twist on the arm.

JACK. I've er . . . I've got this funny illness y'know – it comes on in times of stress.

SECOND MAN. How funny is it? I mean, is it worth hanging about for a laugh?

JACK. It's a sort of fit I go into. Spasms. Takes three men to hold me down.

ROBBER. (*To the second man.*) Get on the blower to Slasher.

JACK. (*Quickly.*) It's all right – I don't feel one coming on.

ROBBER. Tell him we're bringing someone in.

The second man gets the telephone out of his pocket and presses the buttons without taking his eyes off Jack.

SECOND MAN. Hello Slash, it's Chalfont.

JACK. Chalfont?

A glare silences Jack.

SECOND MAN. We're bringing someone in. Just a little duffing up. A sort of deterrent, know what I mean?

GRUFF VOICE. My pleasure, guv.

The second man puts the phone away. Jack cringes.

ROBBER. (*Switching the engine on.*) Right, let's go then. (*He starts to reverse up the alley.*)

As he is doing so, Jack's van slowly crosses the exit. It stops – blocking their car in the alley.

Inside Jack's van/the robbers' car, in the alleyway

Adrian is at the wheel of Jack's van. He's shivering with fright. He climbs into the back of the van and gets under a blanket. He is terrified.

ADRIAN. (*Terrified, in the van.*) Oh my God, what am I doing – what am I doing?

ROBBER. (*Turning to Jack, in the car.*) How did that get there?

JACK. I don't know.

SECOND MAN. (*Shouting.*) Liar.

JACK. It's probably my brother. We've all got keys to each other's cars. He won't do anything – he's an estate agent.

The robber holds his hand out behind him for the van keys. Jack fishes around in his pocket.

ROBBER. Move it!

SECOND MAN. Yeah – move it – liar!

The robber takes the keys, rushes to the van and moves it out of the way. Then the robber rushes back to his own car. Just as he is about to start up again, Billy's car comes thundering along. It stops and blocks the exit of the alleyway, just as the van did.

ROBBER. (*To Jack.*) Which is it – a lot of brothers, or one brother with a lot of cars!

JACK. A lot of brothers, and a lot of cars.

ROBBER. (*Getting out of his car.*) I'll soon finish this one off. (*To the second man.*) Keep hold of him.

He stands looking at Joey who is getting out of the car. Joey gives the car door a special push and it squeaks open. He gets out with great dignity. He then slams the door shut in one go.

JOEY. Greetings.

The car window falls down with a sharp thud. Joey does not wince, but walks slowly towards the other car. He stares at the robber, who stares back. Joey puts his hand in his breast pocket. The robber now looks petrified. Joey pulls out a little notebook – the robber is noticeably relieved. Joey turns the pages.

JOEY. Now then – one radio, twenty quid – one chess set, twenty quid – one carriage clock, twenty quid – one consignment of hats, twenty-five quid – I make that eighty-five quid. Oh, and fifteen quid inconvenience money.

ROBBER. (*Turning to the second man in the car.*) We've got a faulty brain box here, Jacko.

Joey gets out of his pocket a small telephone – he does not take his eyes off the robber.

JOEY. Now let me see – what's that number again? Oh yes – 9 – 9 – 9. (*To the robber, charmingly.*) Excuse me, I have a call to make. (*To the man in the car.*) Excuse me.

He pushes two buttons.

ROBBER. (*Shouting loudly.*) Wait!

JOEY. (*With charm.*) Oh – did you wish to say something?

The Boswells' kitchen (early evening)

Some of the family are around the dinner table. Mrs Boswell is just putting peas into a colander and filling dishes with various vegetables for the table.

JACK. (*Lowered voice – to Joey.*) How's the face?

JOEY. All right.

ADRIAN. He didn't half come at you, didn't he?

JOEY. He did, yes.

ADRIAN. Still, we sorted things out didn't we? (*Pause.*) Well you did. (*Pause.*) I'm better at mental things than physical things. (*Pause.*) I've discovered.

BILLY. Sorted who out?

JOEY. (*Pointing to his mouth.*) Shut it. (*He points to Mrs Boswell.*) OK?

BILLY. Oh – it's a secret.

JACK. Hopefully yes.

MRS BOSWELL. You ought to go to the doctor with that face, Joey.

JOEY. It's all right. Mam – it's nothing.

MRS BOSWELL. I've told all of you never to try and fix Jack's van – putting your head under that bonnet is like putting it in a guillotine. (*She passes Joey a dish of vegetables.*) Here.

He puts it on the table, takes another dish, and another. Billy immediately lifts the lid of each dish to peer in.

MRS BOSWELL. Get your nose out Billy – now I know who the dog got his habit of going round the bins from.

BILLY. I can't do anything in this house. I can't do anything, I can't say anything.

MRS BOSWELL. You can *say* what you like – and you can *do* what you like as long as *we* like it.

JOEY. (*Bringing out the form he got from the DHSS.*) Oh – this is for you Billy. I forgot I had it.

Billy takes it and looks at it.

It's a form – from the Social Security Office. I'll explain it to you later. (*Billy look reluctant.*) You promised – remember?

BILLY. Oh yeah. Hey it was great in the Jag – everybody looked at us. You can't hear the engine – you can actually talk while you're driving. Hey – and we didn't have to keep jumping out and nailing the wing back on. It was great. The only thing was, we couldn't find the ashtray. (*Joey looks horrified.*)

MRS BOSWELL. Right.

She takes the lid off the pot. Joey, as usual, is the first one to put a ten-pound note in.

BILLY. (*Putting a pound in.*) I bust my guts for that.

ADRIAN. (*Putting a pound in – they look at him.*) I have lost my job.

JACK. (*Holding up a five-pound note, then putting it in the pot.*) When I've got it – you can have it.

MRS BOSWELL. You don't often have it though, do you?

Jack puts another five-pound note in.

Oh, Aveline sent five pounds. (*She puts it in the pot, gets the note out of her pocket and reads.*) Dear Mam, this is all I can afford. It cost me four quid for a new loofah today. (*She folds the note up and puts it back in her pocket.*)

ADRIAN. Oh God, another painting and decorating job on her body.

MRS BOSWELL. Right – prayers.

They all put their hands together, and she looks at them all.

It's been a good day.

JOEY. A good day indeed.

MRS BOSWELL. (*Keeping her eyes open.*) We thank Thee, oh Lord, (*they all close their eyes, then so does she*) for another day of reaping the harvest. And whilst giving thanks Father, we also ask forgiveness for the little things, Father, like never going to church. (*They all shift uncomfortably.*) Like teasing Grandad with his egg. (*Jack looks embarrassed.*) Like indulging in the more *earthly* physical pleasures of life. (*Both Billy and Adrian open their eyes, glance at each other and close them again.*) Instead of the spiritual – and like lying through the teeth about Joey's face. (*They all keep their eyes shut. Mrs Boswell looks around the table.*) Amen. You can all come out now.

They still don't open their eyes.

Aveline and Adrian

Episode Four

Inside the DHSS building (*afternoon*)

People are waiting as usual. The places at the counter are occupied. Adrian is sitting amongst others on a chair. He is wearing dark glasses, his coat collar is turned up and he is clutching his briefcase. A man gets up and walks away from Martina's (the usual girl's) desk.

MAN. (*Muttering.*) Bloody Nazis.

MARTINA. Next!

No one moves.

Next! Who's No. 49 please? (*She sees Adrian.*) Excuse me, Elton John, are you No. 49?

ADRIAN. (*Giving a start.*) Oh yes, it's me. Sorry. (*He sits on a chair opposite her and smiles charmingly.*) I'm not used to being called a number.

MARTINA. It'll grow on you, Mr Boswell, it'll grow on you. (*He takes his dark glasses off.*) Oh – there you are.

ADRIAN. I brought the form you gave me to fill in.

Martina looks at it.

MARTINA. You haven't filled in your date of birth.

ADRIAN. No. well, I regard that as personal. I mean, it doesn't really matter, does it, how old I am.

MARTINA. Oh but it does matter, Mr Boswell. How old you are is how long you live, and how long you live is how long we pay you and how long we pay you Mr Boswell (*pause*) matters.

ADRIAN. You read in the papers 'Mrs Ida Jones, aged fifty-three, was dragged across a roundabout by a runaway horse'. Well it's irrelevant isn't it – her age. I mean, it doesn't convey anything. And they never mention how old the horse is and . . .

MARTINA. Could I stop you please, Mr Boswell? There are other people waiting and the pubs are due to close. (*Pause.*) There's nothing personal in this building, Mr Boswell, nothing private, nothing sacred. It is something free provided by the state for those who wish to benefit from it. We don't provide saunas, sunbeds, organic cakes and decaffeinated coffee. We supply money. People who come here are broke, devastated, destitute. And the law is, Mr Boswell, if you're getting something for nothing you obey the rules. Age?

ADRIAN. Twenty six-ish.

MARTINA. Before twenty-six or after twenty-six?

ADRIAN. A long time after and just before twenty-seven. I'm afraid that's all I can divulge.

MARTINA. July?

ADRIAN. No, September.

MARTINA. The twenty-ninth?

ADRIAN. No, the seventeenth.

MARTINA. (*As she writes.*) Seventeenth of the ninth 1960. (*She looks at him.*) When you walk in here, Mr Boswell, you might as well be naked.

Adrian clutches his briefcase.

Outside the Boswells' house (*the next morning*)

Grandad's door is open and his chair is outside. Joey comes out. He is carrying a breakfast tray for Grandad.

JOEY. (*Calling into Grandad's house.*) Are you there, Grandad?!

> *His attention is drawn. He looks up the street and sees Grandad tottering very precariously up the street, going away from the house. He is quite a distance away.*
> *Joey watches for a moment, then puts the tray down and gets into his Jag. He reverses up the road and stops when he reaches Grandad. He winds the window down.*

JOEY. Hey – (*A little whistle.*) – come on – in you get. Your breakfast's ready.

GRANDAD. I'm all right – let me be.

> *Joey just sits waiting. Grandad begins to get very shaky on his feet. Then he stops – breathless. Joey gets out of the car and goes to him.*

JOEY. I've told you haven't I – if you want to go wandering, I'll take you – in the car.

GRANDAD. I don't want to go in the car. I want to go *when* I want to, *where* I want to, under me own steam.

> *Joey guides Grandad to the car, opens the door for him, and stands with his arms folded. Grandad looks at him.*

JOEY. Go on then – get in – under your own steam.

> *Grandad clambers into the car, all legs and bother. Joey finally closes the door, looks through the window, pulls an 'Oh my God, where is he?' face, and gets into the car. He drives back to the house, pulls up, gets out and opens the car door again.*

JOEY. OK, Grandad, out you get.

A foot protrudes, and Joey prepares for a long wait. A couple of kids are standing nearby, they begin to giggle. Joey looks at them.

JOEY. How high can you jump then?

FIRST KID. (*Giggling.*) Two feet.

SECOND KID. Three feet.

JOEY. He was doing four feet when he was your age. (*Pause.*) With his legs tied. Now on your rocket.

They run away.
Joey looks at the car. Another foot has arrived, he waits.

Boswells' kitchen

Mrs Boswell is washing the breakfast dishes. Jack is sitting by the table – he is carefully writing out something on a piece of paper. Joey comes in.

JOEY. He was off again – Grandad. Halfway up the road, he was.

MRS BOSWELL. Oh no – is he all right?

JOEY. I brought him back – he's fine. We'll have to watch him though, Mam.

MRS BOSWELL. I don't know what's got into him – he used to hate going anywhere. It took me years to persuade him to sit outside the house.

JOEY. Poor old Grandad – his legs were everywhere. Still, he must be feeling good.

JACK. No wonder he's feeling good – all the vitamins you sneak into his food. That glass of milk you give him at night is potent enough to save Ethiopia.

MRS BOSWELL. It's our way of looking after him. He doesn't know about the vitamins.

JACK. He's bound to suspect something – when we're all dead and he's still legging it up the street at 110.

The phone rings. Mrs Boswell answers it.

MRS BOSWELL. Hello? (*Joyfully.*) Aveline! (*To the others.*) It's our Aveline.

She hands the phone to Joey.

JOEY. Hi, princess. (*He hands the phone quickly to Jack.*)

JACK. Hello there. (*He blows a little kiss and hands the phone back to Mrs Boswell.*)

MRS BOSWELL. Tell me all your news, love.

AVELINE. I'm in a hurry Mam – I'm going modelling. Listen Mam, I've met a nice chap.

MRS BOSWELL. Oh? Where did you meet him, love?

AVELINE. In the street.

MRS BOSWELL. In the street? You mean he picked you up, outside, in the street!

AVELINE. We bumped into each other. It was lovely. It was like one of those body spray commercials.

MRS BOSWELL. (*Handing the phone to Joey.*) Oh God, why do I let her out of the house. Letting her go through that door is like putting a tadpole in a shark tank. (*Into the phone.*) The world is a bad place, Aveline. It's full of bad people, with bad thoughts.

AVELINE. I don't see how you make that out – it's full of us. Well, we are part of it, aren't we? I mean we can't be the only six good people in the world.

JOEY. We're the only six that come with a guarantee – OK? Look, just bring him home – we'll check him out.

AVELINE. I'd hate to be checked out by this family – it's easier to get into the Masons.

JOEY. Just take care – keep in touch, OK?

AVELINE. I've got to go. I'll ring tomorrow. Tarra everybody.

JOEY. Bye, princess. (*He holds the phone out to Jack.*)

JACK. Tarra, kid.

MRS BOSWELL. Tarra, love.

JACK. That's it! (*He reads.*) 'Mr Amadeus would like to buy anything from the days of your grandad (or his grandad, or his grandad before him) – pictures, trinkets, furniture. Ring 920 8112.' I'll ring my advert up. Can I have the cordless phone, Mam? I'll do it while I'm in the bath.

MRS BOSWELL. (*Hands it to him.*) Don't be long with it, I can't stand those tethered ones.

Jack goes upstairs.

JOEY. I haven't seen our Adrian this morning – where is he?

MRS BOSWELL. I can't get him out of bed. Go up Joey – tell him this cafe closes at nine o'clock.

Joey goes and Mrs Boswell starts wiping down the kitchen.

Honestly – since our Billy started his sandwich-making business, there's egg mayonnaise everywhere. (*She shouts upstairs.*) Switch the immersion off Joey – before it starts heating the Atlantic.

Upstairs at the Boswells' house

Joey approaches the door of one of the bedrooms. There is a sign hanging on the door which says 'Shitty Days are Here Again!!' Joey knocks.

JOEY. Adrian!

He knocks again, then goes in. There are three beds in the room, each one luxuriously sheeted and covered. There is a TV in the room, a radio and a telephone. Adrian is in the bed nearest the door. He is lying on his back, eyes closed.

JOEY. Hey – come on sunshine – what do you think this is the Chapel of Rest?

Adrian is silent, Joey looks at him.

Adrian – I know you're awake – I can see your mind on your face.

Adrian opens his eyes.

It's ten to nine.

ADRIAN. I'm not getting up today.

JOEY. Not getting up? Why?

ADRIAN. There's nothing to get up for, is there?

JOEY. (*Going to the window.*) There's the sky – the trees – the rain – the wind. (*He turns to Adrian.*) There's fate – destiny. They're all out there, son.

ADRIAN. I thought to myself – in the middle of the night – I thought – I have made a major discovery – I have come face to face with fact. I have uncovered an insurmountable truth – *I* am a wimp.

JOEY. (*Gently joking.*) Well, there has to be one doesn't there – in a family this size.

ADRIAN. I can't cope with any of the things the rest of you do. I sat cowering in the van when you and Jack confronted that robber the other day. I've lost me job, I trundle around, hugging my briefcase, like a child with its teddy bear. (*Pause.*) My life is hanging by a thread – hanging by a thread.

JOEY. Hey, come on, you're suffering from 'job loss' – it's a new illness.

We've all had it. The only way to cure it is to open the window, lean out and stick two fingers in the air.

ADRIAN. Who to?

JOEY. The world, sunshine, the world.

ADRIAN. I'm no good – I'm no good at anything.

JOEY. I'll bet Carmen doesn't think that.

ADRIAN. (*Quickly.*) I'm no good at that either.

Joey looks at him.

It doesn't go right somehow. I think part of me is missing.

Joey looks shocked.

I mean – mentally.

JOEY. Oh – thank God.

ADRIAN. I worry.

JOEY. About doing it right?

ADRIAN. About doing it – just doing it.

JOEY. 'Job-loss'.

ADRIAN. I appreciate your fancy name for it – but my word seems more appropriate. Wimp.

JOEY. You see Adrian, when a man loses his job, he loses other things – confidence, security, his sense of 'wholeness'. You've got to geel good (*indicating his head*) in this half of the body, to get any sense out of (*pause*) the other half.

ADRIAN. It's no use – I'm not a free spirit. I need regime, I need order – a time to get up, a time to take lunch, a time to go home. I like rules, regulations, notice boards, memos. I actually like saying 'Yes sir'. And besides, there's the Social Security. I hate going there. I feel demoralised. She called me No. 49. Oh God.

JOEY. Listen Adrian, when there's no work you can become several things. You can become a criminal, you can become depressed, or you can become bonkers. Now we, our family, are none of those things. We don't mug people, we don't take drugs, and we don't take up a space in the funny farm. We collect our dues – and then we go out and 'gently shake life's money box' until the rent falls out. A harmless occupation, wouldn't you say?

ADRIAN. I still feel demoralised – I still feel a cheat.

JOEY. We're all cheats – the rich cheat the tax man, the poor cheat the DHSS. The government cheats us all. *I* don't want pollution, insecticides, nuclear weapons, acid rain and colourants in my food – do you? But we get them, don't we? Those clever bastards in charge of the world don't ask us, do they? They'll either poison us to death, or blow us right off the bloody planet! So let's make hay, sunshine, while we're here. OK?

Adrian thinks about this, then nods his head.

ADRIAN. OK.

JOEY. Go in there, son. Don't be humble – you're a Boswell.

A street

An old van is parked outside the shops. It is smaller than Jack's and it has written across it 'Billy's Quality Sandwiches' – only the 'd' in sandwich has been missed out and inserted above.
 Billy comes out of a shop. He is carrying a huge basket which has packed sandwiches in it. He goes into the shop next door. Whilst he is there, about four ladies congregate at the back of the van, waiting for him.
 Billy comes out.

FIRST LADY. Any egg mayonnaise, Billy?

BILLY. I've got enough egg mayonnaise, darlin', to repair the Mersey Tunnel.

FIRST LADY. Two packets, love, and a cheese and pickle.

Billy opens the van doors, reaches in, gets the packets of sandwiches and gives them to the lady.

SECOND LADY. (*As the first lady pays him.*) Did you do any cottage cheese and peanuts, Billy?

BILLY. I ran out of peanuts, so I had to use dates, and I ran out of cottage cheese, so I had to use bananas. So I've got banana and date.

THIRD LADY. That's a funny mixture isn't it – bananas and date – you'd think we were gorillas.

FOURTH LADY. I'll have a packet love – it's for my old man. He *is* a gorilla.

SECOND LADY. Any cucumber, Billy?

BILLY. You name it – I've got it.

SECOND LADY. Oh listen to him. Give us one chicken, one smoked salmon and one caviar then, love. (*She smiles at the others.*)

BILLY. (*Reaching into the van.*) There you go – one chicken, one smoked salmon, one caviar!

The lady looks amazed.

Hurry up now, ladies, I've got all the offices to do yet.

There is a lot of giving of money and change. The ladies go.

FIRST LADY. Tarra, love.

BILLY. Tarra.

He turns to the back of the van and starts filling his basket with more packets of sandwiches. Martina from the Social Security walks up. She stops beside him. He is too busy to notice who she is.

MARTINA. How much are the sandwiches, please?

BILLY. Sixty pence the ordinary ones, and seventy pence the de-luxe ones.

MARTINA. I'll have a de-luxe sago pudding one please.

BILLY. (*Mechanically.*) Certainly Madam. (*He stops.*) I'm sorry, I haven't thought of that one. P'raps tomorrow. (*Then he realises, sudden change of tactic.*) The only problem is, things aren't going too good. I'll have to close down soon. Nobody's eating, you see. I'm losing a lot of money – it's – it's – impossible to make a living doing this. Still, it was an experience – and the family will all club together to pay the bread man.

MARTINA. You know Mr Boswell – *Junior* – when I used to lie in my worried bed, thinking and fretting about the paraphernalia of life, I consoled myself with the thought that one day your brother, Joey Boswell, might evaporate, or bestow himself upon Hollywood, or take up his rightful position on the British throne. But now, I see that he has a stand-in – an understudy – a *clone!*

She walks away.

The entrance to a very grand house

This is a house which stands in its own grounds. Jack's van comes up the drive. It stops by the main entrance. Jack gets out and looks in wonder at the house. Then he goes to the door and rings the bell. After a moment, a butler comes to the door. He just stands, rather stuffily, looking at Jack.

JACK. Er – I'm Mr Amadeus. I received a call at my residence from this estate. Apparently the owner has unfortunately fallen off his perch, and you wish to dispose of some of his possessions.

BUTLER. This way sir.

He steps aside for Jack, who goes in.

Julie's living room (*lunchtime*)

Julie is sitting nursing her baby. After a moment, she carefully places her in her crib. Just as she is covering her up, Billy comes bursting in.

BILLY. Julie!

JULIE. Shhh! (*She mouths* 'She's asleep'.)

> *Billy stops, mouths the word 'Oh'. Then tiptoes to her. He kisses her, goes to the crib and starts to bend down to see the baby.*

JULIE. Don't breathe all over the baby Billy – you've got all the germs of the world on your face.

BILLY. (*Stopping, looking at her.*) *You* kiss her.

JULIE. I'm her mother.

BILLY. I'm her father.

JULIE. She's not from your body, is she?

BILLY. (*Looking confused.*) I thought she was.

JULIE. You know what I mean – you didn't share your body with her for nine months, did you? We're compatible.

BILLY. Oh. (*He doesn't understand, so he drops the subject.*) Hey – guess how much I made this morning.

JULIE. I don't like guessing games, Billy. Men are not supposed to come home and do a panel game on their wages. Just tell me how much.

BILLY. Thirty quid! I've put thirty quid in the bank just now. (*He takes a deep, proud breath.*) I'm a changed person, Julie. (*He feels in his pocket and brings out a sandwich packet.*) Oh – and I brought your lunch.

JULIE. Aren't I a lucky girl then? (*She pushes the sandwich away.*) I've got better in the pedal bin.

BILLY. It was only fun, Julie. Why don't you smile at things – at life?

JULIE. Because, Billy, I am one of those unfortunate people. Instead of being born with a silver spoon in my mouth, I came out with a gob full of truth. And the truth is that every cloud has a shitty lining.

BILLY. But we're nearly there Julie – a few more weeks and we'll be able to talk about getting married.

JULIE. Oh, we're going to talk about it when you're rich, are we? Let's get the conversation over before your van blows up.

BILLY. You're a pessimist, Julie. Pessimists grow to look old quickly. (*Pause.*) I'm an optimist.

JULIE. Oh good – you can always pass me off as your mother. (*She starts to leave.*) I'll make some coffee.

BILLY. (*About the baby.*) Does Samantha need anything?

JULIE. Yes she does.

BILLY. Name it – I'll get it.

JULIE. She needs a father who can remember her name.

BILLY. Oh.

JULIE. It's Francesca – not Samantha.

BILLY. I get mixed up.

JULIE. She's a baby – not a Siamese cat. (*She goes.*)

Pause.

BILLY. (*Calling.*) I love you, Julie!

Pause. Then Julie peeps into the room.

JULIE. (*Provocatively.*) Black or white? Only with you saying you're a changed person . . .

BILLY. (*Smiling.*) I'm coming in there Julie – so watch out.

She gives him a naughty glance, then goes. He follows her.

The dogs' home (early afternoon)

Joey's car is parked outside. Dogs are barking in the background. Then Joey comes slowly out of the gates. He is putting his wallet back into his pocket. He goes to his car and gets in.
The attendant comes rushing out through the gate carrying a sweeping brush in one hand and some money in the other.

ATTENDANT. Mr Boswell, there's three notes here, did you know? Two of them were stuck together.

JOEY. Findings keepings Tom.

He switches the engine on.

ATTENDANT. Why, Mr Boswell? Why do you come in here and rescue all these dogs?

JOEY. It's a long story, Tom. It's in my guts.

He drives off.

A street

Joey is driving along. He has the stereo on – it is playing a tape of an opera aria. Joey sees Yizzel pushing his boss in a wheelchair. It's a very up-to-date and modern one. Joey slows down and drives along beside them. He lowers his window and laughs loudly.

YIZZEL. Shall I burst him, boss?

BOSS. No, no, Yizzel, it's a lovely day. We'll do it some other time when it's raining.

Joey stops the car and gets out.

JOEY. (*To boss.*) What have you been up to then?

BOSS. It's me legs, isn't it, Yizzel?

YIZZEL. Yeah – his legs.

BOSS. Nasty accident.

YIZZEL. Yeah – nasty.

BOSS. Leaving the casino in the small hours, weren't we, Yizzel?

YIZZEL. Yeah – the small hours.

BOSS. In haste, so to speak, hey Yizzel?

YIZZEL. Yeah.

BOSS. Faulty pavement, bad workmanship. Sued the council, didn't we, Yizzel?

YIZZEL. Yeah, gave them the business.

BOSS. Very understanding, very co-operative, isn't that right, Yizzel?

YIZZEL. Yeah – right.

JOEY. Listen, when you've finished with the chair – how much?

BOSS. Well now, let me see – this is a de-luxe model, electrically powered (*nodding towards Yizzel*) – for when you want to be alone.

JOEY. Okay, okay, got you – how much?

BOSS. Five hundred. (*Joey starts to speak.*) Nearly two grands' worth, one owner, hardly used, only two blocks on the clock.

JOEY. Let me know then, let me know. (*He is about to walk away.*)

BOSS. (*Leaping up.*) Speaking of miracles—

Joey looks in amazement. The boss looks at Yizzel.

There's always another pavement, isn't there, Yizzel?

YIZZEL. Yeah – another one.

Joey puts his hand in his wallet and walks towards them. He gives the boss the money. The boss takes it silently and he and Yizzel walk away. Joey goes to his car, gets out a small handphone and presses the buttons.

JOEY. Hello, Mam, is Jack there? (*Pause.*) Billy then?

Outside the Boswells' house

Billy comes rushing out of the house. He is drying his hair with a towel. Mrs Boswell is following him, she carries a plastic cone. Grandad is in his chair outside his house.

BILLY. (*Handing Mrs Boswell the towel.*) Thanks, Mam. (*He jumps into his van and zooms off.*)

Mrs Boswell puts the cone in place, then looks at Grandad.

MRS BOSWELL. Are you all right, love? (*She goes into the house.*)

GRANDAD. (*Calling.*) There's nothing wrong with me that dinner wouldn't put right!

Outside the grand house

Jack's van is still parked, it is loaded with stuff. Jack comes out of the house pushing a rather posh wheelchair. The butler follows him to the van.

JACK. Sad isn't it – wheelchairs are rather sad.

BUTLER. It rather depends on whether they are full or empty. Sir Hugh was happy enough in this one. (*He looks upwards.*) I can't vouch for him now.

A street (later that afternoon)

Joey is standing by his car waiting for Billy. The van appears and pulls up. Joey strolls over to Billy.

JOEY. (*Indicating the wheelchair.*) Grandad's wings, sunshine.

BILLY. Oh – yeah – great.

JOEY. Well – come on – shift it.

Billy starts to speak.

Somebody's got to conduct the orchestra – OK?

Billy gets out, pulling a protesting face.

The Boswells' kitchen

Mrs Boswell is sitting at the table peeling potatoes. A neighbour sits in the chair next to her. An oven timer is on the table.

NEIGHBOUR. Did Julie get stretch marks after the baby?

MRS BOSWELL. I don't know – she doesn't tell you anything that girl.

NEIGHBOUR. I got them. Marched all over me they did – like the army.

MRS BOSWELL. Yes – well – we've got to pay up somewhere, haven't we?

NEIGHBOUR. A woman seems to pay up everywhere – she has to carry the baby, give birth to the baby, look after the baby. Her chest sags, her mind leaves home, and she's left with her stomach lolling about like a pound of tripe.

MRS BOSWELL. The scientists will alter all that, you'll see. Soon we'll have pregnant men. The pubs will be full of fellas wearing wrap-over shirts and Mothercare trousers.

NEIGHBOUR. The world is going to be a funny place, isn't it? I can't remember what it was like before yoghurt.

MRS BOSWELL. When I was a girl, there were still horses and carts round here. There were cows grazing up the street. Rows of little cottages with Nelly Askwith selling her lettuces at the front door; and Maggie, the mad milk maid, serving your milk out of big urns – still warm it was, straight from a cow that had eaten untainted grass. If I'd known there was going to be radiation and all that nuclear business, I'd never have had all my children.

Mr Boswell appears suddenly at the door, Mrs Boswell jumps.

MR BOSWELL. But she met me you see – and I was irresistible.

NEIGHBOUR. Freddie Boswell – it's you, you devil.

MRS BOSWELL. You gave me a fright Freddie Boswell – creeping in like that. (*She looks at him.*) I suppose you'd give anyone a fright, anyway.

NEIGHBOUR. (*To Mr Boswell.*) Sit down, love.

MR BOSWELL. No – no – I never sit down. Not unless I'm invited by the head of the house (*Nothing from Mrs Boswell.*) Old iceberg face here. (*Nothing.*) Just passing – that's all.

MRS BOSWELL. Well, make it quick.

MR BOSWELL. You're a dark grey woman Nellie Boswell – a dark grey woman.

MRS BOSWELL. And get something done with your hair – you look as if you've been electrocuted.

MR BOSWELL. I've been to see my grandchild – Francesca. (*Pause.*) Our Billy with a bonnet on.

MRS BOSWELL. You keep away from that child – after sweeping the streets all day.

MR BOSWELL. She's got to walk in them one day, hasn't she?

MRS BOSWELL. Anyway – you didn't bother with your own for three years – why bother now?

MR BOSWELL. You don't allow for change, do you? You don't allow for 'I'm sorry – I regret – I wish – if I had my way again'.

MRS BOSWELL. (*Shouting.*) I haven't heard you say any of those words.

MR BOSWELL. (*Shouting back.*) I haven't said them – I've 'done' them.

MRS BOSWELL. And what about Lilo Lil?

The neighbour shifts uncomfortably

MR BOSWELL. She's got nothing to do with me and my family.

MRS BOSWELL. One look at her chest and you were off – like a bat out of hell.

MR BOSWELL. (*Really angry.*) That's because I'm human.

MRS BOSWELL. That's because you're a bastard!

The timer suddenly starts to ring between them. They stop shouting. A brief silence.

NEIGHBOUR. I'll have to go – me scones are done.

She picks up her oven timer and leaves awkwardly. Mr and Mrs Boswell glare at each other for a moment across the table.

MR BOSWELL. (*Desperately.*) Come back, Nellie Boswell.

MRS BOSWELL. It wasn't me who went, Freddie Boswell.

Outside the Boswells' house

Grandad is sitting on his chair nodding off, when Jack's van comes screeching up. Jack gets out, takes the cone and puts it on the pavement.

JACK. (*Going up to Grandad.*) Wait till you see what I've got for you, Grandad.

GRANDAD. I hope it's me dinner.

JACK. (*As he goes to his van.*) Something better than that, Grandad.

He unloads the wheelchair and proudly wheels it to Grandad who sits staring at it.

How about that then?

GRANDAD. Who's it for?

JACK. You – it's for you – your own little vehicle – fully licensed and MOT'd.

GRANDAD. I'll go in me box before I go in one of them things.

JACK. It's fantastic Grandad – you'll be able to go to the park – and the supermarket. You'll be able to go where you want. It'll be like sitting in your chair – only moving.

GRANDAD. And who's going to move me?

JACK. All of us – any one of us – just ask.

GRANDAD. Oh aye – if I can catch you. You come out of that house like a bullet out of a gun. The only one that saunters out is that Billy, and I can walk faster than him myself.

JACK. Try it – just try it. I'll take you down the street to the river.

GRANDAD. I can go down the street to the river any time I want – in me mind. I can go anywhere in me mind – we don't have to rely on anybody.

At this point, Billy's little van comes along. The wheelchair is tied on to the roof-rack. Joey's car follows. They pull up and Joey smiles through his window. Grandad looks at them.

GRANDAD. And you can tell them to piss off an' all!

The Boswells' kitchen (evening)

Joey and Jack are at the table. Mrs Boswell is putting dishes of vegetables on the table. Joey pours the wine. Adrian comes in and sits down.

MRS BOSWELL. Why are you still wearing your pyjama jacket?

ADRIAN. Because psychologically I'm not up yet.

MRS BOSWELL. (*Placing a roast chicken on the table.*) Grandad's had one leg.

ADRIAN. Oh good – I'll have the other.

JACK. You had a leg last time – I was seven when I last had a leg.

MRS BOSWELL. Shurrup the lot of you – until the scientists come up with a six-legged chicken you'll have to take turns. And judging by the information it's Jack's turn. (*She sits down.*) Where's that Billy?

JACK. He's gone to the money machine. It's his first time.

JOEY. Couldn't wait.

ADRIAN. (*A sob in his voice.*) I used to do that. I used to go down with my little card, and my secret number, and out it came – money.

MRS BOSWELL. You'll do it again love – where there's a money machine there'll always be a Boswell.

Outside a bank

Billy's van draws up and Billy gets out. He goes to the machine – he is smiling and excited. He puts his card in, presses the buttons, takes his card out and (with complete amazement) takes the money out. He stands there gazing at it.

BILLY. I've got money – and it's mine. I've earned it. (*Pause.*) I'm a business person.

Two youths come by – one grabs the money out of Billy's hand. They run away. Billy stands staring at his empty hand.

The Boswells' kitchen

The family are still seated round the table (except Billy) with their hands together, ready for prayers.

MRS BOSWELL. We thank Thee, oh God— (*The phone rings.*) Don't move. (*She answers it.*) Hello – yes – just a moment love. (*She hands it to Adrian.*) Carmen.

ADRIAN. (*Into phone.*) Hello.

They all sit, hands together.

CARMEN. Wasn't it wonderful last night?

ADRIAN. Yes. Look could I call you later – only we're mid-prayer here.

CARMEN. Will I see you later?

ADRIAN. Yes – yes.

CARMEN. It'll be wonderful again, won't it?

ADRIAN. Look – Carmen . . .

CARMEN. I read this article in a magazine – and it said a man should talk about things. You never talk about it Adrian – if you talk to me about it then next time it really *will* be wonderful. The magazine said so.

ADRIAN. I'll talk about it later – OK? Bye. (*To the others.*) Sorry about that. (*He puts the phone down and puts his hands together.*)

MRS BOSWELL. We thank Thee, oh Lord, for another day. (*Billy comes in.*) Oh good, you're here, Billy, just in time for prayers. Sit down, love. (*He does so quietly. She continues the prayer.*) For the food on the table, the thoughts in our heads, the DHSS, the money in our pocket (*she glances at Billy who shifts uncomfortably*) and all good things. Amen.

THE REST. Amen.

Mrs Boswell lifts the lid off the pot. Joey puts a ten-pound note in.

JACK. It cost me twenty quid for the wheelchair.

JOEY. We're all out of pocket on that one.

Jack puts a fiver in.

ADRIAN. (*Putting a pound in.*) When my redundancy money has gone, my thread will be hanging by a thread.

MRS BOSWELL. It doesn't get any easier getting money out of you lot, does it? It's like getting orange juice out of an apple.

She pushes the pot towards Billy – he gazes at it.

JACK. Hey – not bad is it – getting pound notes out of the wall.

BILLY. No.

JOEY. I meant to tell you Billy – be careful. What you do is, you grab your money straight into your pocket and away. Don't wave it about, OK?

BILLY. (*Quietly.*) OK. (*He looks at the dish for a few more moments, then leaps up shouting.*) I was robbed! I was mugged!

JOEY. Oh Billy.

BILLY. I was standing there—

JACK. With the money in the air, we know.

BILLY. And I was standing there, planning, making plans, in my head, and I was—

JOEY. Talking to yourself, we know.

BILLY. And these two fellas came along—

ADRIAN/JACK/JOEY TOGETHER. And nicked it, yeah we know.

BILLY. And they nicked it. (*He sits.*) Yeah.

MRS BOSWELL. You're money unconscious, aren't you Billy? Come day, go day, start again Monday.

JOEY. (*Opening his wallet.*) It's like having Dad back – he was always losing money. Remember, Mam, the rows we had? (*He puts money in for Billy.*)

MRS BOSWELL. Well, we'll have two of them to cope with, won't we?

They all look at her.

He's coming back, your Dad.

Freddie Boswell

Episode Five

Inside the DHSS building (*late afternoon*)

The office is empty. It is closed. Martina is working behind the partition. She checks some papers and takes them into another office.

When she returns, Mongy the dog is sitting on a chair in front of her partition. He has a note in his mouth. Martina opens the partition.

MARTINA. You're late. We're closed. (*She relents, takes the note and reads it.*) My name is Mongy, Mongy Boswell. (*she pulls an 'Oh God' face*) and I wish to complain about my allowance. At the moment I'm not collecting enough to buy best quality meat and the economy size aristocratic doggy bickies, even though I'm engaged in protecting the house and family from robbers and thieves, risking my life and suffering extreme job tension – all I get to eat is crap.

Joey comes in.

JOEY. (*Charmingly.*) There you are, Mongy. (*To Martina.*) I've searched everywhere for him. (*To Mongy.*) What are you doing here, son?

MARTINA. He's doing what you told him to – scrounging.

JOEY. (*Tut tutting to dog.*) She's like this all the time. (*To Martina.*) I'll take him home – he's probably over-taxed.

MARTINA. Makes a change in your house.

JOEY. Only, it's not easy you know, guarding our home and Grandad's home. While he's chasing them away from the front, they're coming in at the back, and while he's chasing them away from the back—

MARTINA. They're coming in at the front, I know.

JOEY. (*To the dog.*) Come on son, back to the grindstone. (*To Martina.*) He's looking a bit thin, you know. It's occupational anxiety, due to the spiralling down of society and the excess number of redundant robbers. Still, he's only a dog – you wouldn't be interested.

MARTINA. (*Plonking a form down.*) Fill that in.

JOEY. You know, beneath that frosty-faced exterior there beats a magnanimous heart.

MARTINA. I'm out to get you, Mr Boswell, and this might be my big chance. You've learned all the tricks, found all the loopholes, studied all the booklets. *He* can't read.

The Boswells' living room (*late at night*)

Adrian, Jack and Billy are sitting watching TV. Billy is falling asleep in a chair. Joey walks in and turns the TV down.

JOEY. Mam's trying to sleep, OK?

Billy gives a big yawn.

ADRIAN. Oh God, when he yawns he makes the Mersey Tunnel look insignificant.

BILLY. I'm tired, that's why.

JACK. No wonder you're tired – all that bonking.

BILLY. It's Julie – I was going to leave at ten o'clock, but she was in a funny quiet mood. I remember when all we used to do was talk, talk, talk.

JACK. Now all you do is bonk, bonk, bonk.

ADRIAN. Is that the only word you can find to describe Nature's most uplifting experience?

JACK. Uplifting? In my bonking days I was too weak to uplift my cup.

ADRIAN. Making love, that's what it's called.

BILLY. That's soppy, bonking's better.

ADRIAN. Yes, well it might describe what you do, but it certainly doesn't describe Carmen and me!

JOEY. Eh now come on – what does it matter? Making love describes the emotions, bonking describes the logistics. It's good fun either way.

ADRIAN. Fun?

JACK. Oh God, we're back at the beginning again.

JOEY. What about Dad coming back, eh?

JACK. The rows will start now. We'll have Dad sitting like a little hamster trying not to make a noise with his toast, and Mam dropping the vegetables on to our plates like a dump truck.

JOEY. Yeah, well let them sort it out, no taking sides. And you, Billy, keep it shut, OK?

BILLY. Why don't you all club together and buy me a muzzle? (*He yawns.*)

JOEY. Look, why don't you go to bed if you're so tired?

BILLY. (*Half asleep.*) I'll have to get washed and clean my teeth, won't I?

They hear the dog barking outside.

There's Mongy – he wants to come in.

ADRIAN. (*Getting up.*) Yeah, well I'm off, I've got a long day of nothing tomorrow.

JACK. (*Getting up.*) And me.

JOEY. (*Turning the TV off and going to the kitchen door.*) You'd better let him in now Billy – if you're not there on the third bark he'll be off again. (*He pauses at the door.*) Don't forget to switch the TV off. What you do is you grab the little knob and you turn it. OK? 'Night sunshine.

The Boswells' kitchen (early morning, the next day)

Billy is seated by the table with his head resting on his arms, his face buried. After a moment Mrs Boswell comes in. She is in her dressing-gown. She gets a surprise when she sees Billy.

MRS BOSWELL. Billy! What are you doing up? (*She pokes him.*) Billy!

Billy raises his head – he looks very sleepy.

BILLY. What?

MRS BOSWELL. (*Peering at him.*) Have you been there all night? (*She gets on with setting the breakfast table.*) Honestly, Billy – you'd fall asleep on a level crossing. I've heard of people who sleep a lot – but you're ridiculous. You're supposed to have young blood in your veins – where is it?

He moves his arms and she sees an open letter on the table.

BILLY. It's a note from Julie. She must have pushed it through the door on her way to the station this morning. I thought she was acting funny last night.

He hands it to her.

She reads.

JULIE'S VOICE. Dear Billy, I have been worried lately – about us living here – about the future for our baby – about the world. I know you try hard. But something in me can't wait. I told you about my friends in London. Well I've gone down there to see what it's like – p'raps the streets are paved with hope. I'll phone you when I'm settled. Don't worry about the baby. Love Julie.

Mrs Boswell puts the letter down and sighs.

MRS BOSWELL. It all happens in this family, doesn't it? I'm frightened to open my eyes in the morning in case the house has gone.

BILLY. (*Standing up and shouting.*) She has no right. I'm the father of that baby. She's kidnapped my child.

MRS BOSWELL. (*Coaxing him to sit down again.*) Now don't be over-dramatic Billy – she's gone away for a bit, that's all. God bless and save us, it's like watching the big film.

BILLY. If I was married to her, I'd be the boss – I'd be in charge – she wouldn't be able to do these things.

MRS BOSWELL. I know love – that's why you're not married.

BILLY. Now what do I do? I've got me sandwich business – I'm running round like a blue-arsed fly – for what?

MRS BOSWELL. (*Sitting him down.*) For her, love, and for your baby.

BILLY. (*Scathingly.*) London – what's in London? They're all precaucious snobs down there.

MRS BOSWELL. Pretentious, Billy.

BILLY. They don't even call on one another, they have to make phone calls. You can't go 'Yoo-hoo, is the kettle on queen?' in London.

Joey comes into the room. He is in his bathrobe.

JOEY. What's all the shouting then?

MRS BOSWELL. (*Handing Joey the letter.*) It's from Julie.

Whilst Joey is reading it, Billy stands up again and yells.

BILLY. She has no right! (*He sits down again.*)

JOEY. (*Silently reads the letter.*) Ah – well – yes – she's ambitious isn't she Billy? She wants to try the world on – like a pair of shoes – until she finds a pair that fit her. There's no harm in that, now is there, sunshine?

BILLY. What about the baby?

JOEY. She's a mother isn't she? You know about mothers, Billy.

MRS BOSWELL. (*Busy in the kitchen.*) You'll get an extra tomato for that, Joey!

BILLY. But I'm a father!

JOEY. Of course you are – and fathers are providers. So what you do is you go out there, and you provide.

BILLY. What for?

JOEY. Them – your girl – and your baby. Be ready for when they come back – meet them at the station, with a suit on, and a van that goes.

BILLY. I didn't know she was like this.

JOEY. Of course you knew she had character, courage, truth – that's why you love her.

BILLY. No it isn't. I love her because she has a lovely body and silky hair and—

JOEY. All right, Billy.

BILLY. And when she laughs her eyes close – and her mouth—

JOEY. Opens, Billy – I know – they all do that.

BILLY. It goes all sexy – and—

JOEY. Billy . . .

Billy stops.

What you've got to do is carry on, OK? And when she comes back – be nice to her.

BILLY. I am nice to her.

JOEY. Not just ordinary nice, Billy. Women are strange creatures – you've got to be 'extra' nice.

BILLY. I bring her one of my best sandwiches home every day.

Joey is almost giving up.

Well, men who make cars don't bring their women a car home every day, do they?

JOEY. What I mean is – it's got to be right Billy – perfect even. (*Pause.*) You know, like when you comb your hair, and there's just a little piece that's not right, your whole image is wrong.

Billy gets up.

BILLY. I'm not ready for all this. (*He walks out.*)

MRS BOSWELL. It's no use being profound with him Joey. Anyway, he doesn't comb his hair.

JOEY. Funny thing life, isn't it, Mam? Aveline and Julie have left the fold and Dad's on his way back. Every day something new.

MRS BOSWELL. I hope I'm doing the right thing about your Dad, Joey.

JOEY. Of course you are – it's natural, he's family.

MRS BOSWELL. He travels through life like Coco the Clown – give his mind something serious to think about and it liquidises it.

JOEY. We'll shape him up, Mam.

The Boswells' street

Mr Boswell is pushing his yellow cart, his radio is playing and he is whistling happily to it. He wears a suit, a shirt and a bow tie – a happy, jaunty figure.

As Mr Boswell goes along the street, a lady is brushing the pavement outside her house.

MR BOSWELL. Mind me shoes, girl, mind me shoes.

She looks up.

LADY. Freddie Boswell – it's you again. Ooh – all dressed up. Been promoted, have you?

MR BOSWELL. In a way, sweetheart, in a way.

He arrives outside the Boswells' house and parks his cart. He switches off the radio and picks up a plastic bag. Then he sees Billy sitting sulking in his car. He goes to him.

Hello, son.

BILLY. Hi, Dad.

MR BOSWELL. You're very dark grey, aren't you? What's up?

BILLY. Julie's left me – she's gone to London.

MR BOSWELL. Gone looking for rainbows, has she? Well, I've got news for her – they do a U-turn at Watford.

BILLY. (*With tears in his eyes.*) She's taken the baby.

MR BOSWELL. Move over.

BILLY. It won't open – I've slammed it.

MR BOSWELL. Well listen – there comes a time in all our lives when we have to go. We can't explain – often we leave good for bad. But we have to go – it's part of the learning process. You'll be driving along the road and suddenly you want out – you want to stretch – the field over there (*indicating*) always seems to have the sun shining on it.

BILLY. I'd never leave Julie.

MR BOSWELL. We'll see son – we'll see. (*Pause.*) Hey – and the good news is – we often come back.

They look at each other for a moment. Then Mr Boswell knocks on the front door of the house. While he is waiting, Grandad opens his door – he is in a dressing-gown.

GRANDAD. Is me breakfast coming or not?

MR BOSWELL. I will place your order immediately, Grandad.

GRANDAD. And I don't want honey – them bees is radioactive. I've got enough on with me lungs trying to fight off the stuff that comes out of his (*meaning Billy's*) car. (*He slams the door.*)

The house door opens. Mrs Boswell is there. She stands, frozen. Mr Boswell gives her a quick little kiss on the cheek – which she receives without emotion. He proffers her his bag, which she ignores, and she goes into the house, followed by Mr Boswell.

The Boswells' kitchen

Mr and Mrs Boswell come in. The table is almost set now. As he passes the table, Mr Boswell picks up the large packet of cornflakes.

MR BOSWELL. (*In fun.*) Can I have the cut-out?

Mrs Boswell gives him an intolerant look, then starts to prepare toast. Mr Boswell is still clutching his plastic bag. There are two trays prepared.

MRS BOSWELL. You can put your luggage down, Freddie Boswell.

He puts the plastic bag down. Mrs Boswell hands him some cutlery. He takes it and puts it on the table while she finishes the toast. He is smiling happily.

MR BOSWELL. Back home, eh? (*He counts the place settings.*) One, two, three – how many kids have we got?

MRS BOSWELL. Three upstairs – one left home and one in the car outside.

MR BOSWELL. Oh yes – our Billy. I had a word.

MRS BOSWELL. Well, you are an authority, aren't you? On people leaving people.

MR BOSWELL. You're like a dog with the postman's trousers, aren't you?

He puts a knife and fork down in the wrong order. Mrs Boswell changes them round.

MRS BOSWELL. You don't expect me to forget Lilo Lil, do you? You don't expect me to forget that morning when you walked out of this house to go to that – tart! I have lain in my bed at night with Lilo Lil's name burnt in my brain. I have lain there and made elaborate plans to go out and machine-gun the entire city in the hope that I might blow Lilo Lil right out of her shameless knickers.

MR BOSWELL. Can't we forget Lilo Lil?

MRS BOSWELL. Don't you dare mention her name in this house.

Jack comes wandering in, yawning.

JACK. How are we fixed for breakfast then? I'm going on a call.

MR BOSWELL. Morning son.

JACK. Hi, Dad – you're back then.

MRS BOSWELL. It won't be a minute. Has Joey finished his bath yet?

JACK. I don't know – but his aftershave is seeping under the door and poisoning us all.

MRS BOSWELL. (*To Jack.*) Take these trays, Jack – one to Grandad, and one to our Billy, he's sulking in the car.

JACK. Oh that's great, isn't it? We could all do that. I'll have me dinner in the van tonight.

MRS BOSWELL. He's emotionally disturbed. And besides he's trapped – the car door won't open. Go on.

Mr Boswell is still helping with the table. Mrs Boswell snatches a dish of butter up after he has put it down, and places it elsewhere. Adrian comes down – he smiles broadly when he sees his dad.

ADRIAN. Oh – Dad – when did you move in then?

MRS BOSWELL. He was here with the milk – sit down.

ADRIAN. Welcome home, Dad, welcome home.

MR BOSWELL. Thanks, son.

ADRIAN. Where do I sit?

MRS BOSWELL. Nothing's changed. We sit where we sat.

Jack returns and sits down. Mrs Boswell goes to the stairs and calls.

MRS BOSWELL. Joey!! Breakfast!

MR BOSWELL. (*To the others.*) Still the same, isn't she? Got a loud hailer for a gob!

Mrs Boswell goes on with her work. Mr Boswell gets a brochure out of his pocket and hands it to Jack.

MR BOSWELL. Have you seen this, son?

JACK. The Body Centre?

MR BOSWELL. It's smashing – it's got a sauna, and a sun-bed, shower, massage. Four quid for the lot. I go every week – hence the golden look.

JACK. Are they open this afternoon?

MR BOSWELL. They're open all the time, son, all the time. Well, they've got to cater for the unemployed, haven't they? Being out of work is one thing, but being out of work and pale . . .

MRS BOSWELL. It doesn't matter what colour your body is if your brain's lying on its back, does it? They've got work to do.

ADRIAN. (*Taking the brochure.*) I must say I'd quite like to get a tan. It's nice to be brown all over, isn't it? And my body's a bit – patchy.

MR BOSWELL. (*In fun.*) Ah well, there has to be a runt in every litter.

MRS BOSWELL. (*Turning on Mr Boswell.*) There's no runt in my litter – every one born strong and whole – the only runt was their father.

MR BOSWELL. (*To others.*) No sense of humour – no sense of humour. She'd put years on a Ming vase, she would.

Joey comes in. He stretches out his hand to shake his father's.

JOEY. Dad – another chair at the family table eh? Great. (*He sits down.*)

MR BOSWELL. Hello son, thanks.

Mr Boswell draws out Mrs Boswell's chair and sits in it. Mrs Boswell turns to put a dish of food on the table. She stops and stands looking at him. They all look at him. Eventually, he gets up slowly and moves out of her chair.

ADRIAN. Sit here, Dad.

MR BOSWELL. Thanks, son.

Mrs Boswell puts her hands together. The rest do too, but not Mr Boswell. They close their eyes, but Mrs Boswell sits glaring at Mr Boswell. The others, sensing the hold-up open their eyes. Jack gives Mr Boswell a little kick.

JACK. We're waiting for you, Dad.

MR BOSWELL. Oh – er – leave me out if you don't mind.

MRS BOSWELL. But we *do* mind.

MR BOSWELL. I don't pray any more.

JACK. You used to pray.

MR BOSWELL. Yeah – well a lot has happened since then. (*Pause.*) Oh – I believe in God – but in a different way.

JACK. I know what Dad means – you can still believe in God without chatting him up all the time.

MRS BOSWELL. Not you too, Jack.

JACK. There's no need, Mam. And anyway – with things the way they are – I don't see how he's got time to listen.

ADRIAN. I must say, it has been hard to keep believing, what with losing my job, and my redundancy money ebbing away and – other things of a private nature – my faith has been hanging by a thread, hanging by a thread.

MR BOSWELL. I'm more of a Proddy now.

MRS BOSWELL. A Proddy! (*She crosses herself.*)

MR BOSWELL. Well, it got a bit boring, you know, confessing my sins and then going home and doing it again.

Joey is sitting quietly with his hands clasped and his face against his hands.

MRS BOSWELL. (*Gravely.*) I see. So the rot's setting in, is it – the sheep are beginning to scatter. (*She turns to Joey for help.*) Joey?

Pause.

JOEY. Those who want to pray, pray – those who don't, don't.

Mrs Boswell puts her hands together, Joey next. The others sit somewhat ashamedly.

MRS BOSWELL. We thank Thee, Oh Lord –

Suddenly Mr Boswell thinks better of it – he puts his hands together and closes his eyes. The others immediately do the same.

– for (*a pause*) all the good things in life. Help us to cope with the bad. (*She glances at Mr Boswell.*) Amen.

In the confessional box (*later the same day*)

Mrs Boswell is sitting in the box. She is talking to Father Dooley.

MRS BOSWELL. The thing is, Father, it's him – my (*pause*) husband . . .

Father Dooley is about to open his mouth.

And before you start pontificating about lost souls returning, I think I ought to tell you – he has sinned.

FATHER DOOLEY. The Lord is full of sweet forgiveness, my child.

MRS BOSWELL. Not an ordinary sin, Father, a dreadful sin.

FATHER DOOLEY. There are no good sins, no bad sins, only sins, my child.

MRS BOSWELL. I hardly know how to say it, Father.

FATHER DOOLEY. The Lord will forgive.

MRS BOSWELL. It's such a – a – (*pause, then emphatically*) a *sin*.

FATHER DOOLEY. Fear not, my child. If a man repenteth, the Lord will forgive him – for anything.

MRS BOSWELL. He's turned Protestant, Father.

FATHER DOOLEY. (*In the same tone as if he had not been interrupted.*) Except for turning Protestant.

Croxteth Estate (early evening)

A large country area, once owned by Lord and Lady Sefton, now open to the public. Adrian's motorbike is lying on the ground. The main house is in view, and the lily pond. But Adrian and Carmen are somewhere in the bushes.

CARMEN. It was – (*pause*) – ecstatic.

ADRIAN. Thank you.

CARMEN. When I'm old I'll think of these moments – with you – in a cornfield, in a little room behind a shop, on the sand dunes, in the bushes by a lily pond.

ADRIAN. Where will I be when you're thinking these things?

CARMEN. You'll be old too – and you'll be thinking about them.

ADRIAN. So we won't be together?

CARMEN. We might.

We hear the sound of her giving him a little kiss.

We don't know, do we?

ADRIAN. (*Hurt.*) You'll be with Alan Wentworth, no doubt.

CARMEN. It's no more likely than you being with Helen Pope.

ADRIAN. (*Angry now.*) You're like all women after all. You *deliberately* bump into me in the street, then you deliberately find out where I'm going to be – and get there before me. Then you taunt me – with your – with your— (*he can't say it.*) Then you *steal* my body!

CARMEN. Steal it!

ADRIAN. Yes – steal it.

Adrian comes storming out of the bushes, tucking his shirt in.

Then, after lulling me into a state of adoration, you plan – yes, plan – in front of my very naked self – *your* future – without me. (*He looks at her and shouts louder.*) Since I met you, Carmen, my body is hanging by a thread – hanging by a thread.

Carmen stands up, revealing her head and shoulders as she parts the bushes.

CARMEN. (*Lovingly – panting.*) You were wonderful, Adrian.

ADRIAN. Not to mention your lies. (*He begins to cram his helmet on.*)

CARMEN. (*Shouting.*) All right – they were lies!

Adrian looks at her, and loses all his fight.

You are not wonderful – you are not a great pulsating tiger – the earth does *not* move!

Adrian looks at her pathetically – then picks up his bike. He gets on it, and starts the engine. Carmen shouts above the noise.

You don't even know how to do it!

Adrian pulls his visor down and zooms off, right across a rose garden, round the house and away.

Julie's friend's flat in London

Julie is just rocking the baby to sleep in a carrycot. Her friend Alice is making up at a mirror. Alice peeps over the mirror and watches Julie.

ALICE. Are you coming tonight then?

JULIE. No.

ALICE. My friend Janice will babysit.

JULIE. I'd rather not.

ALICE. Tomorrow night then?

JULIE. We'll see.

ALICE. I thought you came down here to find things out. All you're going to find out is what it's like to sit in every night.

JULIE. I can't leave the baby.

ALICE. She won't know, will she? She'll be asleep.

JULIE. She might wake up and see a strange face.

ALICE. It's time her mother woke up and saw a strange face.

JULIE. You go. I'll be all right.

ALICE. Ralph Connelly will be there.

JULIE. Who's he?

ALICE. We met you at the station – Ralph, Roland and me.

JULIE. Oh, him.

ALICE. He fancies you.

JULIE. He's always smiling. I can't stand fellas that are always smiling. It's as if the corners of his mouth are hooked on to his ears.

ALICE. And Roland – he'll be there.

JULIE. I don't like him either.

ALICE. He drives a Porsche.

JULIE. Oh well he must be all right if he drives a Porsche. Hang on, while I choose me wedding dress. (*She looks at Alice.*) What's a Porsche got to do with it?

ALICE. Well you can tell a fella's ambitions by the car he drives. I mean, it's like reading his horoscope.

JULIE. In that case there's no hope for Billy. Every time he starts his car up it sheds its skin like a snake.

ALICE. Why didn't you marry Billy?

JULIE. He's not ready for it.

ALICE. They're never ready for it. You have to take them by surprise.

JULIE. (*Sitting down now.*) He'd go up the aisle with that daft look on his face. It'd be like putting a sparrow in a little cage.

ALICE. Catch me caring. If I found someone I loved I'd cram him in that cage even if he was a bloody eagle.

JULIE. He comes from a big family. They're very close. I think the mother's related to God. She's only got to nod her head and the universe goes into reverse.

ALICE. How many are there?

JULIE. There's their dad, and grandad. There's Jack and Adrian, and Aveline. Then there's Joey. He was put on this earth to keep the delicate balance of nature – if it wasn't for his leather gear we'd be overrun with cows. (*Thoughtfully.*) And amongst them all there's Billy (*with a little smile.*) He's got curly hair and he hardly ever laughs.

ALICE. He sounds dull to me.

JULIE. He puts his socks on inside out, gets his shirt buttoned wrong, bumps into things, talks through the earpiece on the phone.

ALICE. Instead of marrying him, why don't you adopt him?

JULIE. I've only told you the bad bits.

ALICE. Oh – there are good bits then.

JULIE. Yeah.

ALICE. So why aren't you up there with him?

JULIE. I had to find things out, didn't I?

Outside the Boswells' house

Jack, Mr Boswell and Billy are playing football in the street. There are two cardboard boxes set apart to indicate the goal area. Mrs Boswell appears at the door with Grandad's dinner tray. Jack, Mr Boswell and Billy are all laughing, all having fun. Mrs Boswell goes to Grandad's door and knocks. It opens and Grandad's hands do the usual snatch. The door closes. Mrs Boswell calls again.

MRS BOSWELL. This is the third time you lot – your dinner's ready.

They are too busy enjoying themselves. She goes inside.

The Boswells' kitchen

The table is laid in abundance as usual. Mrs Boswell comes in – she is despondent and disappointed. She is not used to the family disobeying her. She walks slowly to her place and sits down, then puts her hands together.

MRS BOSWELL. I thank Thee, oh Lord, for what I am about to receive – and I ask Thee to forgive me for anything which may follow. Amen.

She serves herself some vegetables and some cold meat, and carefully sprinkles salt and pepper on the food. Then she gets up and systematically empties every dish on to the centre of the table – vegetables, salad, cold meat, calmly and coldly – followed finally by the trifle which she empties on top of the rest. She takes the empty dishes, puts them down on the draining-board, then sits down to have her meal.

After a moment, Adrian comes in. He stops short when he sees the scene.

MRS BOSWELL. You're late.

ADRIAN. Yes, I'm sorry. I was with Carmen.

MRS BOSWELL. She's more important than the family, is she?

ADRIAN. Well – I am entitled to a private life.

MRS BOSWELL. And what am I entitled to, I wonder?

ADRIAN. Why have you done this, Mam? (*He sits.*) What's the matter?

MRS BOSWELL. He's only been here five minutes and he's destroying us already.

ADRIAN. Oh come on – they're having fun out there.

MRS BOSWELL. I know. Jack hasn't done any work, and Billy went out on his sandwich round this morning with the most revolting sandwiches I've ever seen.

ADRIAN. Well he's upset isn't he, about Julie. We're all upset about something.

MRS BOSWELL. You're right – we're all upset about something – and what does *he* do about it? *Nothing!* He doesn't say 'Off you go Jack, you've got a call to make.' 'Off you go Billy – but not until you get those sandwiches right.' No – he says 'When in doubt, get the football out.' (*She begins to sniff.*)

ADRIAN. (*Near to tears himself.*) Don't cry, Mam.

MRS BOSWELL. You try to do things right, Adrian. You try to please people.

ADRIAN. I know, I know.

MRS BOSWELL. You put all your heart and strength into it.

ADRIAN. I know, I know.

MRS BOSWELL. And what do they do?

ADRIAN. (*Emotionally.*) They tell you you're no good at it.

MRS BOSWELL. (*Looking at him.*) You're a clever boy, Adrian. You know nothing about life and yet here you are all warm and wise.

> *Joey comes in – he sees the mess on the table and immediately understands the situation.*

JOEY. Greetings.

MRS BOSWELL. I called them Joey – I called them at least four times.

JOEY. It's OK, Mam, it's OK.

MRS BOSWELL. I'm sorry – I didn't put something aside for you.

JOEY. No sweat, no sweat. (*He draws a chair out and sits down.*)

MRS BOSWELL. I should never have let him come back.

JOEY. He's all right, Mam, he'll settle down. He's like a kid let out of school, isn't he?

MRS BOSWELL. More like he's been let out of a nut-house. (*Pause.*) It's taken us three years to build this family into some kind of strength again – we've

wanted for nothing, we've pulled together, obeyed the rules. And now –
we're all tossing about on a destructive sea – with my Aveline overboard, and
him at the helm.

*Jack, Mr Boswell and Billy come in. They are pushing each other and
laughing.*

MR BOSWELL. (*To Jack.*) You couldn't kick a hole in a blancmange, you!

JACK. Well, at least I didn't go down with bronchitis every time I kicked it.

MR BOSWELL. Years of bringing a family up does that to you, son.

*They all suddenly stop and look at the mess on the table. They glance at
each other, then at Joey who, with his stare, commands silence. They each
draw out a chair and sit down. Joey takes the lid off the pot. He puts two
ten-pound notes in, then looks at Billy, who puts two pounds in, then Adrian
who puts a pound in. Then at Jack who looks awkward as he pats his
pockets.*

JOEY. You'll have to make yesterday's money go round a bit more won't you
sunshine?

*Jack takes out a five-pound note and puts it in the dish. Mrs Boswell feels in
her pocket and brings out a note with five pounds in it.*

MRS BOSWELL. (*Reading.*) Dear Mam, I . . . (*She gives it to Joey.*)

JOEY. Dear Mam, this is my last fiver – I had to buy a face steamer today,
love Aveline. (*He drops the five pounds in the pot.*)

*Mr Boswell smiles, then brings out two ten-pound notes, screws them up and
drops them in.*

JOEY. Thank you. (*He looks at Mrs Boswell.*)

MRS BOSWELL. I've said prayers.

JOEY. (*To the rest.*) Right – shall we begin then?

*He takes a piece of lettuce off the pile and puts it on his plate as if nothing
was wrong.*
They all start, with a great deal of distaste, to do the same.

Adrian, Billy, Joey, Aveline, Jack, Mrs Boswell, Grandad

Episode Six

The Boswells' living room (*morning*)

Jack is sitting on the settee polishing an ornate silver picture frame. Joey, in his dressing-gown, is reading the paper.
  In the kitchen Billy is making his sandwiches for the round. Mrs Boswell is trying to get breakfast prepared.

MRS BOSWELL. How long will you be, Billy? They are all waiting for their breakfast. It's half-past nine.

BILLY. Nobody called me, did they? I'm late.

JACK. (*Calling to kitchen.*) Hurry up Billy – there's a queue here.

MRS BOSWELL. I don't know why you need calling. There are five alarm clocks going off in the house between 7.30 and 8.30 – surely one of them gets through to that brain of yours.

BILLY. I need a voice, don't I?

MRS BOSWELL. At least three radios come on.

BILLY. I mean, a proper voice, a live voice.

MRS BOSWELL. The dog barks when the milk comes and when the post comes.

BILLY. Not a dog's voice – a person's voice.

MRS BOSWELL. And who's going to waken the person whose voice has to wake you?

BILLY. Well, they've got alarm radios and dogs, haven't they? What more do they want? (*He packs the last sandwiches into one of his large baskets.*)

MRS BOSWELL. Have you got the cottage cheese and banana for the people in the hairdressing salon?

BILLY. Yes. (*In despair.*) I wish Julie was here – there's no point.

MRS BOSWELL. She will be here, Billy, one day. That *is* the point. (*She calls.*) Jack, feed the dog, will you?!

Jack comes wandering in. Mrs Boswell hands him a huge bowl with 'OUR DOG' printed on it.

Feed him in the yard – there's no room in here.

Jack gets a spoon and goes to the bottom of the stairs. He bangs on the bowl with the spoon.

JACK. (*Calling.*) Mongy! Food – come on! (*Pause.*) Mongy! (*He looks at Mrs Boswell.*) Where is he?

MRS BOSWELL. As far as I know he's where he always is – on Joey's bed.

JACK. Mongy!!

MRS BOSWELL. (*Joining him.*) Mongy – come on love!

Joey comes into the room.

Was the dog on your bed last night, Joey?

JOEY. No – I thought he was on Jack's.

JACK. He wasn't on mine.

BILLY. He wasn't on mine either.

MRS BOSWELL. Well Adrian won't let him on his bed – and he won't go on Aveline's bed because her talcum powder used to get up his nose.

BILLY. (*As he cleans up.*) P'raps he's gone out.

MRS BOSWELL. He *never* goes out before he's fed.

JOEY. Hang on – I'll go and look. (*He goes upstairs.*)

MRS BOSWELL. (*Going to help Billy clear up.*) There's more salad cream on the ceiling than in your sandwiches, Billy. Can't you remember to put the top on before you shake it?

BILLY. I can't remember everything, can I?

MRS BOSWELL. I don't want you to remember everything, do I? I just want you to remember to put the top on the salad cream before you shake it.

Joey comes down.

JOEY. He's upstairs – in the airing cupboard.

Mrs Boswell is about to speak.

I don't think he's very well, Mam.

MRS BOSWELL. Oh God. (*She automatically gets out the telephone and dials.*)

JOEY. I thought he was a bit quiet yesterday – there was a woman with a French loaf sticking out of her bag and he didn't bother to pinch it.

MRS BOSWELL. (*Into the phone.*) Hello – is that the veterinary clinic? Yes – can the vet come out please? Our dog is not well. (*Pause.*) I don't know whether it's an emergency or not, do I? That's why I want a vet. (*Pause.*) Look – don't bother – we'll go private.

Joey takes the phone from her.

JOEY. Hang on, Mam. (*He speaks charmingly.*) Hello – who am I speaking to please? (*Pause.*) I see – yes – yes. No, of course he can't leave in the middle of an operation – I understand. We'll bring the dog to you – yes – in half an hour. Thank you. (*Pause.*) The name is Boswell – Mongy Boswell. Thank you.

Joey hands the phone to Mrs Boswell.

MRS BOSWELL. Honestly – you've got to fight for everything. The kid up the road fell and broke his arm last week. By the time they saw him at the hospital it had set – he looked like a windmill.

JOEY. OK everybody – just carry on as normal. I'll get Mongy to the vet. (*He goes upstairs.*)

MRS BOSWELL. And remember, Joey, we want a proper consultant. And if they keep him in, we want a private kennel.

JACK. He's a dog, Mam. It's not the same.

MRS BOSWELL. What do you mean – it's not the same? He'll get what we get – he's family.

Billy picks up his baskets.

BILLY. OK – I'm off. (*He calls.*) I'll see you at the vet's Joey. I'm around there.

MRS BOSWELL. What about breakfast, Billy?

BILLY. (*As he walks out.*) I don't want any breakfast. I'm looking at sandwiches all day, aren't I?

MRS BOSWELL. (*Calling.*) People who sell wash-basins don't stop getting washed, Billy!! (*Pause.*) So how many is it for breakfast? Jack – Adrian.

Mr Boswell walks in. He is in his pyjamas, still half asleep.

And nightmare over there.

MR BOSWELL. Morning.

Joey comes down with the dog wrapped in a blanekt.

JOEY. OK, Mam. Hi, Dad.

MRS BOSWELL. (*To the dog.*) There – my little baby – we'll get you right.

JOEY. See you. (*He goes out.*)

MR BOSWELL. What's the dog all wrapped up for?

MRS BOSWELL. There's a family crisis – but as usual you slept through it.

MR BOSWELL. I haven't slept through it – it woke me up.

JACK. He's not well. (*To Mrs Boswell.*) I'd better go with Joey, Mam.

Jack goes out.

MRS BOSWELL. What about breakfast!

No reply. Adrian wanders in – sleepy.

ADRIAN. Morning. (*To Mrs Boswell.*) Has Carmen phoned?

MRS BOSWELL. She phoned at one o'clock this morning.

ADRIAN. I know. We like to start the day and end the day—

MRS BOSWELL. The whole street must have heard you.

ADRIAN. Rowing with each other. (*He sits down.*) Where is everybody?

MRS BOSWELL. Gone to the vet's – Mongy isn't well.

ADRIAN. Not well – he's never not well. (*He gets up.*) Why didn't somebody tell me?

Mrs Boswell sighs and raises eyes to heaven. Adrian goes upstairs.

Is my lucky shirt washed?

MRS BOSWELL. The grey one in the drawer.

Adrian comes downstairs again.

ADRIAN. It's not grey – it's blue.

MRS BOSWELL. It's luck's run out, it's grey now.

ADRIAN. Oh God.

MR BOSWELL. (*With a twinkle in his eye.*) So it's you and me for breakfast.

MRS BOSWELL. You can take that look off your face, Freddie Boswell. I took you back because you're *their* father – no other reason.

MR BOSWELL. It would be nice though, wouldn't it? To sit here – on this yellow morning – drinking coffee together – give me something to think about – while I'm brushing the streets.

MRS BOSWELL. You don't want anything to think about – that's why you *are* brushing the streets.

She sits down and pours their coffee. As she puts the pot down, he reaches for her hands.

MR BOSWELL. Has it really gone? All that wildness – all that thunder and lightning. (*Pause.*) Has our storm really passed?

Mrs Boswell looks at him – there is the smallest sign of weakness. Then the phone rings.

MRS BOSWELL. Hello, yes. (*Pause.*) Oh Aveline, love, how are you? Give me all your news. (*She looks at Mr Boswell who gets up and goes out.*)

The reception area at the veterinary clinic

Several people sit with a variety of animals. A lady is at the reception desk.

RECEPTIONIST. Could you take a seat, please?

> *The lady goes and sits. The door of the clinic opens – in comes Joey holding the swathed dog, followed by Jack, Adrian clutching his briefcase, and Billy. They move towards the desk in a group, very po-faced. The girl looks up – and is met with four sullen faces.*

RECEPTIONIST. Yes?

JOEY. Boswell – Mongy Boswell.

RECEPTIONIST. (*Disbelieving.*) Are you all together?

JOEY. Yes. (*The receptionist looks amazed.*)

Grandad's living room (a *little later*)

Mrs Boswell is dusting and tidying up. Grandad is eating his breakfast off his tray.

MRS BOSWELL. Your clean pyjamas are on your bed, Grandad. I notice you've put your foot through the sheets again.

GRANDAD. It's me legs – they won't keep still. Like eels they are, twisting and turning.

MRS BOSWELL. The doctor's given you tablets for that – where are they?

GRANDAD. They don't work. The tablets don't work – newfangled they are.

MRS BOSWELL. They won't work if you don't want them to, Grandad.

GRANDAD. Me legs stopped – but me arms started. Like an octopus I was, twisting and turning.

MRS BOSWELL. I've told you not to watch those underwater films, haven't I? You know what you're like. I hope you didn't see the dolphin picture – you'll start leaping in and out of your bath.

GRANDAD. I've got an active mind, that's what it is.

MRS BOSWELL. I know love, but your body's lagging behind, that's the trouble.

The phone rings. Mrs Boswell gets it out of her pocket.

Hello, yes?

JOEY. It's Joey, Mam.

MRS BOSWELL. Hello love – how's Mongy?

JOEY. They're doing tests.

MRS BOSWELL. Tests! Oh Joey!

JOEY. I'm going back later. Listen, we've all got things to do, so we'll be home for lunch. OK?

MRS BOSWELL. Will you know then?

JOEY. Should do – yes. Don't worry, Mam.

MRS BOSWELL. All right. Tarra, love.

JOEY. Ciao.

MRS BOSWELL. (*Putting the phone away, to Grandad.*) Right, Grandad. I'll clean the canary cage for you – then I'll go and do the lunch. (*She gets the cage down and puts in on the sideboard.*)

GRANDAD. I made me will out yesterday.

MRS BOSWELL. (*Looking at him.*) Whatever for?

GRANDAD. I was in the mood – that's all.

MRS BOSWELL. Oh love – you'll outlive us all.

GRANDAD. Not with me legs and me arms. (*Pause.*) And things.

Mrs Boswell looks at him. Then moves him forward and brings out a medical book entitled The A–Z of medicine.

MRS BOSWELL. Haven't I told you not to read this medical book? (*She flicks through the pages.*) It's full of bad news. Grandad – you've got to be a doctor to understand this. (*She reads.*) Lower backache – swelling of the ankles and sometimes of the hands. Breathlessness – the inability to sleep and physical restlessness.

GRANDAD. I've got all those symptoms, I have. Jumping about I am – like a fish on a slab.

MRS BOSWELL. Yes – well it says here that you're just about to plunge into labour. Now come on – put the tray down and help me with the bird cage. (*She looks into it.*) Oh God – when did you last do it?

GRANDAD. Every day I feed that bird – never a day missed.

MRS BOSWELL. I know you *feed* it – but do you ever clean it? The poor bird needs a pair of wellies. Come on.

Outside Speke Hall

The old house is surrounded by woods. Carmen is wandering through them – we hear what is going on in her head.

ADRIAN'S VOICE. You said very cruel things, Carmen. Like arrows they were – in my heart.

CARMEN. (*In her thoughts.*) I didn't mean it – I was angry – hurt. Please Adrian, let's meet again.

ADRIAN. I think we should start at the beginning Carmen – get to know each other mentally – gently lead up to – to other things.

CARMEN. You're right Adrian, you're right. I was too demanding. It's just that – you're so – wonderful.

ADRIAN. Speke Hall – let's meet there.

CARMEN. London – let's meet in London. I'd love to do it in London.

ADRIAN. You're doing it again Carmen – you're talking about *it*. It's it, it, it – can't you think about anything else? (*Pause.*) I'm tired, Carmen.

   Pause.

CARMEN. All right – Speke Hall then.

ADRIAN. It's historic and intellectual – a meeting place for minds.

   At this point, Adrian appears. He stands by a tree looking at her.

Carmen.

   Carmen turns and sees him. She runs to him.

CARMEN. Adrian.

   They kiss and immediately sink into the bushes passionately.

Inside the DHSS building

The usual number of people are waiting. Joey is on the front row. The three girls are just opening their positions. Then one girl calls.

FIRST GIRL. (*Shouting.*) No. 1!

   Joey gets up and strolls over to her.

MARTINA. No. 2!

Joey sits down but Martina, who is in the next position, sees him.

MARTINA. All right, Mr Boswell – over here. (*To the first girl.*) Take No. 2, will you?

Joey gets up and sits in the chair opposite Martina. No. 2 sits opposite the first girl.

JOEY. Preferential treatment eh? Not bad, not bad.

MARTINA. Not preferential treatment, Mr Boswell – I just like to keep my eye on you. I want to be here, you see, when you make the final blunder.

JOEY. It's about our dog.

MARTINA. Oh yes.

JOEY. Down on your official list as 'Guard Dog'.

MARTINA. Oh yes.

JOEY. A necessary attachment in these violent times, wouldn't you say?

MARTINA. Yeah.

JOEY. Well – he's sick.

MARTINA. I'm getting that feeling of dread Mr Boswell – that doom-laden apprehension that you get when you realise that the lorry coming towards you isn't going to stop.

JOEY. Now we don't mind paying the veterinary bills – but – there might be an operation. Only *might*, but that would be beyond our means, being as we're all out of work.

MARTINA. (*Sweetly.*) Is there anything else you'd like to claim for while you're here – your Grandad's canary, the street cat, the spider under the sink?

JOEY. I suppose your answer to the problem would be 'Have him put down, Mr Boswell, it's cheaper.' But then we'd be burgled, and we'd have to claim for all the accoutrements of life – you know, the little things we've gathered around us.

MARTINA. Like television, microwave and cordless telephones, video, a fleet of cars, and a safe behind the Rembrandt.

JOEY. (*Pointing at her.*) You've got it, sweetheart, you've got it.

MARTINA. And what's more, Mr Boswell, I'm going to hang on to it. (*She shouts.*) Next!

JOEY. (*Standing up.*) Some you win, some you have to postpone.

He takes her hand and kisses it, then walks away calmly.

Outside the Boswells' house (lunchᴛime)

Grandad is sitting in his chair outside. Mrs Boswell comes to the door and peeps out.

MRS BOSWELL. Any sign of Joey, Grandad?

GRANDAD. No – I haven't seen him.

Mrs Boswell goes in. Jack's van comes screeching to a halt outside. He beeps his horn. Grandad totters over, picks up the cone and puts it on the pavement.

JACK. (*To Grandad, through the window.*) Hi Grandad, has Joey been home yet?

GRANDAD. No he hasn't.

Jack parks the van, opens the back and takes out a decorated Victorian lavatory. He carries it into the house.

JACK. It's to sell Grandad – people put plants in them.

GRANDAD. Funny place – the world.

Jack goes in. Grandad sits down again.
Billy arrives in his sandwich van and beeps his horn. Grandad gets up again, picks up another cone and puts it on the pavement. Billy gets out and takes his big baskets out of the van.

BILLY. Hi, Grandad. Seen Joey?

GRANDAD. No – I haven't.

Billy goes into the house.
Adrian arrives on his motorbike. Gives a little beep and points to the cone. Grandad gets up, picks it up and puts it on the pavement. Adrian parks.

ADRIAN. Thanks, Grandad. (*He looks around as he goes into the house.*) I don't see Joey's car – been and gone has he? (*He rushes into the house.*)

Grandad loses his temper.

GRANDAD. (*Shouting.*) I don't know, do I?! How do I know where Joey is?!! (*He kicks some of the cones back into the street.*)

A cyclist passes.

CYCLIST. Go on there, Grandad, give it to them, son!

GRANDAD. (*Yelling at the house.*) Who do you think I am – the bloody doorman? (*He kicks the final cone into the street.*)

The Boswells' kitchen

Mrs Boswell has prepared the lunch. Billy, Jack and Aveline are seated at the table. Adrian is just taking his crash helmet off, ready to join them. Mrs Boswell is placing a dish with a large ham bone on it on the table.

MRS BOSWELL. Joey said he'd be home for lunch along with the rest of you – so we'll just have to wait.

BILLY. (*Seeing some cold salmon on a plate on the side counter.*) Can I have some of the salmon instead of ham?

MRS BOSWELL. No you can't – it's for Mongy.

JACK. Where's me Dad?

MRS BOSWELL. What do you think I am – the Yellow Pages?

BILLY. Did he say he'd be home for lunch?

MRS BOSWELL. He said he would, yes. But his gob makes arrangements the rest of him can't keep, doesn't it? (*She sits down.*)

BILLY. I'm looking forward to seeing Mongy again. It's funny how you take things for granted, isn't it?

JACK. Yeah – I'll never kick him out through the front door again.

ADRIAN. Sometimes I stick his front paw through his collar, and I call him – he comes chundling along on three feet.

They are all staring at him. His voice trails.

It's really funny.

Pause. They are staring.

I won't do it again.

Joey comes in. They all look.

JOEY. I'm a bit late – sorry.

Silence. They all glare at each other, then at Joey.

MRS BOSWELL. (*Gravely.*) Where is he, Joey?

JOEY. He's going to be all right.

Sighs of relief all round.

Just an operation – that's all!

MRS BOSWELL. Operation! On Mongy!

JACK. What's wrong?

MRS BOSWELL. Is it serious?

BILLY. When?

JOEY. Tomorrow morning. The vet took him in because his temperature was up – but that turned out to be nothing. Anyway, while he was examining him, he found a lump.

MRS BOSWELL. Oh my God – a lump! Oh Mongy. (*She crosses herself.*) Is he going to die?

JACK. (*Nervously.*) They can cope with lumps. They just turf them out – it's like shelling peas. (*Pause.*) Isn't it?

JOEY. (*To all of them.*) Hey come on – pull yourselves together. He's going to be all right. The lump can be removed. (*Pause.*) But . . .

ADRIAN. I can't stand that word 'But'. 'The planet is not going to explode – *but*,' 'You're not going to die – *but*'. It means the planet is not going to explode *yet*, and you're not going to die today. *But* it's going to explode tomorrow and you'll cop it then instead.

JOEY. In order to do the operation successfully . . .

MRS BOSWELL. I'll give me blood.

JOEY. In order to succeed, they're going to have to castrate him.

They are all shocked. Joey sits down.

MRS BOSWELL. (*Eventually.*) You mean – deprive him of – take away his . . .

JACK. They can't do that, he'll look daft.

ADRIAN. Never mind how he looks – what about how he feels? He's the king dog round here – he's got them all lined up. It's his right – they're taking his doghood away.

BILLY. I don't know what you're all worried about – it's nothing.

JACK. (*To Billy.*) How would you like it?

BILLY. I'm not a dog, am I? I'd know what it was all about.

JACK. It must be worse for him – he'd know that there was something missing but he wouldn't know what it was.

JOEY. The thing is, it's the only way. If Mongy is going to be free of this tumour, then he's got to part with his bits and pieces.

MRS BOSWELL. He'll get a funny bark – sort of soprano.

JOEY. No he won't. (*He sighs.*) God, where do they get it all from?

MRS BOSWELL. Well something will happen. He won't be the same, will he?

JOEY. He won't be able to procreate, that's all. It's not the end of the world. I mean, he's done it enough times to lie back and reminisce, hasn't he?

BILLY. And anyway, it's better than being dead, isn't it?

JACK. I'm not sure about that.

JOEY. You're thinking like a human. Mongy's a dog – he won't even *know* what's happened.

JACK. Won't he miss them clanging about?

JOEY. (*Sighing.*) Look, if you're going to be morbid about it, it could have been incurable. I could have come home with his collar and lead, couldn't I? Let's be thankful – OK?

MRS BOSWELL. Joey's right. Let's eat our meal and be grateful for the way things are. (*She puts her hands together.*)

They all put their hands together too.

We thank Thee, oh Lord, for the fruits of the earth – and we ask that you bring Mongy safely home to us, no matter what is missing. Amen.

THE REST. Amen.

Instead of grabbing the food as usual, they all sit there looking at it.

MRS BOSWELL. (*Picking up a piece of ham on a fork.*) Jack?

JACK. It's pig, isn't it? I don't see the difference between that pig and our dog.

ADRIAN. It's never stopped you before.

JACK. I haven't had cause to think about it before, have I? Animals are animals. If you eat that pig you might as well casserole Mongy – and have Grandad's canary on toast.

JOEY. Let's just cut out the chat, and have the salad. OK?

Mrs Boswell goes to put the ham back.

BILLY. I'll have it – it doesn't worry me – we have to live, don't we?

Billy takes some ham, then some more.

JACK. Isn't it funny? I wouldn't have felt half so bad if someone had come home and said they were going to castrate our Billy.

MRS BOSWELL. Jack – wash your mouth out.

BILLY. What have *I* done?

A family argument ensues.

JACK. You don't seem to care. (*He mimicks Billy.*) 'I don't know what you're worried about – it's nothing.' That's great coming from you, isn't it? Your spare parts are not in jeopardy, are they? And now you're mowing your way through a cooked pig. (*To the others.*) He's obscene . . .

JOEY. Now look – look – he's just a baby lad.

ADRIAN. He's way ahead of the rest of us, isn't he? He spends most of his time perpetuating the human race. His spare parts will be worn out by the time he's thirty.

BILLY. I've got other worries, haven't I? Julie's gone – she's taken my baby with her.

MRS BOSWELL. Doesn't Mongy matter then?

BILLY. Of course he matters . . .

ADRIAN. You made enough fuss yesterday when he was begging for a piece of your fruit cake.

BILLY. (*Standing up and shouting.*) I wanted the marzipan – that's all – just the marzipan. (*To them all.*) And anyway, none of you ever take him out.

JACK. How can we take him out? He's never in.

MRS BOSWELL. I take him to the supermarket (*pause*) sometimes.

ADRIAN. I've been too depressed, haven't I? I have lost me job.

JOEY. I suppose we all could have tried harder.

BILLY. So don't get at me then!

Mr Boswell comes in, carrying a bunch of flowers. He stops and looks.

MR BOSWELL. Something wrong?

MRS BOSWELL. Mongy has to be castrated.

MR BOSWELL. Oh – poor little sod.

MRS BOSWELL. A lot you care.

MR BOSWELL. I do care. (*To the others.*) What brought this on?

ADRIAN. (*Coldly.*) I suppose the flowers are to get round our mam, are they?

It suits you now, does it? Three years with Lilo Lil, and it's back to the fold for a rest, is it? Until someone else comes along with enormous great big tits.

Mrs Boswell covers her mouth, and utters a moan.

JOEY. (*To Adrian.*) Hey cut it, cut it!

ADRIAN. Sorry, Mam.

MR BOSWELL. Oh aye – it's reprisals is it? It's 'Say what you think' day. (*To Adrian.*) When did you make your mam a cup of tea? When? (*To the rest.*) When did *any* of you make *her* lunch, *her* breakfast, *her* dinner – when did you clean up, when? I wasn't the only one who went out there and did my own thing. You're all doing it – *all* the time – all except her. (*Pause.*) She's the only one who does what she *should* do rather than what she *wants* to do. (*He shouts.*) You'll all come home one day and she will have turned into a bloody hoover! Still, I don't suppose you lot would bloody notice.

Mr Boswell thrusts the bouquet at Mrs Boswell.

Flowers! (*He walks out.*)

Silence.

JOEY. (*Calmly.*) Right – you've all got your frustrations out of the way – let's get back to normal.

BILLY. I haven't got my frustrations out of the way.

JACK. Oh God – will someone bind and gag him?

JOEY. (*Loudly.*) Look, (*they all stop*) we all feel guilty about Mongy – OK. He's just been a dog – coming and going from this house – and we've been too busy to appreciate him. Now we do, and we can put it right, can't we? We can make it up to him – pat him, let him sleep in the chair, give him the cream off the milk, take him for walks.

MRS BOSWELL. Will he be able to walk?

Joey gives up. He raises his eyes to heaven.

BILLY. And what about our dad? He's gone again! Aveline's gone, Julie's gone, the baby's gone, Mongy's gone – everybody is going. I'm beginning to feel insecure.

JOEY. They'll all be back, sunshine, they'll all be back.

Outside the veterinary clinic (*the next day*)

Joey's car is parked and Mr Boswell's yellow cart is parked behind it. Joey comes out of the clinic first, followed by Jack, who is carrying Mongy wrapped in a blanket, followed by Billy, then Adrian, who is carrying his briefcase. After them comes Mr Boswell, who goes and stands by his cart. Joey opens the door of his Jag. Jack and the others get in. Mr Boswell watches.

JOEY. Thanks, Dad. Will we see you later?

MR BOSWELL. Depends what colour my day is, son.

Joey closes the door, then gets into the car. He drives off. Mr Boswell wanders off with his cart.

Outside the Boswells' house

Grandad is sitting outside in his chair. The Jag beeps. Mrs Boswell comes out and picks up the cone. Joey parks the car and opens the door. Jack gets out with Mongy. Mrs Boswell assists him. The rest get out and go into the house. Joey locks his car.

JOEY. (*To Grandad.*) All right there, Grandad!

GRANDAD. Have they taken his balls then?

JOEY. I'm afraid so, Grandad.

GRANDAD. Can't they do a transplant?

JOEY. There's nothing to match his own, Grandad.

GRANDAD. He can have mine for all the good they do me!!

Joey laughs and goes inside.

The Boswells' kitchen (*that night*)

Mrs Boswell is sitting by the table alone. Everywhere is tidy. The table is set for breakfast. She is in her dressing-gown, ready for bed. She gets up, goes to the door of the living room and looks in. Mongy is on the settee.

MRS BOSWELL. Hello sweetheart, aren't you the lucky one? No more hanky panky for you, but we'll have you running about tomorrow.

The phone rings.

MRS BOSWELL. Hello? Aveline, how are you? Tell me all your news.

AVELINE. Mam, I know it's late. I've just finished modelling. How's Mongy?

MRS BOSWELL. It's not good, Aveline. It's not good. Touch and go.

AVELINE. I thought it was a routine operation.

MRS BOSWELL. Well, yes it is, usually. But Mongy was very well endowed. It wasn't easy.

AVELINE. How will it affect him?

MRS BOSWELL. Well, if you suddenly take a cup off a tray full of cups it tips up, doesn't it?

AVELINE. Oh Mam. (*Pause.*) When will he be home?

MRS BOSWELL. I don't know, love, I don't know. They're waiting to see if he pulls through.

AVELINE. When will you know, Mam?

MRS BOSWELL. Eventually, love. I'm just sitting here waiting (*pause*) alone.

AVELINE. (*Near to tears.*) Oh Mam.

MRS BOSWELL. There's no need for you to worry, love. We'll manage. You've got your career to think of. There's no need for you to come home.

AVELINE. There's an early train tomorrow, Mam. I'll see you.

MRS BOSWELL. Aveline, there's no need.(*Aveline puts her phone down.*)

MRS BOSWELL. (*Obviously pleased.*) There's no need.

Joey calls from the kitchen.

JOEY. Mam!

MRS BOSWELL. In here, love.

Joey comes in.

JOEY. (*To the dog.*) Hello Macho – what are you up to then?! Aye! (*To Mrs Boswell.*) What are you doing up? It's nearly midnight.

MRS BOSWELL. I can't sleep.

JOEY. Dad not back then?

MRS BOSWELL. No.

Pause.

JOEY. You know, Mam, it stands to reason he wouldn't stay, would he? OK so he came back, but not as a man, not sleeping in your bed I mean. And you know our dad – he's proud about these things.

MRS BOSWELL. (*Sighing.*) Yes. I suppose that's why he went with Lilo Lil – just to prove himself to himself. (*Pause.*) We were getting closer, Joey. Oh, only the odd word – the odd look – but something was coming back. It was beginning to feel right again. (*Pause.*) He'll be in his flat now, breaking free again. (*She gives a big sigh.*) Still – never mind – let's see what tomorrow brings.

JOEY. That's the spirit, Mam. It can't be worse, can it?

There is a knock on the front door. Mrs Boswell and Joey look at each other in anticipation.

JOEY. I'll go. (*He goes to the door.*) Oh, you're back. Oh great. Me mam's in there, I'm just off. I'll see you.

Julie comes in.

JULIE. Hello Mrs Boswell.

MRS BOSWELL. Are you back?

JULIE. Yeah – a sudden decision.

MRS BOSWELL. When?

JULIE. Just.

MRS BOSWELL. Sit down, love, I'll wake Billy up.

JULIE. No, no, it's all right. I'd rather wait and see him tomorrow. I did try to phone but you were engaged.

MRS BOSWELL. It was our Aveline.

JULIE. Oh.

MRS BOSWELL. How's the baby?

JULIE. Fine.

MRS BOSWELL. And how's London?

JULIE. Not like home. Anyway I'll go – get back to the baby. Perhaps you'll tell Billy I'm back. (*She goes to leave.*)

MRS BOSWELL. It would be nice, Julie, if you liked us, the family I mean. After all there's nothing unusual about us. We're human beings. We've got problems like everybody else – work, money, health. Grandad's getting old, the cost of life is going up, Mongy's lost his balls. It's all ordinary everyday stuff.

JULIE. Yeah. I'll bear it in mind. Tarra.

Outside the Boswells' house (*early the next morning*)

The milkman is delivering milk. All is quiet. Suddenly the Boswells' door opens. Billy comes hurtling out in his pyjamas and dressing-gown.

BILLY. Julie!!

He collides with the milkman.

Julie's back – from London.

He races across the road.

Julie!!

He bangs on the door loudly. After a moment it opens. Julie stands there in her dressing-gown.

BILLY. (*Almost whispering.*) Julie.

JULIE. (*Tenderly.*) Oh Billy – you still look as daft as ever . . . Get in here.

He goes in. Joey is at the door of the house. He is smiling at Billy's antics. Just then, Mr Boswell comes along with his yellow cart, whistling to his radio as usual. Joey is pleased to see him.

JOEY. Hi, Dad.

MR BOSWELL. Hi, son. (*He stops.*)

JOEY. (*Standing aside.*) Right on time for breakfast.

MR BOSWELL. Just passing, son, just passing. (*He goes off.*)

Joey watches sadly. Grandad's door opens and Grandad peeps out.

GRANDAD. Is me breakfast coming or not?

He closes the door again.

JOEY. (*To himself, quietly.*) Yes, Grandad, it's coming.

At this point, the door opposite opens. An attractive lady of about thirty, who is in her dressing-gown, takes in her milk. She lingers and looks at Joey as she does so. Joey smiles at her. She wiggles back in again and closes the door.

JOEY'S THOUGHTS. You know, son, it's time you had some fun.

Joey is thoughtful about this. Then, to himself again, having given it some consideration.

No – not over there. Not Billy *and* me – not on your own doorstep. We'd wear the street out. (*Pause.*) And anyway, we don't want to make Mongy feel inadequate, do we?

MRS BOSWELL. Breakfast, Joey.

JOEY. Coming, Mam.